Psychoanalysis
From Practice to Theory

Whurr Series in Psychoanalysis

The purpose of this series, edited by Peter Fonagy and Mary Target of University College London, is to publish clinical and research-based texts of academic excellence in the field. Each title makes a significant contribution and the series is open-ended. The readership is academics and graduate students in psychoanalysis, together with clinical practitioners, worldwide.

PSYCHOANALYSIS, SCIENCE AND MASCULINITY
Karl Figlio
2000 ISBN 1 86156 203 9 paperback

A LANGUAGE FOR PSYCHOSIS
Edited by Paul Williams
2001 ISBN 1 86156 166 0 paperback

INTRODUCTION TO KLEINIAN PSYCHOANALYSIS
A Contemporary Perspective
Edited by Catalina Bronstein
2001 ISBN 1 86156 226 8 paperback

ORGANISATIONS, ANXIETY AND DEFENCE
Edited by Bob Hinshelwood and Marco Chiesa
2001 ISBN 1 86156 214 4 paperback

OUTCOMES OF PSYCHOANALYTIC TREATMENT
Edited by Marianne Leuzinger-Bohleber and Mary Target
2002 ISBN 1 86156 279 9 paperback

PSYCHOANALYTIC THEORIES
Perspectives from Developmental Psychopathology
Peter Fonagy and Mary Target
2003 ISBN 1 86156 239 X paperback

THE PERVERSION OF LOSS
Edited by Susan Levy and Alessandra Lemma
2004 ISBN 1 86156 433 3 paperback

FREUD: A MODERN READER
Edited by Rosine Jozef Perelberg
2005 ISBN 1 86156 402 3 paperback

Psychoanalysis
From Practice to Theory

Edited by

Jorge Canestri

John Wiley & Sons, Ltd

Copyright © 2006   Whurr Publishers Ltd (a subsidiary of John Wiley & Sons, Ltd), The Atrium, Southern Gate, Chichester, West Sussex PO19 8SQ, England
Telephone (+44) 1243 779777

Email (for orders and customer service enquiries): cs-books@wiley.co.uk
Visit our Home Page on www.wiley.com

All Rights Reserved. No part of this publication may be reproduced, stored in a retrieval system or transmitted in any form or by any means, electronic, mechanical, photocopying, recording, scanning or otherwise, except under the terms of the Copyright, Designs and Patents Act 1988 or under the terms of a licence issued by the Copyright Licensing Agency Ltd, 90 Tottenham Court Road, London W1T 4LP, UK, without the permission in writing of the Publisher. Requests to the Publisher should be addressed to the Permissions Department, John Wiley & Sons Ltd, The Atrium, Southern Gate, Chichester, West Sussex PO19 8SQ, England, or emailed to permreq@wiley.co.uk, or faxed to (+44) 1243 770620.

Designations used by companies to distinguish their products are often claimed as trademarks. All brand names and product names used in this book are trade names, service marks, trade marks or registered trade marks of their respective owners. The Publisher is not associated with any product or vendor mentioned in this book.

This publication is designed to provide accurate and authoritative information in regard to the subject matter covered. It is sold on the understanding that the Publisher is not engaged in rendering professional services. If professional advice or other expert assistance is required, the services of a competent professional should be sought.

Other Wiley Editorial Offices
John Wiley & Sons Inc., 111 River Street, Hoboken, NJ 07030, USA
Jossey-Bass, 989 Market Street, San Francisco, CA 94103-1741, USA
Wiley-VCH Verlag GmbH, Boschstr. 12, D-69469 Weinheim, Germany
John Wiley & Sons Australia Ltd, 42 McDougall Street, Milton, Queensland 4064, Australia
John Wiley & Sons (Asia) Pte Ltd, 2 Clementi Loop #02-01, Jin Xing Distripark, Singapore 129809
John Wiley & Sons Canada Ltd, 22 Worcester Road, Etobicoke, Ontario, Canada M9W 1L1
Wiley also publishes its books in a variety of electronic formats. Some content that appears in print may not be available in electronic books.

Library of Congress Cataloging-in-Publication Data
Psychoanalysis : from practice to theory / edited by Jorge Canestri.
    p. cm. - (Whurr series in psychoanalysis)
  Includes bibliographical references and index.
  ISBN-13: 978-1-86156-494-8 (pbk. : alk. paper)
  ISBN-10: 1-86156-494-5 (pbk. : alk. paper)
  1. Psychoanalysis. I. Canestri, Jorge. II. Series.
  [DNLM: 1. Psychoanalytic Theory. WM 460 P97443 2006]
  RC504.P749 2006
  616.89'17 – dc22
                                                2005028449

British Library Cataloguing in Publication Data
A catalogue record for this book is available from the British Library

ISBN-13 978-1-86156-494-8 (pbk)
ISBN-10 1-86156-494-5 (pbk)

Typeset in Garamond book 10.5/12.5 by SNP Best-set Typesetter Ltd., Hong Kong
Printed and bound in Great Britain by TJ International Ltd, Padstow, Cornwall
This book is printed on acid-free paper responsibly manufactured from sustainable forestry in which at least two trees are planted for each one used for paper production.

Contents

About the editor · vii
Contributors · viii
Series foreword · xi
Acknowledgements · xiii

Introduction · 1
Jorge Canestri

1 Implicit understanding of clinical material beyond theory · 13
   Jorge Canestri

2 The map of private (implicit, preconscious) theories in clinical practice · 29
   Jorge Canestri, Werner Bohleber, Paul Denis and Peter Fonagy

3 Miss R · 45
   Peter Fonagy

4 Discussion of public and implicit theories in Peter Fonagy's case presentation · 61
   Werner Bohleber

5 The failure of practice to inform theory and the role of implicit theory in bridging the transmission gap · 69
   Peter Fonagy

6 Some perspectives on relationships of theory and technique · 87
   William I. Grossman

7 Theory as transition: spatial metaphors of the mind and the analytic space · 103
   Gail S. Reed

8 The analytic mind at work: counterinductive knowledge and
   the blunders of so-called 'theory of science'   127
   Jorge L. Ahumada

9 Infantile sexual theories and cognitive development:
   psychoanalysis and theoretical production   147
   Samuel Zysman

10 The search to define and describe how psychoanalysts
   work: preliminary report on the project of the EPF Working
   Party on Comparative Clinical Methods   167
   David Tuckett

Bibliography   201

Index   213

About the editor

Jorge Canestri: MD, psychiatrist, psychoanalyst. Specialized in linguistics and epistemology. Training and supervising analyst for the Italian Psychoanalytical Association (AIPsi) and for the Argentine Psychoanalytic Association. Director of the Institute of Psychoanalysis of the Italian Psychoanalytical Association (1992–98). Full member of the International Psychoanalytic Association. Chair of the Ethics Committee (IPA), Chair of the Working Party on Theoretical Issues of the EPF, Chair of the 42nd Congress of the International Psychoanalytic Association (IPA), Nice, 2001. Member of the Conceptual and Empirical Research Committee (IPA). Professor of Psychology of Mental Health at the Roma 3 University. Editor of the Educational Section of the *International Journal of Psycho-Analysis*. Member of the Editorial Board of the *International Journal of Psycho-Analysis*. Correspondent of *Psicoanálisis* and of *Revista de Psicoanálisis*. Member of the Editorial Board of *Aperturas Psicoanalíticas*. Author of numerous psychoanalytical papers in books and reviews and co-author of *The Babel of the Unconscious: Mother Tongue and Foreign Languages in the Psychoanalytic Dimension*. Editor (with Marianne Leuzinger-Bohleber and Anna Ursula Dreher) of *Pluralism and Unity? Methods of Research in Psychoanalysis*. Director of the webpage: Psychoanalysis and logical mathematical thought. Mary S. Sigourney Award recipient, 2004. IPA Global Representative for Europe.

Contributors

Jorge L. Ahumada: Supervising and Training Analyst, Argentine Psychoanalytic Association. Honorary Member, British Psycho-Analytical Society. Mary S. Sigourney Awardee, New York, 1996. Editor for Latin America, *International Journal of Psychoanalysis*, 1993–98. Author of *The Logics of the Mind. A Clinical View* (London: Karnac, 2001), and of psychoanalytic papers published in six languages.

Werner Bohleber: DPhil, psychoanalyst in private practice in Frankfurt, Germany. Training and Supervising Analyst. Former president of the German Psychoanalytical Association. Editor of the German psychoanalytical journal *PSYCHE*. Member of the EPF Working Party on Theory. Author of several books and numerous articles. His main research subjects are trauma; adolescence and identity; psychoanalytic theory; xenophobia and anti-Semitism; and terrorism.

Paul Denis: Member of the Paris Psychoanalytical Society. Editor of the *Revue Française de Psychanalyse* until 2004. Author of *Eloge de la bêtise* (Paris: Presses Universitaires de France, 2001); *Emprise et satisfaction: les deux formats de la pulsion* (Paris: Presses Universitaires de France, 2002); and (with Claude Janin), *Psychotherapie et psychanalyse* (Paris: Presses Universitaires de France, 2004).

Peter Fonagy: PhD, FBA, Freud Memorial Professor of Psychoanalysis and Director of the Sub-Department of Clinical Health Psychology at University College London. Chief Executive of the Anna Freud Centre, London. Consultant to the Child and Family Program at the Menninger Department of Psychiatry, Baylor College of Medicine. Clinical Psychologist and Training and Supervising Analyst in the British Psycho-Analytical Society in child and adult analysis. His clinical interests centre on issues of borderline psychopathology, violence and early attachment relationships. His work seeks to integrate empirical research with psychoanalytic theory. He holds a number of important positions, which include co-chairing the Research Committee of the International Psychoanalytic Association, and Fellowship of the British Academy. He has published over 200 chapters and articles and has authored or edited several books. His most recent works include *Attachment Theory and Psychoanalysis* (New York: Other Press, 2001); (with M. Target, D. Cottrell, J. Phillips and Z. Kurtz), *What Works for Whom? A Critical Review of Treatments for Children and Adolescents* (New York: Guilford, 2002); (with M. Target), *Psychoanalytic Theories: Perspectives from Developmental Psychopathology* (London: Whurr, 2003); (with A. Bateman), *Psychotherapy for Borderline Personality Disorder: Mentalization-Based Treatment* (Oxford: Oxford University Press, 2004); and (with A. D. Roth), *What Works For Whom? A Critical Review of Psychotherapy Research* (New York: Guilford, 2004).

William I. Grossman: MD, Training and Supervising Analyst, New York Psychoanalytic Society & Institute, Inc. Formerly Clinical Professor of Psychiatry at the Albert Einstein College of Medicine, New York. A selection of his papers was recently published on the internet by the Internet Press for Psychoanalysis.

Gail S. Reed: PhD, psychoanalyst in private practice in New York City and Salisbury, CT. Training and Supervisory Analyst and Faculty at the Training Institute of the New York Freudian Society. Founding Member and Faculty, the Berkshire Psychoanalytic Institute; Faculty, Cleveland Psychoanalytic Center. Member of the Editorial Board, *The Psychoanalytic Quarterly*, Associate Editor (Foreign Books), *Journal of the American Psychoanalytic Association*. Author of *Transference Neurosis and Psychoanalytic Experience: Perspectives on Contemporary Clinical Experience* (New Haven, CT: Yale University Press, 1994); and *Clinical Experience* (Northvale, NJ: Aronson, 1996).

David Tuckett: Visiting Professor, Psychoanalysis Unit, University College London, and Training and Supervising Analyst, British Psychoanalytical Society. President of the European Psychoanalytic Federation (1999–2004). Editor-in-Chief, *International Journal of Psychoanalysis* (1988–2001). Founding Editor, New Library of Psychoanalysis (1985–88). Principal of the Heath Education Studies Unit, University of Cambridge (1977–83). He works as a psychoanalyst and is currently Chair of the EPF Working Party on Comparative Clinical Methods.

Samuel Zysman: MD, Faculty of Medicine, Buenos Aires University. After practising as a paediatrician, he moved into child psychiatry and went for psychoanalytical training at the Argentine Psychoanalytical Association. Currently Training Analyst and Professor at the Psychoanalytic Institute of the Buenos Aires Psychoanalytical Association. He teaches the theory of psychoanalytical technique and child analysis. He has written 30 papers, on these subjects and others at the interface of psychoanalysis with ethics and with literature. His current focus is on the psychoanalytic study of actions, especially on psychoanalysis, cognitive processes and the meta-psychological status of scientific theories.

Series foreword

After the first hundred years of its history, psychoanalysis has matured into a serious, independent intellectual tradition, which has notably retained its capacity to challenge established truths in most areas of our culture. The biological psychiatrist today is called to task by psychoanalysis, as much as was the specialist in nervous diseases in Freud's time, in turn-of-the-century Vienna. Today's cultural commentators, whether for or against psychoanalytic ideas, are forced to pay attention to considerations of unconscious motivation, defences, early childhood experience and the myriad other discoveries which psychoanalysts brought to twentieth-century culture. Above all, psychoanalytic ideas have spawned an approach to the treatment of mental disorders, psychodynamic psychotherapy, which has become the dominant tradition in most countries, at least in the Western world.

Little wonder that psychoanalytic thinking continues to face detractors, individuals who dispute its epistemology and its conceptual and clinical claims. While disappointing in one way, this is a sign that psychoanalysis may be unique in its capacity to challenge and provoke. Why should this be? Psychoanalysis is unrivalled in the depth of its questioning of human motivation, and whether its answers are right or wrong, the epistemology of psychoanalysis allows it to confront the most difficult problems of human experience. Paradoxically, our new understanding concerning the physical basis of our existence – our genes, nervous system and endocrine functioning – rather than finally displacing psychoanalysis, has created a pressing need for a complementary discipline which considers the memories, desires and meanings which are beginning to be recognized as influencing human adaptation even at the biological level. How else, other than through the study of subjective experience, will we understand the expression of the individual's biological destiny, within the social environment?

It is not surprising, then, that psychoanalysis continues to attract some of the liveliest intellects in our culture. These individuals are by no means all psychoanalytic clinicians or psychotherapists. They are distinguished scholars in an almost bewildering range of disciplines, from the study of mental disorders with their biological determinants to the disciplines of literature, art, philosophy and history. There will always be a need to explicate the meaning of experience. Psychoanalysis, with its commitment to understanding subjectivity, is in a premier position to fulfil this intellectual and human task. We are not surprised at the surge of interest in psychoanalytic studies in universities in many countries. The books in this series are aimed at addressing the same intellectual curiosity that has made these educational projects so successful.

We are proud that the Whurr Series in Psychoanalysis has been able to attract some of the most interesting and creative minds in the field. Our commitment is to no specific orientation, to no particular professional group, but to the intellectual challenge to explore the questions of meaning and interpretation systematically, and in a scholarly way. Nevertheless, we would be glad if this series particularly spoke to the psychotherapeutic community, to those individuals who use their own minds and humanity to help others in distress.

Our focus in this series is to communicate the intellectual excitement which we feel about the past, present and future of psychoanalytic ideas. We hope that our work with the authors and editors in the series will help to make these ideas accessible to an ever-increasing and worldwide group of students, scholars and practitioners.

Peter Fonagy
Mary Target
University College London

Acknowledgements

The editor and authors of this book would like to greatly thank the European Psychoanalytical Federation for the substantial support they gave to this project.

Introduction

JORGE CANESTRI

The proliferation of theories in post-Freudian psychoanalysis – whether partial integrations of the original Freudian theory or alternative theories – was a major preoccupation for many theorists of psychoanalysis in the 1980s (e.g. Robert Wallerstein). At the time, they attempted to find a common ground that would conceptualize the divergences, thus avoiding the need to speak automatically about the existence of 'many psychoanalyses'. This meant exploring the internal coherence of every theory and subsequently measuring its compatibility with the others. These theorists also hypothesized the possibility of integrating them into a unified theory on which they would all depend, conceiving them, therefore, as sub-groups.

These conceptual operations were carried out at the theoretical level, but in many cases neglected a simultaneous confrontation with clinical practice. When analysts are at work with a patient – and the question became even more pertinent when contemporary analysis began to deal with more serious, borderline or para-psychotic patients – does their work faithfully reflect an official theory to which they claim adherence? Or do they integrate concepts deriving from different theories, or create new ones, usually preconsciously?

Some of the 'implicit' concepts or models that the analyst uses or creates in clinical practice have, over time, acquired theoretical status and have been integrated into official theories. Many of the concepts elaborated by Bion, Winnicott, Kohut, etc., followed this path. Sometimes it has been possible to trace their origins in clinical practice through the narratives of the protagonists – for example, Ferenczi's *Clinical Diary*, Bion (1992), and so forth.

All analysts certainly reflect on the use they make of the theories at their disposal or to which they adhere: the reports of analytic processes and supervisions of clinical material – regularly an integral part of psy-

Psychoanalysis: From Practice to Theory. Edited by J. Canestri. © 2006 Whurr Publishers Ltd (a subsidiary of John Wiley & Sons Ltd).

choanalytical and psychotherapeutic training – allow for the exploration of these applications of theory to practice. Essentially, this is done in order to improve our understanding of the patient and to perfect the analyst's technique.

However, little has been done to investigate systematically and analyse with an appropriate instrument all that occurs in the relation between practice and theory from the viewpoint of the creation of new 'theoretical segments' in clinical work – i.e. the heuristic role of clinical experience in psychoanalysis – and of the use of 'implicit', 'private' or 'preconscious' theories to which the analyst at work turns very frequently, often without knowing it.

The title of this book, *Psychoanalysis: From Practice to Theory*, reflects this orientation. It analyses in detail all that *really* happens in clinical practice in order to link it subsequently to the knowledge we acquire from official theory. These analyses allow us to highlight the divergences and/or convergences with the theory to which the analyst adheres, but they can also reveal outlines for new models that could subsequently acquire 'rights of citizenship' within the discipline.

To make this type of analysis of clinical material possible, it was necessary to devise a suitable instrument. This instrument, *a map of private, implicit, preconscious theories in clinical practice*, is the result of many hours' analysis of clinical material in clinical workshops, in groups of ongoing training for members of different psychoanalytical societies, and in working meetings with analysts from various societies. All this work was carried out by a conceptual analysis group of the European Psychoanalytic Federation (the Working Party on Theoretical Issues), and all the analyses were conducted with the active participation of the analysts who presented the clinical material.

The concerns that motivated this research – to explore the relationship between clinical psychoanalysis and theories of psychoanalysis – are shared by the majority of the psychoanalytical community. There is an increasing awareness of the problematical relation between clinical work and theory, regardless of which psychoanalytical theory is invoked.

For this reason, some of the analysts who participated in the creation of this qualitative research project and who developed the abovementioned instrument were invited to collaborate in the preparation of this book, as well as some well-known analysts from the three IPA regions who offer their contributions in order to widen the horizons of this problem.

In Chapter 1 (Canestri), the reasons and the bases of the project, and its epistemological foundations, are explained. Besides questioning the scientificity of psychoanalysis based on a scientific model suitable for disciplines that concern calculus and/or are able to propose repeatable verification experiments, the epistemology of logical neo-empiricism in Karl Popper's hands makes a sharp distinction between the context of discovery and the context of justification. This distinction was introduced by Hans Reichenbach (1951; see also 1938) who said:

> the act of discovery escapes logical analysis; there are no logical rules in terms of which a 'discovery machine' could be constructed that would take over the creative function of the genius. But it is not the logician's task to account for scientific discoveries; all he can do is to analyze the relation between facts and a theory presented to him with the claim that it explains these facts, in other words logic is concerned with the context of justification.

The context of discovery implies the production of a hypothesis or theory, or the invention of a concept. In this context there are various factors that influence the gestation of the discovery: psychological, social, political circumstances, etc. The context of justification instead concerns the validation of the hypothesis: how we know whether it is true or false, and what evidence we have to corroborate it. Many epistemologists presently consider that this distinction is neither legitimate nor useful.

Besides debating the general inadequacy of this distinction, this chapter aims to underline the particular incongruence that this could provoke in clinical psychoanalysis. Clinical experience is the ideal place in which the analyst constructs, together with the patient, those intermediate theoretical segments (hypotheses of conjunction between the observable and theory) that allow for the creation of a shared narrative that is, moreover, specific to the given situation. Clinical experience is therefore the place for invention, for the 'procedures for finding', for what in epistemology is called the context of discovery. Disassociating it from the context of justification, or radically separating the official theories from private or implicit ones, would alter the analytical process itself.

In order to challenge Popper's formulation, we started with certain positions that, in epistemology, contradict the radical schism between the context of discovery and the context of justification. We also mentioned similar research, such as that carried out in the field of mathematical invention, which offers interesting stimuli for our reflection.

Every discipline implements 'research strategies' in accordance with its set goals. Psychoanalysis is no exception, and in this chapter we also attempt to describe which research strategy characterized the path taken by Freud when he invented psychoanalysis, as well as suggesting another strategy that could be complementary.

The exploration of the important heuristic role that the implicit ideas of the analyst acquire in the psychoanalytical experience is in line with

Sandler's (1983) proposition that analysts' implicit, private, preconscious theories guide their *real* clinical practice. These implicit theories are the result of multiple factors that analysts can metabolize. These range from the official theories received and internalized, to unconscious determinations, and to whatever they may gradually learn from their own experience in relation to the numerous stimuli deriving from their relationship with patients.

One of the theses of this project is that implicit theories offer considerable heuristic potential if we are able to formulate them and provide them with scientific dignity, because they are closer to the reality of clinical experience. We also want to show that by identifying the implicit theories that guide what the analyst *really* does in clinical practice, one can proceed to a concise confrontation between theories and models in our discipline, with significant advantages from the point of view of the teaching of the theories themselves.

Chapter 2 (Canestri, Bohleber, Denis and Fonagy) is a presentation of the instrument we have developed. We use a three-component model as it functions in the analyst's mind: public-based thinking + private theoretical thinking + the interaction of private- and public-based thinking (the implicit use of explicit theory).

When constructing a map of the theories used in clinical practice, we must include an examination of how analysts' theories that are completely private and of different origins are influenced and transformed from the public (official) theory they have internalized; of how their private and public theories influence their comprehension and use of the official theories; and of how the private and public theories interact with each other. The result of this integration could alternatively be described as 'lived theory'. The process of integration that leads to the 'lived theory' may undergo many vicissitudes and be submitted to various tensions; these will definitively determine the degree of integration between the public and the private theories and the major or minor harmony or coherence that the product will have.

Inasmuch as we are convinced that knowledge must be organized along dimensions, and that there can be no observation without classification, in order to report our observations we have adopted a categorization for heuristic purposes *which has no status beyond that*. This is why in 'The Map' we describe six different vectors: topographical, conceptual, action, object relations of knowledge, coherence versus contradiction, and developmental. The instrument we present – 'The Map' – is organized around these six vectors (or dimensions), which in turn comprise different sections. They attempt to cover the conceptual dimensions present in clinical practice: for example, the action, including analytic listening; the formulation of the interpretation and the way in which it is enunciated; or, which developmental theory the analyst uses when considering the patient's material during the session.

In the next two chapters we offer a concrete example of the use of 'The Map'. It is an instrument in constant evolution, inasmuch as its use continuously increases the possibility of extending and perfecting it. Working 'from practice to theory' necessarily implies being open to learning from what every new clinical experience teaches us. Chapter 3 (Fonagy) is a detailed description of a psychoanalytical session and provides a reflection on the possible implicit theories of the analyst. In Chapter 4 (Bohleber), the clinical material presented in Chapter 3 is analysed by applying the instrument presented in Chapter 2, which the reader will easily be able to consult.

In Chapter 5 (Fonagy), the author analyses the fragmentation of psychoanalytical theory, which in contemporary literature is euphemistically called 'pluralism'. He hypothesizes that the fragmentation of psychoanalytical theory may be the consequence, at least in part, of the problematic relationship between psychoanalytical theory and psychoanalytical practice. This fragmentation could put the clinical application of the theories at risk and lead to an implosion of the theories themselves. In order to challenge this progressive disassociation between the reality of clinical work and the theories destined in principle to explain it, he advocates a more pragmatic use of theory, based on 'implicit' psychoanalytical knowledge. This orientation would have epistemological consequences: it would place psychoanalysis, as previously discussed in Chapter 1, in harmony with a more modern concept of the sciences, liberating it from the burden of neo-empiricist epistemology.

The author argues that *the value of theory in psychoanalytical practice is that of helping the analyst to construct models that explain behaviour in terms of mental states*, which can subsequently be communicated to the patient. Perhaps from this point of view the difficulty of the relationship between theory and practice is determined by the over-specification of psychoanalytical theory, i.e. in the attempt, beginning in Freud's work and geometrically increasing with time, to create exclusive links between the unconscious conflict ('core theory') and specific manifestations that can be explained by one theory or another (early envy, narcissistic trauma, environmental defect, etc.).

Paradoxically, this same over-specification is justified by the need to capture and communicate the complex system of human subjectivity. From this point of view, the theories appear to be metaphorical attempts to come as close as possible, at a subjective level, in both the patient and the analyst, to the extraordinary complexity of the experience.

This leads the author to favour the elimination of the separation between 'public' and 'private' theories. The latter can be discerned only by observing the clinician at work. And this brings us directly to our research project and to the 'Mapping'.

Chapter 6 (Grossman) confronts a problem similar to that found in the previous chapter, but from a slightly different angle. The author argues that technique cannot be entirely deduced from our theories of the mind and of the therapeutic interaction deriving from clinical experience; nor can it be deduced from considerations derived from interdisciplinary studies. It is therefore necessary to produce some intermediate ideas in order to create a bridge between theory and practice. Inevitably, the therapist will provide the meeting point, in the relationship with both his patients and with his colleagues.

From this perspective it becomes necessary to point out the role that the analyst's unconscious phantasies play in the construction of the theory. This aspect was underlined by Joseph Sandler (1983) when he stated that the implicit or private theories that the analyst used in clinical work were preconscious (descriptively unconscious), but that preconscious phantasies had their roots in the dynamic unconscious.

A deeper exploration of the role of unconscious phantasies does not entail neglect of the intervention of conscious reasoning and of the learning of theory in the analyst's training. During this learning process, which also includes the articulation of theory with technique, a multitude of elements comes into action: the emotive connections of the therapist with theory; inter-generational transmission; the relationships between colleagues; the special modalities of training in every institution; the characteristics (democratic, authoritarian, favourable to criticism or, on the contrary, submissive repetition, etc.) of the psychoanalytical institutions.

The importance of the community in determining how objective a certain theoretical principle is – and how relevant it is to the comprehension or explanation of a clinical fact – derives from accepting the principle that affirms the relativity and transitory nature of truths obtained through the application of a particular scientific method, in all scientific disciplines. Psychoanalysis is no exception to this principle; in fact, in our discipline the creation of 'communities of thought' is probably more important and necessary than in other fields. This may be partly due to the isolation that characterizes the work of the psychoanalyst and to the strong influence that the analyst's own subjectivity has on it. This is why the author emphasizes the need to study the processes of dialogue, affiliation and separation that characterize every stage of the psychoanalyst's training and of his subsequent 'permanent training', with special attention to the emotive aspects that come into play in these processes.

Introduction

Grossman defines implicit theories as what an observer can deduce and subsequently formulate from what the therapist does, says or writes in order to describe or explain a clinical case. This is fully in accord with the methodology and philosophy that has been used in constructing 'The Map' illustrated in Chapter 2. His careful analysis of the factors that intervene in the psychoanalyst's training and his relationship with the community of his peers represents a significant contribution to the understanding of the phenomena that we study in this book.

Similarly, his conclusions regarding the development of the science and on what psychoanalysis could contribute to the epistemology are in harmony with the general epistemological argument of Chapter 1. If we abandon our preconceived ideas (mainly derived from logical empiricism) about how knowledge should evolve and progress, we might perhaps better understand how this really happens. The interweaving between subjective and objective, between implicit and explicit, between context of discovery and context of justification, to which psychoanalysis predisposes us, could assume a significant heuristic value.

In Chapter 7 (Reed), the author presents a detailed and interesting clinical example in which an impasse is handled by reorienting the position of the analyst who configures in her mind a different 'spatial metaphor'. By analysing an example taken from a paper by Winnicott (1945) on primitive emotional development, the author illustrates the value of metaphors in clinical experience: the metaphor facilitates the passage from the inner to outer, from the known to the unknown, and allows for the articulation of categories that are neither one thing nor the other, but are together both and none. Reed is thus able to connect metaphors to Winnicott's concept of transitional space.

These 'metaphors of transition' are certainly linked to the countertransference, but their composition and provenance are very complex. The author focuses her attention on spatial metaphors and their role in clinical work and particularly in the case presented; but she suggests that metaphors of various kinds are inherent in all psychoanalytical theories and play a leading role in determining how we use and think of the theory. This is in line with the consideration of the role of metaphors in determining what the analyst thinks about the therapeutic action, about what can facilitate the analytical process, about the objectives of the cure, etc., in 'The Map' presented in Chapter 2.

When analysing spatial metaphors, Reed concentrates on three psychoanalytical models that evoke a certain concept of the psyche and a corresponding conception of the relationship between analyst and patient: a) the classical or conflict model; b) the Kleinian or the paranoid/schizoid position; and c) that elaborated by Green (1975).

In Chapter 8 (Ahumada), we find a comprehensive examination of an argument that the author has been developing for several years and that has been presented in previous works: the psychoanalytic mind at work. This issue is intimately linked to the debate on the epistemic place of our discipline and to the wider issues of theory of science.

Crucial to Ahumada's thinking, and in harmony with the overall argument of this book, is the Freudian conviction of the link between everyday thought and scientific thinking. In this conception, the analytical work was a part of the scientific work.

The close alliance (Junktim) or conjunction between cure and research promoted by Freud (Postscript to *The Question of Lay Analysis*, 1926) is, as we know, a controversial issue that, as Dreher (2000) rightly underlines, probably requires elaboration. However, as the author reminds us, Freud (1933, p. 174) emphasizes that: 'Progress in scientific work is just as it is in an analysis'. Therefore, Ahumada's statement is consequential in the sense that both analyst and analysand are involved in a logic of disclosures and refutations: analytic interpretations are conjectures in search of evidential disclosures.

The logical concept of counterinduction, developed by Georg H. von Wright (1957), thus appears to be a useful instrument for exploring some of the peculiarities of psychoanalytical practice, which, according to the author, is a counterinductive extension of everyday practical logic, subject to observation.

As clinical experience and the development of the infantile mind teach us, every process of knowledge must come to terms with and overcome emotive barriers and processes of disavowal and of false attributions, usually self-referential. A clinical case offers the reader the opportunity to see these concepts at work.

From the point of view of the theory of science, the author reminds us (as we ourselves have done in Chapter 1) that the term 'theory' covers a wide range of meanings: from a system of ideas very close to experience and to common sense, to what Popper defines as formal theory. It is therefore necessary to distinguish between informal background knowledge or informal theories and formal theory operating as a logic. Wanting to unite all scientific activities under the umbrella of the theory of science deriving from the Vienna Circle and from Popper's epistemology, or expecting all theories to assimilate to formal theories, is contrary to the experience of many disciplines, above all to psychoanalysis.

Ahumada, therefore, distinguishes 'formula-theories' (mathematical formulae) from 'frame-theories' (on the model of Darwin's theory of the evolution of species). The latter are not formalized; nor do they allow for a deductive procedure *strictu senso*. They are mainly a framework for thought that will be subjected to modifications according to further observations.

In Chapter 9 (Zysman), the author proposes studying from a psychoanalytical perspective the relationship between the acquisition of knowledge in general, the formulation of theories based on the generalization of such knowledge and the existence of infantile sexual theories whose relevance to the above process he will try to establish. In his work 'On the sexual theories of children' (1908b), Freud discovers that these theories try to cover certain 'primal facts', such as the origin of children, birth, coitus, the differences between the sexes and castration, and that, moreover, they prove indispensable for an understanding of neuroses because their 'imperfection' is instrumental to the formation of symptoms. This extension of the concept of 'theory' is consonant with the very heart of our research, inasmuch as it structurally connects the construction of theories to the existence of psychic conflicts. It is easy to recognize one of the problems that we tried to deal with in 'The Map' elaborated in Chapter 2 regarding the unconscious ramifications of preconscious 'theories'. Freud himself, when speaking of infantile sexual curiosity in 'Leonardo da Vinci' (1910a), authorizes the author of this chapter to link children's curiosity and humanity's spontaneous interest in research, knowledge and creation. As we know, the 'drive' that gives the impulse to research has been conceived alternatively as an integral part of Freud's classical theory of instincts, or as an autonomous element, mainly in the work of Melanie Klein and subsequently of Wilfred Bion (factor K).

This widening of the concept of theory coincides with the definition of theory that we elaborated in the construction of the research instrument ('The Map'), to the extent that child sexual theories are 'imperfect' theories in continuous evolution.

In his work of 1908, Freud attributes a double causal origin to infantile sexual theories. They would depend on both the deceitful replies of adults and the child's spontaneous intellectual activity.

An analysis of the differences between the concept of fantasy in Freud and in the Kleinian School introduces the cognitive aspect of drive activity. The author argues that an examination of the ideas of Money-Kyrle (1971, p. 448), who attempted to 'bridge the gap between psychoanalysis and ethology', would be very useful in order to consider human cognitive development from Darwin's viewpoint, which agrees perfectly with Freud's thought on the same matter. Within the scene of postempiricist epistemology, as outlined in Chapter 1, modern genetic epistemology could play a very significant role in understanding the construction of theories and their development.

This chapter ends with a significant section dedicated to the relationship between psychoanalysis and genetic epistemology, inspired by the work of Jean Piaget and Rolando García on psychogenesis and the history of science.

In the final chapter (Tuckett), we return to the research of the European Psychoanalytical Federation, this time to the research headed by the author of this chapter, about the comparison of the methods actually applied in analytic practice. As he reminds us at the beginning of his text, it has always been difficult to determine what is and what is not competent psychoanalytic work. It is just as difficult to decide when this competent work is applied and when it is not, as we do not possess an adequate and consensual methodology for rejecting theories or techniques. The task that the Working Party on Comparative Clinical Methods has set itself is to consider what could be done to overcome the difficulty of defining what type of psychoanalysis is being practised, and how to communicate what one does to other analysts. The methodological problem raised by this task was dealt with by enquiring what reputable psychoanalysts actually do, and by creating the conditions for understanding the presenters' assumptions (underlying models) and methods and comparing presentations in depth. This meant elaborating an appropriate work methodology, i.e. a methodology that would produce statements capable of creating an 'uncompelled' consensus among those participating in the work and, subsequently, among the psychoanalytic community. The difficulties this Working Party encountered in creating an adequate methodology were similar to those encountered by the Working Party on Theoretical Issues. These can be summarized by saying that among analysts there is a definite tendency to privilege the use of abstract and excessively imprecise definitions, together with a certain reluctance to engage in grounded empirical studies.

The Working Party has elaborated an instrument called the 'typology of intervention' which enables analysis of interventions in two steps. In Step 1, *Classifying interventions*, the researcher determines which of five specified types of intervention each of the interventions taken into consideration could correspond to. The five types are: 1) interventions directed at maintaining the basic setting; 2) interventions aimed directly at facilitating a psychoanalytic process; 3) interventions directed at designating the here-and-now emotional and phantasy meaning of the situation with the analyst; 4) interventions directed at providing elaborated meaning of the here-and-now experience with the analyst of the particular session; and 5) interventions directed at providing elaborated meaning of what analyst and patient are discovering, but not particularly closely based on the here-and-now experience of the analyst in the particular session.

Step 2: *Discerning the underlying model* involves identifying where each analyst could be placed, in relation to other colleagues, according to five 'core components' which are applied to the analyst's work. These are: 1) the analyst's ideas about listening for unconscious content; 2) the analyst's ideas about how to further a psychoanalytic process; 3) the analyst's ideas about the here-and-now relationship to the patient in the sessions studied; 4) the analyst's transformational theory; and 5) the analyst's theory of pathology.

Although the goals of the Working Party on Theoretical Issues and the Working Party on Comparative Clinical Methods are different and the instruments elaborated in their respective researches differ, they utilize similar methodologies of research and epistemological formulations. Readers will also find overlapping areas, especially concerning the underlying models (WPCCM) and the implicit, private theories (WPTI). These convergences can be found through a careful study of these instruments in Chapters 2 and 10 and their application to the clinical examples analysed.

Three interesting clinical cases are analysed using the 'typology of interventions', and the author announces some preliminary results of the work carried out.

To conclude, we believe that this book makes a significant contribution to the debate about some of the most important problems that the psychoanalysis of the twenty-first century presents to both psychoanalysts and psychotherapists.

1
Implicit understanding of clinical material beyond theory

JORGE CANESTRI

> With increasing clinical experience the analyst, as he grows more competent, will preconsciously (descriptively speaking, unconsciously) construct a whole variety of theoretical segments which relate directly to his clinical work. They are the products of unconscious thinking, are very much partial theories, models or schemata, which have the quality of being available in reserve, so to speak, to be called upon whenever necessary. That they may contradict one another is no problem. They coexist happily as long as they are unconscious. (Sandler, 1983, p. 38)

The project

Sandler's words remind us of the particular relationship between praxis and theory in psychoanalysis that characterizes our discipline and illustrates its specificity.

The psychoanalyst, 'as he grows more competent' when listening to the experiences that his patients tell him about, does not apply simple derivations of the theories that he knows because he has learnt them, what we have called 'official theories'. Rather, he constructs, preconsciously and descriptively speaking unconsciously, 'theories' or models adapted to the circumstances present in his clinical work with that particular patient. The quantity of elements of every type and origin that contribute to the construction of these 'theories' or partial models is not to be underestimated.

Psychoanalysis: From Practice to Theory. Edited by J. Canestri. © 2006 Whurr Publishers Ltd (a subsidiary of John Wiley & Sons Ltd).

Among these elements are the specific contents of the analyst's unconscious and preconscious, his *Weltanschauungen*, the psychology of common sense, his connection to a psychoanalytical group or school, the quality of this connection and the relationship he has with the psychoanalytic 'authorities', his scientific and pre-scientific beliefs, his personal re-elaboration of the concepts of the discipline, his countertransference, etc. The list could be much longer and is always open to new influences. If due account is taken of the specificity of clinical practice, it can be seen that concepts in psychoanalysis are never formed once and for all, but are in continuous transformation and re-elaboration.

While psychoanalysis in the 1980s speculated about what we call theoretical 'pluralism' and its consequences, i.e. one or more psychoanalyses, and while many theorists of our discipline explored the internal coherence of every theory or model and hypothesized the level of congruence between them, a confrontation with the *reality* of clinical practice was missing. If this had been analysed seriously, it would have been readily apparent that the analyst at work, notwithstanding his declared adherence to a particular theoretical model, was actually allowing his comprehension and interpretation to be guided by what Sandler called partial theories, models or schemata, which were for the most part constructed with concepts deriving from different theories integrated unconsciously.

It is not only a question of the normal re-elaboration that concepts undergo merely because they are being used, inasmuch as they inevitably pass through the meshes of the user's language. A more complex operation comes into play; although it certainly includes this re-elaboration of the concepts of theory, it also, and perhaps above all, includes the integration of concepts drawn from different theories, in a mixture that incorporates, as mentioned above, many other elements of different origin. It is important to remember that all of this usually occurs, as Sandler hypothesizes, within the descriptive unconscious of the analyst. These implicit, private, preconscious theories may have a strong heuristic power and lead to the creation of new theoretical segments. They can subsequently become part of the official theories, or even a new theory or model. Many examples can be found in the history of psychoanalysis – in Ferenczi, Bion, Kohut, to mention but a few.

However, we must not overlook the negative potential that these implicit theories or models may contain: that is, the increased babelization of psychoanalytical language, increased conceptual laxity, the proliferation of the narcissism of small differences. Moreover, a greater integration of the phenomena observed in clinical work is not automatically ensured, and the multiplication of the theories can seriously obstruct the possibility of eliminating rival theories, as happens regularly in other disciplines.

We think that it is important to keep in mind this double aspect (the positive and negative potential) of implicit theories. If we wish to find an interdisciplinary example that has affinities with our case, we could mention present-day research in economics. The *homo oeconomicus* of neoclassical economics responds, in accordance with the theory, to strictly rational motivations and possesses extremely articulated information and decision-making capacities. The theory is consequently normative and prescriptive. Contemporary research, carried out with the help of cognitive and experimental psychology, has redesigned the neoclassical paradigm. If studied at the level of what he *effectively* does when taking decisions, the *homo oeconomicus* proves to have a more limited rationality than that hypothesized in neoclassical theory. His treatment of information reveals a different capacity from that hypothesized, his motivations are much more variegated, affectivity can lead to decisions that violate the axioms of rationality. All this may sound obvious from the point of view of psychoanalysis, but not from that of the theory of economics. The inclusion of psychological factors and the subsequent revision of the idea of absolute rationality, together with the creation of a methodology suitable for analysing what *really* happens in economic behaviour, have brought about a paradigm that is complementary to that of neoclassical economics.[1]

It is important to emphasize the positive and negative potentials of this type of research: the analysis of what *really* occurs in practice – whether clinical or economic – must be complementary in respect to the normative capacities of the 'official' theories. Therefore, if we want to investigate this particular movement *from practice to theory* it appears necessary to work out a programme that could enable us to confront some major problems of psychoanalysis so that they can be explored *within* our analytical practice. It is equally necessary to elaborate a specific methodology that allows for conceptual research, but that also has a solid empirical basis.

This chapter sets out to explain the rationale of the project that the Working Party on Theoretical Issues (WPTI) of the European Psychoanalytic Federation has been working on since the end of 2000, and that has led to the creation of the 'Map of implicit (private, preconscious) theories in clinical practice' (Chapter 2).

---

[1] This contribution to the comprehension of the functioning of decision-making processes through cognitive and experimental methods has been recognized through the award of the Nobel Prize to Daniel Kahneman and Vernon Smith (2002).

In constructing this 'Map' we have provided a piece of qualitative systematic research based on the study of: a) clinical reports of analytic work; b) our own clinical experience; and c) our own negotiation of public theory in a wide range of contexts. On the basis of these experiences we have identified a number of categories (vectors) that appear to us to be relevant in understanding the way concepts are used in practice in psychoanalysis. The aim of this piece of qualitative research was to provide a fresh perspective on the relationship of theory and practice in psychoanalysis. The 'Map' we are providing is a somewhat organized delineation of current patterns of analytic thinking about clinical material, which are either not publicly discussed or are literally outside the individual's awareness.

The title

Three words appear alternately in the title of 'The Map', as well as in our considerations about this matter: *implicit, private and preconscious*. We would like to explain briefly the reasons for our oscillation between these three terms.

Implicit derives from the Latin *implicitus*, past participle of *implicare*, meaning 'enveloped, fused together'. According to the *Istituto dell'Enciclopedia Italiana*, it is a 'judgement or concept or fact that, without being formally and expressly enunciated, is however contained, by inference, in another judgement or concept or fact'. This definition corresponds precisely with the significance we would like to attribute to these theoretical constructions in clinical practice. The idea of envelopment, of being fused with the other, is pertinent to the definition of theory that we present in 'The Map'.

We distinguished three components of 'theory': *public theory-based thinking + private theoretical thinking + interaction of private and explicit thinking (implicit use of explicit theory)*.

Mathematics can contribute to a further investigation of the meaning to be given to 'implicit theories'. In mathematics an 'implicit function' is a 'function that is not assigned directly, but indirectly through a connection between the independent variables and the function itself'.[2] Analogically it is what the previous definitions of 'theory' refer to, as we shall see. These models, or theoretical segments, remain *private* until, as

---

[2] For example: if the function $(f) f(x_1, x_2, \ldots x_n, y)$ is a function of $n + 1$ independent variables, the equation $f(x_1, x_2, \ldots x_n, y) = 0$ serves to define y as a function of the remaining n variables. One then says that the equation $f = 0$ defines y as an implicit function of x inasmuch as, with a fixed value for x (between -1 and 1), y is obtained by solving the written equation. Explicitly: $y = \pm \sqrt{(1 - x^2)}$.

Sandler notes, they find the right conditions to emerge in a 'plausible and psychoanalytically socially acceptable way' (Sandler, 1983, p. 38).

It is evident that what is private cannot be the object of scientific research until it is made public. Bion proposes facilitating a transformation in the analyst 'that enables [internal, unconscious processes] to be communicated to another . . . this process, which I call publication . . .' (Bion, 1992, p. 119). With this project the WPTI has tried to design an instrument that would allow implicit theories in the psychoanalyst's clinical work to be identified and made public.

The third term that appears in Sandler's text and in ours is *preconscious* (descriptively unconscious). In the last chapter of her excellent book *Foundations for Conceptual Research in Psychoanalysis*, Anna Ursula Dreher (2000) raises some valid objections to the use of 'preconscious (descriptively unconscious) theories'. She emphasizes that the use of the Freudian topographical method may be misleading (since it could suggest an equivalence between implicit and unconscious) and supports the concept of 'implicit knowledge', following the observations made by Michael Polanyi, in *The Tacit Dimension* (1966). We agree with Dreher's objections, but think that the use of 'preconscious' must not be completely eliminated, for reasons that will be explained later.

Dreher suggests differentiating this implicit knowledge of the analyst into three components:

> 1. the socially shared implicit 'theories' of the psychoanalytic *milieu* in which the analyst was trained and its respective collegiate environment; 2. the individual thoughts of the analyst that arise during his own clinical practice – that is, his own personal mixture of explicit theories and tentative reflections, which can certainly carry within themselves creative elements and thus contain the potential for conceptual change; 3. the unconscious ideas, motives, and values embedded in the analyst's personality and personal history. (2000, p. 171)

Dreher believes that the first two components allow for conceptual research, while the third would require a form of conceptual research assisted by psychoanalytical methods. The third component would discourage the use of the word 'theory', inasmuch as it would be a question of aspects connected to the dynamic unconscious, not the unconscious 'descriptively speaking' of Sandler. There is no doubt that the use of the word 'theory' is inadequate in the case of the third component, yet one could raise an objection to its *tout court* use in the phenomena we are dealing with. It is not purely by chance that, in the text mentioned above, Sandler speaks of partial theories, models or schemata.

The word 'theory' is in itself polysemous and has various meanings in the epistemological field. We believe that it is possible to distinguish at least four different meanings of the word:

1. A group of hypotheses that are the starting point of any given research. In the group are included the deduction of the deriving hypotheses and the consequences of the observations.
2. A group of all the initial hypotheses and of those that can be deduced from them. This responds to the Aristotelian necessity of ensuring that the logical consequences of the initial hypotheses of a scientific theory belong to the theory itself.
3. A group of pure theoretical hypotheses, i.e. of enunciations that do not include empirical elements (Campbell, 1920). A formal structure of this kind requires rules of correspondence to be applied to a determined empirical basis (these three meanings of the term are proposed by Klimovsky, 1994).
4. A group of elements (hypotheses, models, schemata), more or less clearly defined and characterized, implicit or explicit, that can represent a starting point for the layout of a research if one succeeds in making the group (or, alternatively, some of its elements) explicit. Such a definition would probably not be approved by epistemologists, but is really what is most adapted to the type of project we are illustrating.

Paraphrases and extensions of Sandler's ideas

Sandler believes that there is a 'conservative' attitude in psychoanalysis, the utility of which lies in carrying out a stabilizing function. From this derives a 'standard', 'public', 'official' formulation of the concepts. But we know that conceptual terms in psychoanalysis are strongly polysemous; it is not by chance that all attempts at 'logicization' (Bion, Lacan) have yielded poor results. It is not certain, however, that polysemy is completely negative. In fact, Sandler states that the variation of the meaning of the concepts in relation to the contexts in which these are used, that is, their elasticity, plays a very important role in keeping psychoanalytical theory together and in subsequently favouring theoretical change. Implicit tensions in theories would be absorbed until new and more organized theories manage to develop and are successful. These functional modalities apply in all scientific activities: it is normal to patch up a precarious theory by adopting *ad hoc* hypotheses, before substituting it *in toto*. It is, nevertheless, very doubtful whether in psychoanalysis there are any real theoretical substitutions (following the example of physics or astronomy).

Regarding the configuration of 'sets of dimensions of meanings', Sandler proposes that 'it is also possible to look with profit at the dimension of meaning of a theoretical notion or term *within the mind of any individual psychoanalyst*' (1983, p. 36; emphasis added). This would transform the psychoanalyst into an 'instrument', and the careful study of the analytical situation into a laboratory for studying the 'formation of unconscious theoretical structures' in *status nascendi*.

The author says:

> Such partial structures may in fact represent better (i.e. more useful and appropriate) theories than the official ones, and it is likely that many valuable additions to psychoanalytical theory have come about because conditions have arisen that have allowed preconscious part-theories to come together and emerge in a plausible and psychoanalytically socially acceptable way . . . It is my firm conviction that the investigation of the implicit, private theories of clinical psychoanalysis opens a major new door in psychoanalytic research. (1983, p. 38)

We have just mentioned the alternative use of terms such as 'unconscious (descriptively), preconscious', 'implicit' and 'private'. The above quotation accurately describes the reasons for the direction our research has taken.

The logic (or context) of discovery

Studying the 'formation of unconscious theoretical structures' means entering the world of the context of discovery. In the epistemologist Karl Popper's well-known 1934 formulation (also the date of the publication of his *Logik der Forschung*, extended and reprinted in English under the title *Logic of Scientific Discovery*, 1959): 'If we make a distinction, as Reichenbach does, between a 'procedure for finding' and a 'procedure for justifying' [a hypothesis], then we have to say it is not possible to reconstruct the former rationally.' It is equally well known that this definite distinction and exclusion of discovery from the field of rationality has been the object of much criticism.

Those contained in Thomas Kuhn's epistemological proposals are well known, even though, since he was dealing with social and cultural aspects, matters connected with the history of science and with the coming into being of scientific practice, they are only relatively useful to our reasoning. However, the point of contact is in Kuhn's objection to the effective, real correspondence in proceeding with research using the parameters described by Popper.

In a field that is closer to Popper's (the enlarged framework of the falsifying conception), Lakatos (1976), analysing the logic of mathematical discovery, reveals a certain short-sightedness in Popper's approach. He says that when Popper divided the aspects of discovery into psychological and logical aspects, in such a way as not to leave any room at all for heuristics as an independent field of enquiry, he did not notice that his 'logic of discovery' was more than a merely *strictly* logical reconstruction of scientific progress. He adds that Popper did not notice that the nature of his enquiry was neither psychological nor logical, but was of an independent discipline, heuristics, and therefore proposes an 'intrinsic unit of logic of discovery and logic of justification' as an attempt to understand better the strategies of research in the scientific practice.

Other objections from yet another different and contemporary epistemological area are useful for our case. E. Bellone, Professor of the History of Science, writes in *La stella nuova. L'evoluzione e il caso Galilei*:

> The insuperability of the obstacles [interpretative of the real course of scientific discoveries for those who believe that the development of a science is upheld by rules of the method] has even generated a kind of historiographic dogma according to which the contexts of discovery are so opaque and inscrutable as not to admit any rational reconstruction. This dogma is however the source of pseudo-problems. An excellent example of pseudo-problem can be seen in the thesis by Popper relative to the question: 'How do we reach our theories?'
>
> Popper's reply is that the question is of a historic, factual and psychological nature. As such, it is of minimum importance from the logical, methodological and epistemological point of view about the validity of the theories.[3] The behavior of the individual scientist is, therefore, outside the framework of the real problems . . . But the opinion that the moves made by an individual are without interest, and that only the questions about the logical value of the solution are worthy of serious argumentation, cannot be reconciled with an evolutionary Darwinian type of hypothesis. If we admit that knowledge evolves, we must also accept that the selection acts precisely on what an individual does, that the appearance of a new solution – of a mutant – does not obey a preconstituted and valid form of logic for each evolutionary process, and that the affirmation or otherwise of the mutant depends on what, *a posteriori*, we individuate in terms of adaptation. (2003, pp. xxii and xxiii)

From a heuristic viewpoint, the intrinsic unity of the logic of discovery and the logic of justification proves to be essential: 'concepts in growth are vehicles of progress . . . the most exciting developments come from the exploration of the boundary zones of concepts, from their tension and from the differentiation of previously undifferentiated concepts' (Bellone, 2003, p. 183). The operation of submitting a concept to

---

[3] Bellone refers to Popper's *Realism and the Aim of Science* from the Postscript to *The Logic of Scientific Discovery* (W. W. Bartley (ed.), Part I, Ch. 1, 3, II), where we read: 'In fact, the historic, factual and psychological question, "How do we reach our theories?" although it may be fascinating, is irrelevant for the logical, methodological and epistemological question of validity.' Notwithstanding this, Popper quotes in a note 'an extremely interesting book on the topic', J. Hadamard's *The Psychology of Invention in the Mathematical Field* by (Princeton, NJ: Princeton University Press, 1945).

tension proceeds surreptitiously, also widening the scientist's reference system.

This situation is very similar to that described when speaking about implicit theories in psychoanalysis. In clinical work, the analyst, driven by situations of participation when working with the patient, and under the pressure of problems that may derive from the particular pathological conditions of a certain analysand or as result of personal restructurizations, submits to tension those concepts arising from official theories. Conceptual change, or the creation of new concepts that result from the interaction of official theories with one's own, can remain at the preconscious level or manifest themselves to consciousness. Moreover, they can prove to be totally inadequate or can acquire a theoretical dignity and become part of the official theories.

On the one hand, this description reflects more faithfully the way in which an analyst truly proceeds; on the other, it introduces heuristic elements for our consideration. An anti-dogmatic epistemology should favour those theories and programmes that display a greater heuristic power, and from this point of view, Freud seems to offer a good example.

But why choose Lakatos's book on the 'logic of mathematical discovery' to consolidate arguments in the psychoanalytical field? Mathematics is a non-empirical discipline, even though Lakatos's thesis is that it can become 'quasi-empirical' through the method of demonstrations-confutations. The greater and most important part of what occurs takes place in the mind of the mathematician. This would allow us to find analogies with our work that is always already a shared mental experiment. But what makes mathematics suitable for contemplation about our discipline is, on this occasion, the attention that mathematicians, unlike other scientists – including psychoanalysts – have paid to creative work and invention, to all that happens in the mind of the mathematician when he does mathematics. What happens on a mental level is subsequently matched on a level of 'objective' heuristics; it establishes a dialectical relationship with the methodology of research and with its products.

'Normally scientists do not consider the motivations that inspire scientific activity, or the aesthetic basis of such activities, as being arguments worthy of serious discussion' (Chandrasekhar, 1987, quoted Giorello, 1993). There are exceptions, and some of these belong to the history of mathematics. In 1937, at the Centre de Synthèse in Paris, the 'Neuvième Semaine de Synthèse' was held and dedicated to *L'Invention*. Among the speakers those who stood out were Paul Valéry for poetic invention, Louis de Broglie for experimental sciences, Edouard Claparède for psychology and Jacques Hadamard for mathematics. It was Hadamard – defined by G. H. Hardy as 'the living legend of mathematics', outstanding not only for his vast output in the field of mathematics, but also for his dedication to civil and political teaching – who, in exile in the United States, produced a book that is a classic on the subject: *The Psychology of Invention in the Mathematical Field* (1945), written in English (and mentioned by Popper, see fn. 3).

In his reflections Hadamard was inspired by the work of another French mathematical genius, Henri Poincaré, who also stimulated Bion. Hadamard writes: 'This study, like any other thing that can be written about mathematical invention, has been inspired by the well-known conference held by Poincaré at the Société de Psychologie de Paris'. This was 'L'Invention mathématique', subsequently published as Chapter III in *Science et méthode* (1908), which begins: 'The genesis of mathematical invention is a problem that must stimulate much interest in the psychologist.' It is difficult not to give in to the temptation to recommend the reading of this chapter to psychoanalysts.

Elected to the Collège de France, Hadamard writes: 'following scientific fantasy in absolute freedom: this is the tradition and the honor of the Collège de France'. This suggested direction is not very different from that written by Freud (1933) for the obituary of Sandor Ferenczi in reference to 'Thalassa': 'It is a vain attempt to seek today to distinguish what can be accepted as a genuine discovery, from that which tries, through scientific fantasy (*wissenschaftlichen Phantasie*), to be future knowledge'; or from the observations on the fantasies to be hosted, which appear in his letters of 1915.

Hadamard sets himself the task of constructing a credible mathematical heuristics, derived from observations – some guided, others spontaneous – of the mental activity of mathematicians at work. He recognizes that he is indebted to Raymond de Saussure, who provided him with other useful indicators and who informed him about the unconscious work and on the possibilities of 'educating the unconscious through the very powerful means supplied by the methods of psychoanalysis' (1945, p. 51).

Poincaré was already certain that the creative mathematical process requires the contribution of a lengthy unconscious effort. In the personal testimony that he provides about the theory of groups and the Fuchsian functions (an understanding of the problem is of little importance, but Poincaré's description of how he came to discover it is fascinating) he writes: 'What strikes one at first is this semblance of sudden illuminations, evident signs of a previous lengthy unconscious effort; the role of this unconscious effort in mathematical invention seems to me to be indisputable' (1908, p. 40). This is part of a *stage of preparation* that reveals a deep dialectic between conscious and unconscious work. Once again, Poincaré provides a metaphor for the possible combination of ideas by comparing them with the 'hooked atoms of Epicurus', which pass from immobility to 'flashing through space in various directions' and do not return to the state of primitive repose, but continue their dance. Hadamard emphasizes that 'In these new combinations . . . lie the possibilities of apparently spontaneous inspirations' (1945, p. 43). It is an activity that has its roots in the work of the unconscious and that can be assimilated to the 'surreptitious' activity of Lakatos, to the 'tacit' activity of Polanyi or to the 'combinatory play' of Einstein. It is the controlled news of this activity provided by mathematicians that allows for the 'rational reconstructions' outlined by Lakatos in the epistemological field.

Something similar could be suggested in relation to the implicit theories in psychoanalysis: to try to explore the 'combinatory play' that develops in the reverberation of the three levels of the Freudian topic. The analyst's capacity to allow for and favour an adequate, effective and creative 'combinatory play' proves to be essential for orienting the work of transformation in the analytic process.

Hadamard says that the discovery cannot be the result of mere chance in itself, even though he admits that chance will inevitably intervene in the process; it is the 'combinatory play' of the instances that will be decisive. Polanyi (1958) speaks of 'intellective passions' (Bion's K), which constitute 'the force that drives us to abandon an accepted interpretative schematism and commits us, by overcoming logical discontinuity, to use a new schematism' (quoted by Giorello, 1976, p. xiii). This dynamism also orients the work of transformation that the analyst manages (or not) to promote in the analytic process.

All these considerations lead to the conclusion that knowledge has a personal component which, as heuristics demands, is the result of the combinatory play of the three psychic instances (unconscious, preconscious and conscious) and is metabolized in the 'space of proximal development' of Vygotskij or in the 'preconscious' of Freud and Sandler, and an intersubjective component that survives every process of objectivization.

We could enrich these epistemological quotations with others from the vast production of 'post-empiricism' epistemology, but we can also consider the problem from other points of view. Taking into due account the nature of the object we are dealing with, it is reasonable to observe it from several viewpoints. Sandler himself promoted the study of psychoanalytical theories in the light of a 'developmental-historical dimension'. But we do not think it necessary to prolong our discourse further because, at this point, we are not involved in an epistemological discussion, but wish only to offer small support to the direction that our research has taken and to its legitimacy.

Research strategies

The earlier quotation from Lakatos mentions the existence of research strategies in scientific disciplines, and also in the mind and the projects of single individuals. It is possible to distinguish some of the main lines of the strategy followed by Freud during the course of his long career. We have attempted to specify some of the parameters we considered relevant on previous occasions (Canestri, 1993; 1999; 2003) and we will not propose them again here. We will only mention, as an example, Freud's much-quoted letter to Ferenczi of July 1915, since this alone summarizes a formulation of research in harmony with what we are saying. Freud writes: 'Dear friend, in the preparation of *Übersicht der Übertragungsneurosen* [a text that the careful research work of Grubrich-Simitis (1986) has returned to us] I find myself dealing with fantasies that disturb me and it will be difficult for them to have any result for the public' (see the relationship between the fantasy that comes to light and its 'publication', mentioned above). In a subsequent letter he writes: 'I must state that one must not make theories; they must turn up like an unexpected guest in the house, while one is busy enquiring into details.'

The normative indication ('they must turn up...') that can be deduced is that the theories have been treated in the same way as fantasies. They appear like an unexpected guest who has to be made welcome. This must be followed by an examination of their effective validity. In fact, Freud describes the mechanism of scientific creativity in 'Synthesis', as a 'succession of audacious fantasy and ruthless criticism carried out by reality'.[4]

Briefly, what is being objected to in Popper and other epistemologists is certainly not their need to ensure that a theory demonstrates its validity within the field of justification, but the fact that the exploration of how the theories are *de facto* produced in scientific practice and, in our case, in psychoanalytical practice, is excluded from the epistemological field.

The French philosopher Louis Althusser, in *Philosophie et philosophie spontanée des savants* (1974), made a proposal that in some ways is similar to ours: to study, within the work of certain scientists, the 'spontaneous' ideas they had (with major or minor levels of awareness) about their activity and their science. He identified, in several cases, the existence of one element of intra-scientific origin (the convictions and beliefs that scientists derive from their daily practice) and another of extra-scientific origin (reflections on scientific practice linked to the philoso-

---

[4] Sigmund Freud (1915 [1985]) *Übersicht der Übertragungsneurosen*. Frankfurt am Main: S. Fischer Verlag.

phy of science). Very frequently these two elements had a contradictory content.

Althusser thought that the first element, the intra-scientific, could be a source of theories and models if it undergoes elaboration, supporting what we have said above about its heuristic potential. If there is a definite point of agreement in contemporary psychoanalysis – traversed as it is by a growing and, at times, unsettling theoretical pluralism, accompanied by an increasing babelization of the conceptual language and a sometimes inordinate broadening of the 'set of dimensions of meaning' that Sandler spoke about – it can be identified in the awareness of the complexity of our clinical experience. If today we were to enunciate a normative indication in the style and (following that of Freud) from the point of view of our project, it would be as follows: we must come closer, as close as possible, to the reality of our clinical experience in all its complexity, with its inherent and irreplaceable subjectivity, with the use we make in it of our person and of our 'implicit, private, preconscious' theories.

Therefore, the challenge is that of studying a methodology that would help us to identify, in our clinical work, the implicit theories of the analyst at work, publicizing them when possible and giving value to their heuristic potential, if this is the case.

In his previously quoted paper Sandler writes: 'It is my firm conviction that the investigation of the implicit, private theories of clinical psychoanalysis opens a major new door in psychoanalytic research . . . What determines the emergence of new theories on the basis of clinical experience is a matter for further research' (1983, pp. 38, 39). We have tried to move in this direction. The result – provisional and in progress – is 'The Map', an instrument we will briefly describe. But let us first return to the question of the preconscious.

The preconscious, 'zone of proximal development'

In our earlier discussion of Dreher's valid objections to the use of the term 'preconscious' when speaking about implicit theories, we intended to say something more about why we thought it useful, in spite of everything, to retain the term. If we read Sandler's previously mentioned work, together with another of the same year written in collaboration with A.-M. Sandler, 'The 'second censorship', the 'three-box model' and some technical implications', we can see that the authors are attempting to articulate the Freudian concepts of the topographical and the structural theory of the mind. The second box of the three-box model includes 'parts of the unconscious (structural) ego . . . as well as unconscious parts of the superego; and it [the second box] embraces the Preconscious system of the topographical model' (1983, p. 420). This second box is charged with the elaboration of the derivatives of the unconscious. The preconscious fantasies-theories sink their roots in the dynamic unconscious, even though they obey the rules of the secondary process. This system has a high tolerance of contradictions, even though it is not of the same nature as the non-contradiction that dominates in the unconscious. The system is oriented towards the present in its search for adaptive solutions, and is defined as the creative centre of fantasies and thoughts.

We have utilized a concept introduced by Vygotskij, in *Thought and Language* (1934, the same year as the publication of Popper's book), in relation to the conceptualization of the role of the preconscious relative to the implicit theories (Canestri, 2003). This is the concept of the 'zone of proximal development'. In short, Vygotskij thinks that in infantile cognitive development, the interaction between the spontaneous concepts of the child and the non-spontaneous (learned) ones is relevant – contrary to what Piaget maintains. The zone of proximal development represents the area of what the child can do with the collaboration of the adult in the process of learning.

Vygotskij's thesis is that concepts, including scientific ones, are developed, that between the spontaneous representations and the acquired ones there is a reciprocal influence, and that the psychic process in question is complex, continuous and is not concluded with the assimilation or the formation of a concept. What is valid for the cognitive development of the child is just as significant for the cognitive life of the adult. At the cognitive level this 'transitive' area, of *conceptual negotiation*, has many affinities with the role attributed by Sandler to the preconscious as 'creator' of part-theories, models and schemata.

It is interesting to note the difference between Vigotskij's thesis (and the one we ourselves are proposing) and Popper's about the existence of world 1, world 2 and world 3. World 1 includes physical objects or states, world 2 corresponds to mental states and world 3 is that of objective thought contents, especially scientific thought. Popper (1979) believes that there is a very important feedback effect from world 3 to world 2, but without there being a reciprocal effect from world 2 to world 3. This explains why he cannot include heuristics within the field of rational research.

Landscape and/or mapping

It is important to point out the need to organize knowledge along dimensions, however artificial these might appear at first sight. There can be no observation without classification, so in order to report our observations we have adopted a categorization that we use as a heuristic and that has no status beyond that. This is why in our 'Map' we have included six 'vectors' (explained in detail in Chapter 2) that organize the various theoretical and motivational elements and the structures of knowledge: topographical, conceptual, action, object relations of knowledge, coherence versus contradiction, and developmental. The risk, as always, is of reification, i.e. that our topographical vector, used to describe an aspect of implicit theory in terms of the degree of consciousness, may suddenly be considered as if it were something real.

'Landscape' and 'mapping' are two terms mentioned in 'The Map'. In the vector regarding Action (which considers what the analyst actually does in listening, formulating and articulating an interpretation), we try to describe the difference between making 'landscapes' and 'maps'. In the psychoanalytic process 'The Map' could be conceived as 'finding' the old theory in the material, or as applying the known theory to the material. The landscape could be thought of in terms of creating implicit theory in the relationship with the patient, preconsciously (descriptively unconsciously) using the stimulus that the patient produces in the unconscious thinking of the analyst. From this point of view, a map is public or official theory, and a landscape is implicit or private theory. However, from what we have said, it is evident that we conceive these two organizations as being interdependent, reciprocally influencing each other. A smooth passage from one organization to the other could be the sign of a secure and flexible structure of the mind of the analyst at work.

In order to survey the metaphorical landscape of the analyst in his clinical practice we have created 'The Map'. We believe it can be used in the analysis of sessions, and that it is particularly useful in training candidates and in the ongoing training of analysts. We can affirm that, based on our experience, it is useful both for the examination of implicit theories and for proceeding towards a comparison of the different 'official' models and a deepening of the 'set of meanings' of the concepts used by the analyst.

From our experience of applying this instrument in many working groups, seminars and congresses, we think that it is sufficiently flexible and open to the continuous inclusion of new parameters. This has in fact already happened: 'The Map' grows every time it is applied. It is the result, always provisional, of continuous 'work in progress'.

For the same reason it is difficult to recognize an author of 'The Map'. All of those who in one way or another have participated in the discussions, workshops, seminars and email exchanges or who have written reports on the meetings in which it was used have contributed to it. From this point of view, we can consider that one of the objectives of this project – creating a dialogue between colleagues from different societies who are interested in producing something in common – has already partly been achieved.

Acknowledgements

My personal thanks, as Chair of this project, go to all those who have collaborated in its growth. They are so many that I cannot name them all. I would, however, like to thank in particular the consultants, Werner Bohleber, Paul Denis (previously Gilbert Diatkine) and Peter Fonagy. Without their collaboration, intelligence, knowledge and friendship, none of this would have taken shape.

2
The map of private (implicit, preconscious) theories in clinical practice

JORGE CANESTRI, WERNER BOHLEBER, PAUL DENIS and PETER FONAGY

As we demonstrated in Chapter 1, we have explicit or public theories in our minds implicitly, and so we have trouble separating the two levels. We would therefore like to propose a more accurate definition of this reality: a *three-component model of theory*.

> Theory = public theory-based thinking + private theoretical thinking + interaction of private and explicit thinking (implicit use of public theory)

We are charting the private aspects of theoretical work, in which we include both entirely private theories and the way public theory is integrated into an analyst's daily work. This work is influenced by private theories with a range of origins, and private theories are influenced in turn by public theories. A better term than private theory might be 'live theory' or 'lived theory'. It is descriptively not conscious. For the most part, private or implicit theories could be conscious or preconscious, but preconscious theories have unconscious influences.

Psychoanalysis: From Practice to Theory. Edited by J. Canestri. © 2006 Whurr Publishers Ltd (a subsidiary of John Wiley & Sons Ltd).

Our preconscious ability to let colleagues and authors come into our minds gives us the opportunity to check key questions, such as the oedipal situation, the function of the working ego of the analyst, etc.

Private theory could be conceptualized as play, like a transitional tool, a way of playing for the patient, but also as a metaphor for what we are doing when we are working.

The study of the analyst's clinical activity through the application of this instrument ('The Map') has entailed the accurate analysis of a great quantity of clinical material carried out with the collaboration and feedback of the analysts who provided the material.

The analysis of any reality requires the use of categories. We outlined six different categories – 'vectors' – in order to trace some trajectories along which to organize our research. These vectors are not completely independent of each other; in fact, many of the elements found by applying one can be found while applying another. It is essential to remember that the function of the vectors is heuristic and that they have *no* specific status outside this function. This avoids the temptation to reify the vectors by attributing to them an existence outside their purely methodological and operative function. The conceptual dimensions that the vectors cover are present in clinical practice, from which we started in order to outline them.

It is also important to remember that 'The Map' is an instrument that is open to integration. This is directly related to the fact that it was constructed by analysing real clinical material reported by the analysts, not from preconceptions about how things *should have been*, but how they really were. Consequently, the quantity of parameters taken into consideration may increase according to what is being observed in clinical practice. To make these pages more intelligible and understandable, we have avoided describing all the items that we have identified in each vector and have chosen to use a narrative style.

Topographical vector (three-box model)

This vector deals with the different levels (conscious, preconscious and unconscious) at which theoretical thinking takes place. We can presume that at the conscious level the analyst's implicit or private theories are well formed and could be enunciated, but they are not publicly recognized.

Conscious but not public

This item refers to all the changes that a theory or a technique undergoes through time, and to the differences that are revealed in theories and techniques according to the geographical region in which they are applied. A British Kleinian, a Latin American Kleinian or a North American Kleinian may present variations that are easily recognizable although not expressed. This applies to other theoretical currents too.

Some private theories may be accepted by an analyst, but he or she would not acknowledge them publicly. One example is the supportive action of the analyst, an action that is very frequent but is rarely expressed, probably because the analyst would consider it not very analytical and closer to a form of psychotherapy (secret supportive therapists).

Preconscious theories and theorization

Preconscious theories and theorization refer to a complex subjective activity that includes a wide variety of elements, ranging from those concerning the analyst's self-understanding to the entire system of values, also culturally conditioned, to which the analyst implicitly refers. We will mention some of these elements at work.

1. Like all human beings, the analyst uses what we can call 'common-sense psychology'. In a sense, psychoanalysis is a scientific theory of self-understanding. Analyst and patient share a basic agreement about the fact that they are attempting to communicate; they are not carrying out a simultaneous translation or decoding of unconscious contents, but are using a common way of thinking about human subjectivity. Paradoxically, the value and role of this common-sense psychology becomes evident when it is not being used. If the comprehension of the theory is 'concrete' and is communicated to the patient without respecting the patient's naïve understanding of the mind, the sessions are dominated by jargon replacing interpretations. If the common-sense theory of the mind is absent, the mind will appear to be working like a machine (mechanical interpretations). Maximizing the analyst's capacity for understanding the patient's understanding (a capacity theorized by Faimberg (1996) with the concept of listening to the patient's listening) goes in the opposite direction. When an analyst loses his listening-to-listening capacity we are faced with a sure sign of an analyst in trouble.

J. O. Wisdom (1967) spoke about 'home truths' that are impregnated by the assumptions of one's native culture. Common-sense psychology is culturally bound and there can be a split between two ways of thinking, one linked to common-sense psychology, the other to scientific theories. Differing models of development can constitute a frequent example: simple models of linear development that can be attributed to a common-sense psychology interfere with the comprehension and use of scientific models that are more complex and also more likely.

2. The 'setting' that the analyst proposes for accomplishing his work, in its turn, is included in a more ample setting. J.-L. Donnet (1995) called this structure *Frame of the Frame*. Ideological restrictions or implicit values of one's culture that are not dystonic may be incorporated without the deriving unconscious presuppositions being perceived. The list of these elements can be extremely long. Some of the most frequent that deserve mention are:

- Psychiatric or psychological training. The psychopathology described by psychiatry has no linear correspondence with that hypothesized by psychoanalysis. However, changes in the psychopathological orientation in psychiatry have more influence on psychoanalysis and have more adherents in some countries than in others.
- Political factors may be relevant, especially in post-dictatorships and in psychoanalytic societies that were created by people involved in different ways with a dictatorship. The history of psychoanalytical societies is usually of great importance regarding the transgenerational transmission of psychoanalysis.
- The implicit relationship to common law changes from one country to another. This has been studied in relation to confidentiality, reimbursements, sexual abuse and other issues, and may impact on how closed or open a psychoanalytic institution might be to the society as a whole.
- There are cultural standards that could generate boundary violations if not respected: handshaking, the use of first-third person or first-second person speaking between analyst and patient in those languages that allow this variation.
- Religious ideas could be very important. Could analytic neutrality be compromised if the analyst is an orthodox or fundamentalist? Has a very strong religious affiliation any influence in the way we listen to our patients, especially when the material regards issues that could be in conflict with the analyst's religious affiliation, such as abortion, euthanasia, etc.?

3. The analyst may use 'borrowed' concepts from other psychoanalytic groups, for example Kleinian analysts adopting defence analysis ideas or ego psychologists adopting views of the self derived from James, Mead or Erickson. Making use of borrowed concepts may be simple enough for some analysts and very difficult for others. Some may avoid using certain concepts of a theory because of loyalty to a current of thought, even if such concepts would be useful on a specific occasion. The theory transforms into an internal objects family one must remain

loyal to. Due to the peculiarities of psychoanalytic training, this conception of theory in terms of an internal family may explain, together with the master–pupil relationship and the transference relationships, the rivalry between psychoanalytic groups.

4. Other preconscious assumptions are linked to the theory of the science or to the theory of the language in which the analyst believes. He may be completely unaware of adhering to one concept rather than to another, but these implicit theories are revealed and manifest their influence in his clinical work. For example, the analyst may consider that in his verbal communication with the patient he carries out an operation of codification–decodification of contents; alternatively, he may think that the communication presupposes inferential processes in the mind of both. He may favour a thesis that says that what is essential in communicating is the content; alternatively, he may think that what counts is, above all, what we do with the words (the pragmatic aspect of language). Or again, the analyst could rely on the polysemy of the language and orient his listening mainly according to this.

From an epistemological point of view, according to the guidelines of logical empiricism, the analyst may be convinced that the clinical data are primitives, i.e. they are always the same, independently of the observer. A dialogical perspective, on the other hand, would consider that the data necessarily imply two people and the theories that they sustain in order to confront the data.

5. The analyst may use an implicit eclecticism: he may use concepts from different theories creating a patchwork of convenience. This integration can assume very different characteristics. We should remember that eclecticism is mainly an individual phenomenon and is normally disapproved of, while pluralism is a cultural phenomenon and is permitted. Integration between theories, models and concepts can function in the service of omnipotence and of perversion or, on the contrary, can produce an enrichment of the theory if there is a professional ego able to amalgamate the theory coherently, according to clinical experience.

6. Metaphor plays an important role in both the listening and the interpretative wording. Every analyst uses metaphors, which he creates according to the situation he faces in his clinical work. There are also some common, shared metaphors, which may reveal implicit theoretical formulations. A frequently encountered one concerns the relationship between deep = genuine and surface = superficial. A metaphor of this kind could force analysts into a mental stance of looking behind everything, rather than trying to understand by looking at the surface.

Unconscious influences on the use of theories

The unconscious influences on the use we make of theories are many and, as we anticipated in Chapter 1, are much harder to perceive. We all agree with Dreher's observations that unconscious influences on the use of theories must be perceived through conceptual research backed by psychoanalytical methods. However, an accurate analysis of the clinical material with the analyst's feedback allows us to hypothesize some of the unconscious influences that may be at work in clinical practice, just as normally occurs in supervision. We have singled out three examples:

Repressed ideation (a neurotic quality of unconscious influence on the use of theories)

This item includes the use of *theory as countertransference*: aggression against the patient might be displaced onto theory or we might sublimate sexual feelings about the patient through theory. The patient's narrative may evoke some intolerable anxiety in the analyst which is sidestepped by introducing protective theory to apply in that case. The theory may protect by reducing the experience of the patient's disturbance. For example, anxiety about the patient's madness or paranoid-schizoid destructive tendencies might be alleviated by giving a depressive anxiety interpretation. In this case the theory 'normalizes' the patient. Theory may act as a protection for the analyst's narcissism, when the analyst is not aware of having missed something. In a similar sense theory may function as a response to the analyst's sense of helplessness or hopelessness.

Theory may also operate as superego or have the value of a primary object equivalent. It is possible to hypothesize in this case the existence of an insufficient ego-ideal or a deficit in the psychoanalytic identity.

Splitting of theory (a borderline quality of unconscious influence on the use of theories)

This is a much more serious case of a wrong influence and it becomes manifest in the analyst's action. Despite the fact that we may be convinced of the strength of a theory, we may also not believe it. Although it does not concern an analyst, an example drawn from everyday life may serve to illustrate this. A physicist was working on the construction of a powerful beam of potentiated X-rays. As he was in the process of starting up the prototype, he commented with amazement to a colleague that an invisible ray such as that could penetrate dense matter almost without limit. At the same time, he placed his hand in the trajectory of the X-ray, thereby causing it to go gangrenous so that it had to be amputated. The splitting between theoretical knowledge and the act was total.

Theory as resistance

This type of unconscious influence is very common in clinical practice. From a certain viewpoint, getting to know someone through theory is the only way not to get to know patients, yet it is also the only way you can get to know them. Another method of resistance could be that of not applying an obvious theory because of implications for the relationship, not getting to know someone because of anxieties about over-involvement or boundary issues. (This anxiety might be present in the interpretation of erotic transference or negative transference.) Normally, the use of theory as a tool is aimed at producing something new in the patient's mind. The use of theory as defence does not produce anything new in the patient's mind; rather, it functions by trying to reduce the analyst's anxiety.

Conceptual vector

This vector includes various kinds of worldviews, ideologies, general clinical attitudes, the analyst's implicit theories on the psychoanalytical process and implicit theories of change or envisaged aims of the analytic treatment. We describe next the issues involved in this vector in more detail.

Worldview or cosmology

Worldviews (*Weltanschauungen*), or cosmologies, can be *social*, *private*, *theoretical*, *scientific* or *philosophical.* Many examples of each kind can easily be proposed. For instance, as far as a scientific worldview is concerned, we may recall the ideas that implicitly oriented Freud in his construction of the 'Project for a Scientific Psychology' (1895), and the change of paradigms that have been produced in the twentieth century by quantum theory, chaos theory, biological theories of auto-organization, etc. New metaphors enter into theory formation and in the way we conceive our scientific activity. Let us consider, for example, the incidence of philosophical differences in the conceptualization of the 'other' in psychoanalysis; or the diversity introduced by a tragic, guilty or romantic concept of existence in relation to our conceptions about Oedipus, reparation or the significance of desire in the theory. Arguably, the influence of these worldviews is much greater in our choice of a particular theory than we are aware of, and their implicit presence in our clinical work can be clearly demonstrated.

Clinical concepts

Clinical concepts are used to manage a clinical situation, e.g. envy, false self, loss of objects in infancy, abandonment, depression, etc. At this level it is possible to apply concepts from other groups and work with them, e.g. try to decide between separation anxiety and castration anxiety. Working with middle-level concepts that can be combined is common. Concepts may be articulated in a meaningful way, but it is equally possible to create a meaningless patchwork.

Clinical generalizations

Clinical generalizations may be conceptual, technical or general interpretations or stances to clinical material. Each of these categories has many examples that illustrate them and are of current use in clinical practice. We will mention a few for each issue:

1. Conceptual generalizations include both general 'diagnostic' concepts such as homosexuality, trauma, narcissism, etc., and metaphors that the analyst can use in reference to some of these diagnoses. For example, a frequent metaphor referring to a narcissistic patient can be implicitly formulated in the analyst's mind as: 'You have to break through the narcissistic shield.'
2. The origin of technical generalizations is often linked to the analyst's training, and are applied without much reflection on their nature or rationality. They can be thought of as the 'recipes' of clinical practice and are handed down in the transmission of psychoanalysis through supervision. Heinrich Racker liked to compare the experience of the psychoanalytic session and the work of interpretation to a Viennese cake. His 'recipe' consisted in recommending that the interpretation, like a Viennese cake, should operate in 'layers'; i.e. interpretation of the prevailing defence, of the transference, of the unconscious conflict present at the moment, of its relationship with the patient's history, and so on.

Some of the technical generalizations that we can mention have been taken from the examples of clinical material that we analysed. They are:

- The first dream a patient recalls contains a complete panorama of his problem; always privilege the dream if it is present in the material of a session.
- Any dynamic described by the patient is likely to refer implicitly to the analyst and consequently reveals something about the patient's current feeling towards him or her.

- The patient mentioning a person's internal state may refer to the patient's current state in the analysis and is related to the analyst (broad interpretation of the notion of transference).
- Asking questions or clarifications must be avoided (a frequent justification regards the need to respect free association, not conditioning the patient, etc., but often the analyst avoids asking questions even when he does not have elements for understanding the material). A similar implicit injunction can regard making reference to the external world.
- The analyst speaks in the first person and reveals something about himself, e.g. starting an interpretation with 'I think that' or 'It seems to me that', etc. This could represent a meta-communication of supportive action. The way in which the analyst 'heads' the interpretation can be repetitive and usually derives from his own experience of analysis ('my analyst says this') or from his supervision. Some analysts always begin the interpretation in a probabilistic way ('Perhaps', 'It could be that', etc.). This could imply the wish to enunciate a hypothesis, but could also reveal the analyst's difficulty in affirming something. Others, by saying, 'You are telling me that . . .', reveal an implicit conception of the interpretation as a translation of the patient's communication into another language – that of the analyst.
- The analyst may privilege progressing towards deepening an authentic relationship between patient and analyst or may insist on interpreting defences against more authentic dialogue. He could insist on 'genetic' interpretations as if considering the 'archaic' to be a more convincing proof if compared to the material in the session that appears as a derivation of the unconscious in the here-and-now.
- He or she may prioritize visual images or the polysemic nature of language and may consider dreams mainly in their transference/countertransference meaning or not, etc.

Psychoanalytic process

This item regards the stage at which the analytic process is at and the history of the relationship with the patient in the analyst's mind. We presume that a joint worldview arises with implicit selection of meanings. Therefore, it is important to analyse the implicit in the subjective relationship with the patient – the implicit ways of thinking about the inter-subjective relationship between patient and analyst.

Theories of change

Here we could place the analyst's ideas about what helps to promote change in the psychoanalytic process.

- *What could cause change or be the aims of treatment.* Some of the implicit theories that the analyst might use include: to reduce the violence of the superego; to make the unconscious conscious is therapeutic in itself; it is helpful to communicate to the patient that we are working together by prefacing interpretations; if the analyst informs the patient of the way unconscious mechanisms function, he will get better; if we put the patient in touch with the feelings he is trying to split off, he will benefit, etc.
- *To create a situation where change can happen (safely).* Focusing the patient 'on the mind', as oiling the wheels of change, focusing away from external reality (the external world), to elaborate multiple self-representations for the patient with the aim of gradually helping him to adopt an observing role *vis-à-vis* the self, could help change.
- *Having aims for the patient as outcome* which impact on how the patient is treated. The patient should have real attachments (be able to miss the analyst); the patient should be able to have dialogue between ME and I; a genuine aim is that he should have an authentic self; there is a 'direction of the cure' for the patient; reaching the oedipal stage is essential, etc.

Action vector

In this vector we consider the analyst's actions in his relationship with his patient. We distinguish between 'formulating' and 'wording'. The former means the work that the analyst does mentally to give shape to an interpretation of the material coming from his activity of 'listening'. 'Wording' means the concrete way in which he verbalizes his formulation, i.e. what he concretely says to the patient. 'Wording' includes not only the words used, but also the whole style of the interpretations, which must include the tone of voice, the rhythm and inflexions of the discourse, and also its pragmatic significance in the communication ('how to do things with words').

Listening

Free-floating attention allows diverse theories to play a role in the analyst's mind. The analyst's liberty in listening is conditioned only by his own limitations: personal, deriving from his countertransference, or cognitive. In an analysis, *a posteriori*, it is interesting to single out what the analyst manages to hear (or not hear) in the material, as well as his choice of the 'selected facts' that will help him to give meaning to the patient's communication.

Formulating

Contrary to what happens in listening, formulating has to be coherent and within one theory. We can therefore presume that there is less input from implicit theories. The analyst has to create something coherent for the patient. We have identified a difference between making 'landscapes' and 'maps' in the psychoanalytic process. The 'map' is the finding of the existing theory in the material; 'landscape' is creating the theory in the process of the finding. In the 'landscape' the expression of the private/implicit theories is maximal. From our viewpoint we could say that public theories are maps and private theories are landscapes, but of course the maps may also be implicit to some extent.

Theory may serve to contain the patient *and* the analyst. This can become very evident in some cases where, if theory is not found, the analyst may break down.

Wording or interpretation

Here the influence of theory is wide open. While the content of what people say might be determined by formulation at one level, the precise wording of an intervention is not necessarily related to the formulation work and sometimes it is in contradiction.

One significant issue in wording is the distinction between one-person wording and two-person wording: e.g. describing envy as a characteristic of the person at the moment (a bad part of the patient) versus interpreting that the patient is angry because the analyst makes him or her envious and the consequence is that he or she feels small (as a result of the interaction with the other). It could be a matter of degree of stating the putative repudiated feelings of the patient more or less interactively.

Wording – the choice of words of an interpretation – may signify wanting to be understood versus wanting to be felt to be ambiguous or enigmatic. It is possible to identify implicit theories about the meaning of language and about the relationship of conscious, preconscious and unconscious.

Behaving

Behaviour is more evident when there is a face-to-face interaction. However, as we have seen when speaking about 'the frame of the frame', different cultural standards, together with the personal modalities of every analyst, lead to a certain variety in behaviour.

Object relations of knowledge vector

This vector deals with the analyst's relationship with theories, models and concepts considered as 'internal objects' with which 'object relations' are created. It also includes unconscious relationships to the people who we fantasize originated or held the ideas, therefore generating a psychoanalytic identity.

History of knowledge

This refers to an explicit history of psychoanalytic knowledge and how it has been incorporated. The ways in which the history of ideas is taught in institutes of psychoanalysis and the epistemological principles that guide this teaching determine the internalization of theories and the possibility of a non-dogmatic consideration of the same.

Transgenerational influences

Transgenerational influences, a history of affiliations, lead to more or less successful identifications which are the makers of psychoanalytic identity. The analyst may experience the history of his or her training as a superego influence and may idealize or reject the ideas of prior generations.

Sociology of knowledge

All the ideas that humanity has elaborated can be studied from the viewpoint of the sociology of knowledge. Psychoanalysis is no exception. What are the cultural, social, political, religious and scientific conditions of the birth of a theory? Many examples can be cited, drawn from the history of our discipline and from the history of culture. A careful analysis of these conditionings contributes to a non-dogmatic and more adequate relationship with theory, and challenges any connection to ideas that may have been formed 'on trust'.

Internalization of theory

The way in which the internalization of theories is produced depends on both strictly personal factors and on others linked to the teaching in the institutes and to relationships of 'affiliation'.

Attachment theory

It is important to try to illuminate our relationship to our own theories and to those of others. If we use attachment theory as an instrument, we can hypothesize various types of relationship: a secure relationship with theories that offers the possibility of exploration (it could be easier for those who adhere to a strong and consolidated theory, e.g. a classical Freudian); a dismissing attitude: passion in considering a theory important, relevant or potentially threatening; a preoccupied attitude, e.g. about intrusion of others' ideas or even a disorganization of attachment.

Coherence versus contradiction vector

This vector concerns the ways that contradictions are dealt with theoretically. The analyst must choose at a certain point for the sake of logic, but sometimes he does not want to give up the ambiguity. To tolerate, not to eliminate contradictions, may be a first step in order to find elastic concepts or new solutions to what may appear at first sight to be an unsolvable conflict.

Public where coherence is expected

As we have suggested in vector 3: 'Action', listening allows for a relatively easy tolerance of contradiction. Formulating and wording call for greater coherence. However, on many occasions, the analysts' words and interpretations are not entirely coherent or at all congruent with the theory they say they are applying. The following is a not infrequent example of interpretation drawn from clinical work and constitutes a conceptual 'patchwork': 'Maybe as a child you are feeling much too small to get children [child within, forced into oedipal frame]. Maybe some part of you [splits in ego, topographical mind] would like to be closer to me [prioritizing the transference] but is feeling too small or inadequate somehow [Grunberger, narcissistic injury associated with oedipal conflicts], which makes you angry [Kohut] and gives you a bad conscience [classical, superego]. So you are turning yourself into someone big and rather evil [Kleinian, Winnicottian manic defence against guilt] so you can have control over me and deny your feeling of guilt [here and now].'

On the other hand, on many occasions the analyst manages to carry out a creative work of integration of various theories.

Using metaphors or polymorphous concepts

The analyst may work to maintain contradictions while ensuring that coherence is not too threatened by using metaphors or polymorphous concepts. Metaphors may derive from public-scientific language or from a social-private one. Metaphors and polymorphous concepts avoid absolute or rigid definitions that would not allow the contradictions to be maintained in a coherent way. Metaphors also carry implicit explanatory power in guiding therapeutic action in ways the analyst may only be dimly conscious of.

Creative solutions

Creative solutions necessarily imply a significant tolerance of contradictions, elasticity and the maximum use of metaphors and polysemy.

Developmental vector

This vector is concerned with taking a position on where the patient is from a developmental point of view. It is possible to put emphasis on somatic, non-verbal material, to emphasize a particular stage of development (e.g. libidinal stage – anal/phallic, narcissistic), to be able to shift between developmental levels (or stay the same – paranoid schizoid vs. depressive position), to consider that development is something like a linear series of stages, with the individual moving forward step by step, or to take into account more sophisticated developmental models.

The mental functioning of the analyst can regress from more sophisticated conceptual models to more simple (common-sense) models in his/her clinical practice.

Conclusions

We have suggested that 'The Map' can be viewed as a methodological instrument for analysing the private, implicit and preconscious theories of the analyst at work. The psychoanalytic sessions are the empirical base to which this instrument is to be applied; and the instrument can expand inasmuch as its use allows for new vectors or items to be taken into consideration within them. To the extent that 'The Map' helps to identify the theories or models that the analyst, consciously or implicitly, is using, it has also proved to be a useful instrument for teaching the psychoanalytical theories within analytic training. This teaching modifies the normal orientation because it starts from real clinical practice and ends up at the theories. This explains the title of this book: *Psychoanalysis: From Practice to Theory*. We believe that reversing the perspective in this way helps to identify better the convergences and divergences between rival theories, as well as hypothesizing a future integration or selection between them.

Appendix

Theory = public theory based thinking + private theoretical thinking + interaction of private and explicit thinking (implicit use of public theory)

Vectors
1. Topographical vector (three-box model)
   (a) *Conscious but not public*
   (b) *Preconscious theories and theorization*
   (c) *Unconscious influences upon the use of theories*
2. Conceptual vector
   (a) *Worldview or cosmology*
   (b) *Clinical concepts*
   (c) *Clinical generalizations*
   (d) *Psychoanalytic process*
   (e) *Theories of change*
3. Action vector
   (a) *Listening*
   (b) *Formulating*
   (c) *Wording or interpretation*
   (d) *Behaving*
4. Object relations of knowledge vector
   (a) *History of knowledge*
   (b) *Transgenerational influences*
   (c) *Sociology of knowledge*
   (d) *Internalization of theory*
   (e) *Attachment theory*
5. Coherence vs. contradiction vector
   (a) *Public where coherence is expected*
   (b) *Using metaphors or polymorphous concepts*
   (c) *Creative solutions*
6. Developmental vector

3
Miss R

PETER FONAGY

Miss R, a 22-year-old doctoral student, came to see me about two years ago, on the recommendation of a North American colleague, with whom she had been in psychotherapy for two years. She was short, round-faced, dark-haired and quite attractive. She came expensively dressed, well made up, as if for a job interview. She was cheerful, vivacious and highly eloquent. Her anxiety to be accepted was, however, immediately apparent. We made contact at a superficial level, but I sensed her reluctance to discuss any aspect of her past history, which she felt might risk creating a negative impression. She described a substantial history of past sporting and academic achievements.

She said little about her relationship difficulties, which I subsequently learned were the primary reason behind her seeking treatment. In fact, she has no close friends and has been unsuccessful in establishing an appropriate sexual relationship. There was little to indicate, in this initial interview, any serious or deep-seated disturbance. She seemed to be a pleasant, energetic, engaging young woman, with a determination to achieve prominence in the corporate world. I was struck by the extent of this ambitiousness, verging on grandiosity, but felt that given her past remarkable achievements, and her age, this was understandable.

She was the eldest of four daughters, all quite close in age. Her father was a self-made property devoloper, her mother an ambitious young courtroom advocate who was preoccupied with her career through much of Miss R's early childhood, leaving her in the care of a nanny and a housekeeper. Miss R was extremely successful throughout her school years and was a champion swimmer. She always received a great deal of encouragement and support from both parents for all these activities.

She had some difficulties in making friends even as a child and was offered a psychiatric consultation by her parents, which she refused. However, she had no difficulty in gaining entrance to an extremely competitive university course. At university she made a number of spectacularly unsuccessful relationships, both sexual and social.

Her failure to establish an enjoyable relationship with a person more appropriate to her age, and her sense of isolation, eventually took her into therapy. She had two unsuccessful attempts, one with a college counsellor, the other with a college psychiatrist, neither of whom, she felt, understood her, and eventually she found her way to her first analyst. She valued this relationship very much, but was aware that it could continue for two years only. She preferred not to use the couch, and was conscious that her analyst had decided to address only a selected set of issues in the time they had available. She became very anxious about her examinations, and found him particularly helpful in this regard, but there was no progress in terms of finding more appropriate relationships. At my initial meeting with her, she was keen to establish a similar time-limited relationship with me, but I sensed that her pathology might be more complex than either of us understood at that stage, and suggested that she should think of her treatment in terms of years rather than of months.

Within weeks of beginning the analysis, she confirmed my initial intuitions. This was not because of anything that she said or that could be clearly observed, but more from the overall sense I had of her communications to me. I had, and to some degree continue to have, an uncomfortable impression that something about her is not genuine. Especially when she spoke about her analysis in a glowing way, I was left sceptical or unconvinced. She would speak about the remarkable progress that we were making, or how 'good' a particular session was. In the countertransference, I felt a certain emptiness or shallowness after such remarks, and wondered what it was that needed to be kept at a safe distance by such idealization. I also had an uncomfortable feeling of not knowing her as a person, as if our relationship was at one and the same time a close and a very distant one.

A little later, perhaps two or three months into the analysis, a pattern began to emerge, which clarified this issue considerably. When she felt progress had been made in the session, when she was able to bring material about her childhood or current life that she felt was important to communicate to me, or I made an intervention which 'felt right' to her, she would leave my office full of optimism and excitement. She would then report again and again how her 'good mood' would disappear mere hours after the session, and would be replaced by strong feelings of self-doubt, which over time would intensify into self-disgust. She was plagued by thoughts of being unlovable and ugly, lacking in talent, comparing herself unfavourably to peers and seniors, and envisaging her life as one of isolation and failure. The inability to sustain good feelings, and the experience of relatedness with me turning almost into self-hatred, while not inevitable, became a significant feature of my work with her. Her deep, and to her hopeless, depression was fairly close to the surface of her vivacious and slightly seductive character.

The feelings of shame were most clearly and deeply felt in relation to her body. She has always attributed her failure to establish a long-term relationship to her unattractiveness. The deep ambivalence of her attitude to her body is well illustrated by a peculiar combination of 'dressing up' for her analysis in attractive, fashionable clothes, and then wrapping herself in the couch cover so that she does not have to cope with the thought of me looking at her body. At other times, her pleasure in her good looks and her sense of dress dominate. She often recounts how looking in the mirror can make her feel good about her body, and these occasions coexist uneasily with her apparent diffidence at other times. When feeling confident, she would express contempt for the sloppy way that other students dressed, which was also of course a thinly disguised expression of her disdain for my appearance. Her contempt extended to her view of her teachers and the institution which she attended. Although her achievements and progress, as far as I could observe them, justified most of her high opinions about herself, the inevitability of an intense backlash highlighted her narcissism, and splitting as her dominant mode of defence.

From the earliest stage of her analysis, I was struck by the sometimes painfully denigrating attitude she took to herself. It reminded me of a relationship between a torturing and cruel figure of authority and a submissive and masochistic child, who was unable to appraise reality sufficiently to use it as a protection against such sadistic attacks. I suspected that her early relationship with her parents, now internalized, was at the root of these experiences.

Not surprisingly, Miss R initially described her relationship with her mother in a greatly idealized way. She was her 'best friend', and was devoted to all her children. But it gradually emerged that her early experience of her mother was severely limited; her mother returned to work two weeks after her birth and took similarly short periods of leave following the births of the three other children. It seems that she was hardly a part of Miss R's early life at all. In fact, Miss R has very little recollection of her mother during these early years, but has memories of running away from home and crying herself to sleep at night because her parents were not there when she was put to bed by her nanny. The birth of her siblings she now describes as 'catastrophies'.

Father represents an incongruous figure in Miss R's life. In some ways, he appears to have fulfilled the role left vacant by a busy mother. She has memories of him coming home and making a fuss of her. She also feels that he preferred her to his other three daughters. He sometimes took her to work with him, and showed an interest in her intellectual development. However, it has also become clear that his pleasure in her success was an extremely personal one: for example, he would take her to his workplace in order to show off her remarkable intellectual capacities to his colleagues. He encouraged her in swimming, in part because his own ambitions in a related sport had been thwarted. Thus, there was much to suggest that he was using her to promote his narcissistic needs, and relating to her as an extension of himself. Evidently, at some level, she internalized this perception of their relationship and dreamed of herself as being physically attached to him, as a small Siamese twin or a (? phallic) part of his body.

Miss R, as a child, appears to have submitted to her father's demands of her and accepted these as her own. In many ways, it is difficult to see Miss R's father separately from her sense of herself. For example, when some years ago he went through what seems to have been a severe depressive episode following a major professional disappointment, she also became depressed. In the analysis, she frequently refers to experiencing her body as male, not so much in the sense of possessing a penis, but having no sense of herself as a containing body. She feels 'full', as if there were no room inside her. This may be because there is an unconscious grandiose phantasy that she already has a penis inside her, but most of the time there is a different feel to this material. Strikingly, when she has fantasies about having a baby, this never involves a concurrent phantasy of being pregnant. It is as if she were her father, to whom a baby was born. Her description of her sexual excitement reminds one more of someone seeking gratification and discharge, rather than a more traditionally feminine attitude of seeking to be excited or to excite somebody else. Her homosexual ideation also tends to reflect a phantasy of using another woman's body to obtain gratification. In fact, her sexual fantasies seem strikingly objectless, and her declared desperate wish for a relationship seems far more driven by the acute sense of shame she feels in not having an age-appropriate relationship, rather than a genuine need for real intimacy.

Similarly, in the transference, it is difficult for Miss R to conceive of me as a separate object. She seems to rely on me heavily as an object that provides narcissistic supplies. When she feels ashamed or humiliated in social or other situations, she turns to me, demanding reassurance and encouragement, and a reaffirmation of her as special and superior. In the transference, too, I am but a part of her, or someone with exactly her interests and priorities. She sometimes seems to assume that I have read everything that she has read, that I know everyone that she knows, and that I like the same paintings and photographs that she appreciates. She shows surprisingly little curiosity about my family or circumstances, almost as if she already knew all there was to know. In part also at times she appears to lack the capacity to envisage me fully in any context other than with her.

As working on this aspect of her transference proceeded, she increasingly became aware of a sense of inner emptiness and ignorance of her true identity. She had a dream in which she depicted herself as made out of chicken wire, a kind of wire mesh image. Her associations to the famous experiment by Harry Harlow on monkeys brought up by a wire mesh rather than a cloth 'mother' gave an indication of the early roots of this experience, and I felt at the time was genuine as it was accompanied by real sadness and a sense of loss. We understood this dream, and much other material surrounding it, as manifesting a wish to conceal her inner self so desperately that sometimes she herself loses contact with it. She put to me quite helpfully that she now realized that for her the goal of the analysis was no longer to find a satisfactory relationship or friends, but rather that first of all she would have to establish a secure and substantial sense of herself. It has also become apparent that she is terrified of giving this true sense of herself direct expression.

Frequently, she is able to build on my interpretations, and appears to be constructive in how she takes the material forward. But even this I often sense to be tinged with the wish for appeasement. For example, often I find myself feeling somewhat impatient and wary of her attempts at being 'analytic'. This is not because what she says is overly intellectual, as genuine emotions often seem to follow, but rather my sense is that she is trying to make me submissive and useless, leaving me little to do except agree with her understanding. Increasingly, on these occasions, I tend to challenge her and indicate to her my (reverse transference) feeling that she perhaps feels more comfortable controlling the session, and leaving me to feel the sense of helplessness that is actually hers. However, I often feel wary of imposing my understanding on her, because that in itself may be a collusive repetition of her past experience with her father, when he tried to dominate her with his own interests. Simple empathy with her feeling of bewilderment, her sense of being at a loss as to how she can please me, appears to be at the moment the most valuable use of this countertransference. I attempt to identify the specific reasons which might lead her to be frightened of expressing her true feelings. Yet I continue to feel uncertain about many of Miss R's communications. The interpretations that make most impact on her tend to be my saying that she seems to have no sense of self, of an 'I' or 'ME'.

She recognizes that her current state is like a 'lukewarm bath', where she often refuses to allow either my comments (external stimuli) or her thoughts, feelings and bodily desires to get through to her. Any aspect of her experience of herself which might disturb this state has to be projected out, into me in the transference, with a hollow shell which remains, having to fit around and perhaps identify with, these projections.

Session with Miss R

[*Background to the session*: This is the Tuesday session in the second week following her return from a half-term break when I had been away. In the week that preceded the session she was determined to tell me that she had not missed me and managed, if anything, better in my absence than she does when I am around. When I came back she claimed that she had used the time extremely well and was slightly disappointed that I came back 'too soon'. The day before, there was quite a bit of material about her repeated childhood injuries and she talked of other children who had been physically hurt at a young age. In particular, she described for the first time a traumatic hospitalization. At the age of four, she missed a step and fell down a flight of stairs at her father's office, broke her shoulder and arm very badly, and had to have quite painful surgery in order to ensure there was no loss of function.]

At the start of this session she talked about her current project which involved interviewing children about the circumstances in which they lived. She went into great detail, and it felt as if Miss R was being very repetitive and superior, and a bit boring. She was telling me about the difficulties of her journeys to these families who lived *miles away* and went on to describe in minute detail, but with great intensity, her discussions with the sound recordist about the types of equipment to use to maximize sound quality. She explained the problems of naturalistic recordings – whether digital or analogue recordings would be better, and whether the microphone should be an overhead one, which might be too far away, or one pinned to the child. I found my mind wandering as it sometimes does when she goes on in this way and could feel I was about to switch off. I then remembered the previous session, when she talked to me about her accident with the glass door and described her father's visits to the hospital. According to her account he had visited her regularly (at least every second day and sometimes every day), but would merely listen to her complaints about the treatment she was receiving. Her unhappiness yesterday had been that he could not hear her complaints. I found myself wondering if he, like me, had switched off, perhaps unable to bear the child's suffering, and how she must have felt when her father seemed 'miles away' when she was in pain and frightened. I wondered how to put to her, without seeming to be critical and eliciting a defensive response, my sense that she was almost expecting to bore me because she wanted to prove that I, just like her father, was incapable of listening to and hearing her pain and hence all the material about sound recording. (Of course, I was also aware that it seemed that, in actuality, her mother was miles away from the hospital. But as is often the case with her, mother had not been part of her associations yesterday. I decided to bear it in mind rather than address it directly.)

I then heard her conclude her description by saying: 'Oh I know that this is all just terribly boring for you.' I said: '*I am puzzled about something... I noticed now and at certain other times that you speak to me as if you have no hope of me being at all interested in what you are saying.*' She paused and there was a heavy silence. I had the impression that she even stopped breathing for a moment. I went on: '*It occurs to me that you are treating me at the moment as you used to treat your father when he came to visit you in the hospital. I think you became hopelessly used to him not doing anything about what was happening to you. The fact that you're treating me as if I won't do anything about what you are telling me makes me think that you must be feeling in pain or anxious about something which you aren't telling me about.*'

She was silent for a moment and I had a sense of a sadness in the room. I did not think she was crying but from her movements and breathing I felt that she was very close to it. Eventually, she said that she had had a strange dream. She dreamt that she got into the bath with her clothes on thinking that she was washing them. 'It felt the right thing to do,' she said. In associating to the dream she wondered, in passing, if the clothes would shrink. I wondered out loud if bringing a dream did not 'feel the right thing to do' but it was in fact covering the feelings she was having at this very moment, just like the clothes covered her body in the bath. I also thought (to myself) that the dream seemed to portray her approach to analysis as wanting to be in it, but without taking her mental clothes off. Her anxiety seemed to be that the analysis will diminish or shrink her, and indeed she made *me* inferior with the earlier technical material about sound recording.

She said that she thought I was dangerous for her. I was a monster with big eyes and ears. She had a fleeting thought of my chair, brown, rather old and shabby; an analyst like me ought to have a better chair, she said. I thought she was aggressively and contemptuously diminishing me in her comments about my chair in a defensive way because she felt that I had diminished her somehow. I said that I could understand how angry it made her, that perhaps at the moment she was troubled by thoughts and feelings which she wanted somehow to wash away because they felt so unacceptable and humiliating, that she did not want me either to see or to hear them. I was dangerous to her, big eyes and ears yet shabby and disreputable, and she was in danger of being shrunk and diminished by me. She said that that was not true, that she had learnt that I was a sweet person who never got angry and was very careful about the way I used words, and that the thought about me being dangerous just came into her mind because I mentioned her body. I sensed the seductiveness of her comments about me, and said: '*I think that you are frightened that it is* **your** *responsibility to keep me sweet, that if you tell me some of the thoughts that come into your mind, particularly the sexual or angry ones, it will be* **dangerous**.' I thought to myself that the danger probably came not from the sexual thoughts themselves, but from the threats to the imperative to keep things clean and immaculate in the analysis because her real image of herself was brown, shabby and unacceptable. [Perhaps her seductiveness was also defensive – she felt so bad, brown and shabby, like a piece of shit, and the sexuality was a kind of remedy.]

Apparently without giving herself time to reflect on what I had said, she responded: 'You have no business to go away in the middle of term-time.' I said that it sounded to me that she had in fact minded me being away, but perhaps had been ashamed of feeling this way, which might be why she had not mentioned it until now. To my surprise she agreed. She said she was bored while I was away; she started to feel depressed, ill and was inexplicably sleepy: 'I could not get myself out of bed, when I knew I did not have to come here. I suppose I must have missed you.' I thought that what was being suggested was a partial truth; that she had indeed been depressed at times and unable to use my absence as efficiently as she would have liked to, but I was less confident that this reaction was due to a sense of loss of me as a person. I thought that if I had suggested that she might have felt a sense of loss, even if this were partially true, she would have been triumphant in the knowledge that I had mistakenly assumed that she felt attached to me. Therefore, I only said: '*I think you still feel angry about my going away because it made you feel that you didn't matter to me; and now you are asking, how could I do this to you?*'

She replied with something like a 'hmm' and went on, as if changing the subject, to talk about her friend, a highly successful editor who had just lost his job with a major Anglo-Indian production company. While on the surface she seemed to be sympathetic to him, she concluded her story by saying, rather derogatively: 'How the mighty fall! He is so depressed now he does not even answer the telephone when people may well be pursuing him with new projects and offers.' It became clear to me that what had been so unbearable about my absence was the envious thought that, in her mind at least, I was wanted by somebody whereas she was not, leading to her virtually undisguised, envious retaliatory wish to cause my downfall. I said: '*You know, I think that so often you feel bad about yourself, and sometimes you get quite depressed, because you feel belittled by someone else's success; you feel bad and furious with me for making you feel small.*'

She went on to talk about her editor friend's depression. He was sacked by his company because he was a 'troublemaker', telling them ceaselessly that the films they were making were not of real life and were not of real quality – not surprising that they told him to 'take a hike'. If he had been nicer to them, he would still be working for the company. I thought that this communication in part referred to herself as a troublemaker who might be in danger of being dismissed. However, her apparent enjoyment of this man's predicament made me think that this had already been projected onto me in the transference. I said: '*You know, maybe sometimes you feel like telling me to take a hike because I am a troublemaker who is trying to separate the real from the unreal in you. But I believe you are also frightened that unless you are as you think I am expecting you to be, I might not want to see you.*'

She allowed herself to get uncharacteristically angry with me, and showed her immense sensitivity to this theme. 'Sometimes you are full of yourself, and then I don't like you.' She went on, comparing me to Dr Y, the college psychiatrist she saw for a few months, and her first analyst, Dr X. Dr Y, like me, was an unpleasant mediocre, self-important little man; he looked and behaved like a gnome and was always serious. Dr X was unlike me. He was bright, well educated, erudite; his mind was nimble and he was able to play. I felt that what she perceived as my ability to understand and help her rankled and made her feel vicious. I acknowledged her mood: '*I think you don't want to be serious at the moment because you are frightened it will make you feel unhappy.*' She told me that what I was saying made her think of a German film about a suicidal woman; she noted that she shared the same first name with the woman in the film. She described some of the film, painting a very bleak picture. [I was not sure if the reference to suicide was a provocative one, an admission of how desperate she felt, or both.] I said: '*I think it is very painful for you at the moment; you want to escape particularly from the feeling of being angry with me when you also feel depressed and in need of me. So you try and make yourself feel that you are not really involved in your depression, but both of us are watching a film with someone with your name being depressed.*' It struck me in writing up that the theme of watching other people and distancing herself was not just apparent within the transference relationship, but was an actual theme throughout the session; her making films about other children, film editors, watching movies and, of course, she has an ambition to be a film producer and make films that others will watch. It is as if in her mind feelings become attenuated in this way, as if in a hall of mirrors, each reflection implying another observer and each distancing her more from her feelings.

She was silent for a moment, said 'Yeah', and fell silent again. The silence felt relatively creative so I let it continue for a few minutes. Then she said in a way that seemed to come from quite a real part of her: 'Oh, I don't know. It feels very heavy in here.' She was silent again, then broke the mood by saying brightly: 'I saw a book about coping with depression. Do you know it? Do you think I should buy it?' I thought that she was trying to evade the painful aspect of the transference relationship, for both herself and for me, and replace the therapeutic relationship with one with which she was far more comfortable, the relationship between the book and its reader, or the film and audience, as well as identifying with me as a reader and perhaps as a writer. I said: *'I think you feel that your depression is such a terrible weight, that of course you are unsure if either you or I can really get to know it without being crushed under it.'* She sighed, then said that of course she knew that she did not want to change, she did not need me to tell her that. 'Dr Y told me that already three years ago and you told me hundreds of times.' [This was something of an exaggeration although we had talked about it quite frequently, with her reassuring me that, of course, she wanted to change – she wanted to be brilliant and famous, who would want to stay like her, etc.] I said that I thought that she was in a trap; if the analysis worked she would lead a life which was real but it was also something which she felt was very unpleasant.

She went on to say that she had for a moment been aware of the 'ME' inside herself that I have been talking to her about, but now it was gone. When she felt the ME, she also felt suddenly frightened that she was shutting out her life from being lived. She seemed unhappy during all this. I said: *'I think it must feel frightening that your "Me" (the real you) might take over, and you would lose control and be stuck with something which you don't like at all.'* She replied: 'I never told you but since I was a little girl I have always believed that I have everyone trapped and under my control.' She went on to tell me about how she used to go to sleep every night with the phantasy that she was immortal and could make people do whatever she wanted just by thinking of it. Sometimes, she had the phantasy that her father gave her a magic wand with which she was able to turn people into her slaves and get them to do anything she liked. I was very aware that the need to feel absolute, omnipotent control was a reflection of a deeper sense of total absence of control that she might very well have felt when, as a little girl, her mother, overwhelmed with professional and childcare responsibilities, was experienced as being so dramatically unresponsive to her need to be special and cherished. I have a good sense that this material will emerge, perhaps relatively soon, but in the present context I felt that the anxiety surrounding the repetition of this childhood attitude in the transference needed to be addressed.

I pointed out that she often behaved in the analysis in ways that indicated to us that she still held on to this belief, that she needed to feel that she could totally control me and could do this very very subtly, otherwise I would be a source of danger. She said: 'Oh I know, I even know that you are thinking that I provoked you to say that. But I am pleased that you did not say that the magic wand was the penis I wanted to have – I thought that you would.' This is what often happens, she double-trumps me, maintains the magical, grandiose thought that she has implanted the thought in my mind and I can only say what she had first thought. [Here I am not even permitted to have as my own thought the thought that she is controlling my thoughts.] I said: '*You are in a terrible trap. On the one hand, you feel you need to control me by anticipating my thoughts because you are so scared that we might find the "real unacceptable you" which frightens and depresses you. But another part of you is pleased when I say something you didn't expect, because it gives you hope that the analysis will make you into the person you actually want to be.*' She responded by saying: 'Oh, stop putting your big foot in it.' Although she seemed to find what I said intrusive and rejecting, there was also a relatively rare spontaneity to her exclamation. I said: '*I think you are **very** frightened both of the damage and of the possibility of the change which could happen here, and that is perhaps the main reason why you need to keep absolute control.*' She said: 'I feel frightened of you at the moment.' When it was time, she got off the couch slowly and walked out looking unhappy.

Next session

Uncharacteristically, she started the session in much the same mood as she left the last one. She immediately said that the last session had been a tough one for her, she had been unhappy ever since. 'I hope you enjoyed it because I certainly didn't!' I said that she made it sound as though she expected me to feel triumphant or get some enjoyment out of her unhappiness. Her response was: 'I don't know why I want to please you so much, I don't even like you that much.' A brief pause, and then: 'I don't think I like anyone at the moment.' I thought that she was quickly backtracking on her initial aggression. Generalizing it protected her from my anticipated retaliation. She told me that it had been quite a struggle to get up this morning and she did not particularly feel like coming to see me. I said: '*I think you felt there was movement in your session yesterday, but you didn't feel very likeable when you left. I think you didn't feel like coming this morning because you feared* that *I would not want to see you.*'

Her response was: 'You *must* hate me. I am so boring.' I said that I wondered if she continued to feel disappointed in herself because she couldn't get over the feeling that I would not approve of the real her of whom she felt so ashamed. She then said something that was a genuine surprise to me. 'You know very little about me really, although you know more than Dr X.' I remained silent, wondering what brought about this change of attitude. Then she said, clearly still in some turmoil, that last night she had thought that I had been right about her being stuck and she had made a decision to tell me everything. I wondered silently what the everything was and said that I wondered whether she had continued to think about the 'trap' we had talked about yesterday. She said that she had suspected last night, when I talked about her feeling immobilized (which I could not remember having talked about), that I already knew about her fantasies. Sometimes she thought that I was psychic and could read her mind.

She then gave me a clue to her mood. She was hoping to have a relationship with K, a fellow student. She was apparently somewhat resistant to his advances. She told me she preferred a 'Platonic' relationship, as she put it, to a sexual one. She did not find him sexually exciting. She now found that he had started a relationship with another woman, though he told her that he would still be interested in her and think about her, and would imagine what she was doing and asked her if she thought of him in the same way.

Sometimes it is difficult with this young woman to know if she is thinking of phantasy or reality, a real dream or a phantasy, and perhaps she does not know because phantasy and reality get so blurred for her. But she told me she had a dream the night before where she visited his flat while he was out with his girlfriend and got in using the key hidden in a flowerpot. When K returned he found Miss R already in his bed, she did not see the girlfriend but felt petrified and paralysed, was aware of a terrible humiliation but thankfully at that point the dream ended. In associating to the dream she revealed that she thought that she had called out a warning to K from the bed. In the dream as she heard the two people coming in the front door she had the terrible feeling that she would be asked to leave.

Although the dream seemed clearly oedipal, I felt I should relate to the narcissistic aspect of the phantasy. I said: '*It seems that the terrible secret which you must not give me warning of is something to do with your wish to intrude into a sexual relationship and your fear of the humiliation of being excluded.'* She became a bit evasive and defensive. She said: 'Don't you think I know that!' She went on to tell me that sometimes she felt excluded from her father's relationship with his colleagues, and said that when she was taken to his workplace, she felt a bit lost in the big offices while he was talking with his secretaries, and at times she felt jealous of other women who had permanent boyfriends. I had the impression that she was presenting these associations as if they were the kind of trivia we should both ignore. She ended by saying: 'It's silly because I know that I am more attractive than 95 per cent of other women.'

I felt that in a sense she was clearly indicating to me that her oedipal anxieties were inaccessible because of her infantile grandiosity. I said: *'I think what makes all this a lot harder to talk about is that a part of you secretly feels quite convinced that when K saw you in his bed, he would say that he realized what a mistake he had made and he would send his girlfriend away and welcome you back. I think you know that this is a dream and you feel terribly humiliated when the dream ends.'* I added that I thought yesterday and at other times a similar sort of thing happened between us. That she initially hoped I would go along with her dream of secret triumph, but yesterday we got closer to the reality of the actual her and this made her feel that I was trying to humiliate her by expelling her from the dream where she could at least enjoy comforting phantasies.

After my comments, she seemed less threatened and able to relax a little. She complained that her body had no value for her, she hated it. No man will want to hold it or caress it. She did not know why she was so frightened of sharing her body with a man; after all, it might make her feel better to do so, if only for a little while. But then, men were cruel and insensitive. Equally, she was not sure why she felt she could not share her thoughts with me about her sexual phantasies, when she knew that it would help her not feel so guilty, but she felt very ashamed. I said: *'I too think you feel ashamed of your body and perhaps my analytic distance from you feels like proof that I am disgusted by it. But you are also frightened that I might be interested in you and my possible insensitivity frightens you even more. So, perhaps once again, you just feel trapped.'*

She surprised me by being emphatically in agreement. She said she felt constrained and trapped by most aspects of her life. Strangely, she did not feel too bad about it. I wondered out loud if there was something about this feeling of being trapped and paralysed which both excited and pleased her at some level. She was silent again briefly, then said: 'I knew that you would guess', which I hadn't. She then told me about her sexual phantasy, clearly a very important one for her, of being tied down and forced to have sex with a man who was quite unattractive, while another person, a man or woman, was watching. While I felt that she had overcome her resistance and told me for the first time of a highly embarrassing phantasy, I also felt that she was drawing me into a voyeuristic discussion of her sexual phantasy, in effect being the man or woman watching her, so I simply said: '*In some ways you must feel that you are tied down by your conflicts and I am just looking on, but at times, when a part of you feels you are the observer, I think you also feel quite triumphant.*' In a strange way I thought she also feels triumphant because she has made me tie her down, then she feels in control because she forces me to be the attacker and thus actualize the phantasy of her being forced to accept intrusion.

She then recalled that at school the other girls used to call her a 'spy' because she would always want to look into their affairs. She felt mocked by them, they hated her for being intrusive and taking 'too much of an interest'. She felt that she had to take on this role of the observer from when she was little because there was only the nanny to look after them at home. She felt her mother was quite grateful for her taking on the role of 'inspector'. Although she appeared to recognize her insatiable and intrusive curiosity, and identified with the figure of the onlooker, I thought that her, also evident, identification with the ugly man was at this stage too shaming and unbearable. Of course, while part of her was the one being tied down, while another part of her was looking on, her real self was projected onto and perhaps identified with this unattractive man who forced himself on her. I felt that at the moment her paralysed, helpless self was projected onto me in the transference, as well as the role of inspector. I chose this latter context to take up her anxiety about showing herself in the analysis. I said: '*I think you are very frightened at the moment that I will become the inspector of your mind, and mock you and humiliate you, having discovered your secrets. Perhaps that's why it is so important for you to feel that you can control me almost totally, as in your phantasy.*'

She confirmed this by saying that what made her unhappy the most was that whatever I did as an analyst could not be right for her. She would be unhappy if she thought I was not interested, but was equally unhappy when I was. Triumphantly she added: 'You simply can't win.' After thinking about what she said I interpreted: 'My sense is that you feel unhappy about my situation with you because you know exactly what it feels like, you want to put me into exactly the same situation of helplessness that you feel you are in and perhaps were often in as a child.' She then brought material, obviously not for the first time, about the 'catastrophe' [her word] that befell her when her younger sisters were born, her need to distance herself from the 'family' because she felt so alone and abandoned by her mother. We have been over this material many times and I have become somewhat uneasy about it because it often seems emotionally shallow and well rehearsed. But this time there was a little more depth and feeling in what she said. She talked of her anger with her mother (which she often does), but also about the impact her mother's absence had on her (which she does much more rarely). She talked about having to be mature yet she 'was only two for goodness' sake'. She said: 'I am not surprised that I had all these accidents, there was no other way of knowing anyone cared about me.' [She was referring to Monday's session, falling down the stairs.] I added: *'And it also seems that you knew of no other way of showing how filled with rage you felt, except by hurting yourself, and through that hurting your mother by these accidents.'*

She began to cry as I mentioned the word 'rage'. She was crying quite openly, but also somewhat theatrically – it was once again hard to know how much the affect was genuine and how much she felt I expected this reaction from her. She continued to cry for a while and then confirmed my unease by saying: 'I think I was clinically depressed from the age of one.' I heard myself mentally saying: 'I give up!' But then she added something that I felt was more genuine: 'Unless I think of myself as that child, I just cannot understand why nothing means anything for me sometimes and I feel like an empty shell.' I felt that my earlier countertransference reaction of giving up was very relevant to what she was trying to express and I said: *'I think you are telling me how afraid you are that important things can simply lose meaning for you. It is almost as if from time to time your mind just gives up on keeping in touch with all that is happening to you, here and outside, which is perhaps when you feel like an empty shell.'* She said I was right, but she thought it was getting better. It was time to stop.

4
Discussion of public and implicit theories in Peter Fonagy's case presentation[1]

WERNER BOHLEBER

In his impressive and sensitive report on the analysis of a 22-year-old patient, Peter Fonagy has recounted one session in great detail, sharing with us his patient's remarks as well as her non-verbal and emotional reactions and his interpretations, perceptions, thoughts and insights.

Our task now is to discern in a deductive analysis of the session protocol the underlying theoretical issues that arose during the course of the session, and then consider which were either incorporated or dismissed in the resulting interpretation. In contrast to other case discussions, this will not involve developing alternative hypotheses about the way in which the case is to be understood, which might well strike the reader as strange or at least unusual. I will proceed by first conducting an initial sweep through the clinical material, in which I seek to trace the main contours of the session as it unfolds and to identify the most important theoretical elements that arise. I will return in a second pass by grasping the implicit alongside the public theories and classifying and plotting them on our map.

---

[1] Report for the panel on 'Implicit understanding of clinical material beyond theory' of the Working Party on Theoretical Issues. Second annual EPF conference, Sorrento, 24–27 April 2003.

Psychoanalysis: From Practice to Theory. Edited by J. Canestri. © 2006 Whurr Publishers Ltd (a subsidiary of John Wiley & Sons Ltd).

I

At the initial phase of the treatment it was less the explicit verbally communicated clinical material which allowed for a theoretical assessment of the patient's disturbance than the analyst's perception of the way in which the patient conveyed and presented herself. It was these nonverbal elements that gave the impression that the patient was not 'genuine' and had a problem with her authenticity. Here the analyst has the uncomfortable feeling of not knowing her as a person, of being in a relationship that is both close and yet also very distant. It was the analyst's implicit knowledge of relationships which allowed for this categorization and made him aware of further concepts in the preconscious involving self-concealment and the problem of revealing oneself. This conceptual field also contains the concepts of shame and exhibitionism on the one hand, and that of insufficient self-realization on the other. A few months into treatment, the case material had condensed into a clinical pattern: good moods would dissipate after about an hour and make way for self-doubt, self-accusation and self-disgust. Fonagy understands this pattern theoretically as the expression of a depression lurking behind a superficially vivacious character, a problem stemming from the insufficient availability of the mother during infancy. For his part, the father used the daughter as a self-object for the fulfilment of his own narcissistic needs. In accordance with this, in this stage of treatment the analyst took on the function of a self-object for the patient in order to stabilize her narcissistic fragile self; in this position he was not permitted to differentiate himself from her. The theoretical understanding of the patient's disturbance is then expanded by the Eriksonian concept of 'true identity', of which she is lacking. After a dream – associated with the Harlow experiments – the concept of anaclitic depression and attachment theory comes into play. In response to the realization that her mother was insufficiently available the patient reacted with sadness, which for the first time in the analysis enabled an authentic sense of self to appear. This is described in theoretical terms by the concept 'true self'. At this stage, 'simple empathy' was the analyst's most therapeutically effective use of the countertransference, and interpretations directed towards an inadequate sense of self had the largest impact. Here the concepts 'I' and 'ME' arise, which as long as not understood in the sense of a common-sense psychology, point to G. H. Mead's theory of mind, according to which the concept of 'I' is that which enables spontaneity, and 'ME' represents the socially realized self. Fonagy uses this terminology in order to characterize this inner self-reflexive dialogue theoretically, as well as to communicate with the patient. The patient's condition is again described as that of a self that permits no emotional contact and instead projectively distances itself from everything that could touch her by shifting it onto the analyst in transference. In this context, 'emotional contact' is a clinical-theoretical concept found in theories of self-reflection.

The clinical material of the session proceeds to unfold on the basis of this clinical-theoretical understanding of the case. It is an hour following a break in the analysis that took place a week ago. The patient is quite sensitive to separations. Although she cannot admit that she suffers from them, this topic becomes the focus of the sessions. The break triggers a memory of an accident and traumatic hospitalization in the patient's early childhood. With that, preconsciously, theories of traumatization and its consequences come to the fore alongside those of separation theories. The patient begins the session with a long account of her project involving interviews she conducts with children. She talks in great detail about her difficulties with the recording device she uses. The implicit significance of this material remains latent and preconscious until later in the hour. The analyst becomes bored and is in danger of tuning out. Reflecting on this countertransference, he associatively remembers how the patient had reported on her father, who had visited her in the hospital as a child, but had not understood her emotional state. The analyst uses his countertransference feelings for a biographical reconstruction that the father must have acted similarly in leaving his child alone with her pain and fear. This reconstructive hypothesis forms the basis for the interpretation that follows. A good emotional contact exists pre- and unconsciously between the analyst and the patient. The patient talks of the way in which everything she said must have been very boring for him (good matching). In addition, a suspicion grew out of the analyst's implicit knowledge of the relationship that there was something she was not saying. The patient is emotionally quite touched by the interpretation of a father-transference and of her feeling that the analyst also was not interested in her pain and problems, leaving her with something she was unable to say. The closeness of the session is then interrupted by the report of a 'strange dream', in which the patient talks of stepping into a bath with her clothes on, with the intention of washing them. The analyst interprets this dream as a defence, in that she is covering her feelings just as the clothes cover her body in the bath. With that he touches on a subterranean sexual theme of nakedness. The patient finds the analyst dangerous. He interprets her fear of her sexual feelings in the transference and the defence against it, but then forms the hypothesis that what is more likely to be involved is the desire to be clean and immaculate as a counter-cathexis to her devalued self. The patient, however, appears to have experienced this passage as a defence in another sense, in that she suddenly admits that she could not stand the separation, became depressed and missed her analyst – something she is still unable to express directly. A friend serves her as a side transference figure, whose career failure she describes quite disparagingly.

Fonagy then focuses his intervention on the fact that she cannot openly admit her dependence and understands this conceptually as the consequence of her envy of him and her resulting desire for retaliation by bringing about his downfall. The patient reacts angrily, which can be understood as a battle against admitting to her depression and dependency. Once she is able to admit to this, she flees again a moment later from the recognition of this painful aspect of her relationship to her analyst. Fonagy interprets this as resistance to change. She is able to admit, however, that her true self, her 'ME', as she now calls it, was briefly present and perceptible, but then disappeared again. The interpretation of her fear of losing control if she let her 'real me' take over allows new clinical material from infancy to appear. Her absolute need for omnipotent control over all objects is understood as a reaction to her helplessness in regard to her mother, who was 'unresponsive' to the needs of the child. On the theoretical-conceptual level, it is most likely Winnicott's thesis of the significance of omnipotence in childhood development that surfaces here. In the next step, however, Fonagy proceeds to interpret the omnipotent control in the transference as a defence against her unacceptable self, which the patient has experienced up to this point as an intrusion into her fragile self and affectively rejects. Fonagy understands this reaction to be a genuine spontaneous expression of her self and thereby also an indication of a true self that the patient is trying to guard.

II

We do not have finished theories stored up in our preconscious in the manner of a body of knowledge that we can simply search, call up and apply in accordance with the patient's clinical material and the questions at hand. Sandler (1983), it is well known, has shown that we employ many of our concepts and theories without ever having consciously articulated them. Likewise, Parsons (1992) has described how, in our daily analytical practice, we have in a sense to rediscover ideas and theoretical concepts, even though we already more or less fully know the analytical theories involved. As hermeneutics has long understood, we always already have an initial preconception with which we listen to and absorb clinical material. In order to understand, we must, however, distance ourselves and expose ourselves to the new material in order to deepen our understanding or to bring the material into a completely new gestalt with the help of further, more appropriate concepts. The inner cognitive process involved in searching for terms and concepts, and then comparing and evaluating them against clinical material, proceeds associatively, nested in the understanding of that which the patient presents, and in the analyst's ideas and associations, stamped as well by the respective personality-specific strategies involved. We have attempted to use our map to integrate and plot along various vectors the multidimensional factors involved in these search and comprehension processes.

Fonagy uses his initial intuitive perception to form his first trial hypothesis about the patient's fundamental problem (*action vector, a: listening. The analyst's theoretical perspective determines where he should direct his attention and what he should listen for*). Genuineness and authenticity are not terms stemming from the body of psychoanalytical theory, and the terms 'as if personality', 'false self', 'fragile self' and 'negative identity' do not fit this matter adequately (*conceptual vector: authenticity is a philosophical concept referring to the modern demand for individual identity-formation*). According to current cognitive theories, categorizations such as genuineness spring from implicit knowledge of relationships with which we judge what an emotionally close relationship is and how we are to perceive it. The implicit preconscious theory connected to this could be summarized as follows. The lack of a vivacious emotional contact provides an indication of a deeper disturbance of the self (*topographical vector, b*). Within psychoanalysis various theories have been developed on this issue, beginning perhaps with Theodor Reik's notion of 'listening with the third ear'. As for more recent conceptions, one should mention Betty Joseph's understanding of transference as 'total situation', as well as Daniel Stern's new conceptions of attunement. Contemporary developmental theories have also brought about new knowledge about disturbances in the mother-child interaction which add to our understanding of later personality disorders. In keeping with this, Fonagy conceptualizes the patient's fundamental disturbance to be the 'unresponsive mother', who is unable to grasp adequately, mirror and satisfy the needs of the child, presumably understood in the sense of his own theory of mentalization and self-reflection. The lack of mirroring dialogue led to an inadequately developed or absent self-reflection and to a disrupted contact with one's own self. At this point Fonagy assimilates various theories, which can be seen as compatible here in that they formulate the same matter from various perspectives: Erikson's theory of identity, Winnicott's true self, Kohut's self-object theory, and attachment theory (*topographical vector, b; conceptual vector, b. Here we can see how during the session the analyst integrates various concepts of a middle clinical level (2.b) from differing psychoanalytic theoretical models*). Fonagy rejects other theories, however, such as that of an internalized sadomasochistic object relationship between a sadistic superego and a submissive masochistic self.

The hypothesis that the patient is denying her fragile, depressive, fearful self and has never been in inner recognizing contact with it (*developmental vector*) is the leading hypothesis, which also determines the course of the session presented here (*conceptual vector, e*). Her past separation from the analyst, along with her reaction to it, makes the patient aware of her relationship, although she seeks to deny it. It is finally the interpretation of the patient's various defensive manoeuvres and the acceptance of her fragile self in the relationship to her analyst which is able to lead to an inner recognition of her self (*conceptual vector, e, an implicit theory of change: it is helpful to get in touch with feelings one cannot feel*). This theoretically informed treatment strategy, which can be located in the preconscious and need not be conscious, is repeatedly formulated in various interventions throughout the course of the session. In this way the patient is able to come into emotional contact with and accept her fragile self that is missing the analyst. The aim derived from the theory of self-reflection is to bring about the most authentic inner dialogue possible. In accordance with the theory, the self is conceived as a relationship between two parts of itself: a perceiving self and a real or fantasized self, or a 'ME' with emotions, attitudes and behaviours. This theory provides a type of superordinate frame of reference, into which classical structural theory appears to be inserted, but not without tensions between the various elements of the theory. A different metapsychology resides here, namely that of self and other. The view of the other towards oneself is necessary in order to be able to experience oneself. This model stems from philosophy, as first formulated by G. W. F. Hegel. In a clinical-theoretical sense, this also means: in order to come into contact with one's self, an encounter with the other must take place first.

In all that has been discussed so far, we have been dealing with public theories that arose throughout the session. The course of the treatment allows them to converge, as clinical material and theory confirm each other reciprocally and thereby strengthen the therapeutic strategy applied (*topographical vector, preconscious theorization, b: integration of theories*). At the same time, however, there are two appearances of other theories in the reported session, both brought about by relevant material on the side of the patient, which are activated in Fonagy. He applies them in interventions that the patient either found unhelpful or aggressively rejected. At the beginning of the session Fonagy tells the patient that she treats him as if he were like her father in that she finds him unreceptive to what she was saying; he therefore assumes that something is troubling or hurting her that she is unable to talk about. This is an interpretation resting on the leading hypothesis that insufficiently available primary objects lead to inadequately developed self-reflection. This interpretation clearly touches the patient. After a moment of silence, she relates her 'strange dream', which Fonagy interprets as her covering up her feelings. The dream serves Fonagy as a metaphor and becomes a pictorial image and gestalt for the way in which the patient engages in analysis: she wants to be involved, but without removing her mental clothes. Her fear is that the analysis will make her small or cause her to shrink, like the clothes submerged in water. In the following sequence Fonagy interprets the patient as being angry with him because she is confused by thoughts and feelings she finds unacceptable and humiliating and would like to wash away. He interprets these feelings as sexual or aggressive. The metaphor of the analysis as a removal of clothing, understood as something meant to cover that which is essential and genuine has a momentary seductive appeal for theoretical thought, in that it leads to an implicit unconscious disregard for character and personality formations with a defensive character (*topographical vector, b: preconscious influence of metaphors*). The seduction for thought and evaluation is located in the following strategy: one has to look behind in order to recognize the essential and genuine (*conceptual vector, e: estimation of defences*). Involved here is a preconscious/unconscious theory, which is more likely to be triggered than actually produced by such metaphors. In so far as they remain undetected, they can be quite influential. In Fonagy's case this implicit theory is brought to the fore through the metaphor and leads to an interpretive strategy aimed at making the patient conscious of the sexual impulses and fantasies that she is trying to conceal. This private/implicit theory leads Fonagy at this point into the field of classical psychoanalytic theories of the drive/defence model. The patient, however, is not willing to accept this shift in focus at this point in the session.

The other point I would like to address is located at the end of the session, when the patient suddenly becomes aware of her true self, but then fears that she might no longer be able to realize this self in her daily life. Fonagy goes on to address her fear of losing control if she lets her true self come to life. At this point she first speaks of her childhood belief that she could magically keep everything under control, giving her a sense of omnipotence. Fonagy understands this as a reaction to the circumstances of her infancy: because of her mother's absences and unresponsiveness, she failed to develop the feeling that she was able to control and influence situations. The childhood belief in her omnipotence provided a substitute for the unsatisfied need to be recognized by her mother as someone special and worthy of love. At this point Winnicott's theory about the significance of omnipotence for the development of the child's sense of self comes into play. Fonagy decides not to address this material, however, but focuses first on the repetition of a childhood belief in omnipotence in her attitude towards the analyst, as well as on the need for control which she directs toward him and the fear residing behind it. His theory is not based on Winnicott's theory of omnipotence, which was conceptualized as a transitional phase in the formation of an individual and autonomous self, but on classical notions of defence, in which control is considered a defence. He tells her at one point: 'On the one hand, you feel you need to control me by anticipating my thoughts because you are so scared that we might find the "real unacceptable you" which frightens and depresses you . . .'. The patient finds this interpretation intrusive and reacts emotionally, saying, almost as if to confirm Winnicott's theory: 'Oh, stop putting your big foot in it.' These two theories about the significance and function of control are contradictory (*coherence vs. contradiction vector*). This moment in the session demonstrates what Sandler has already pointed out: quite contradictory theories can easily coexist in the preconscious without our being aware of them. Often it is the patient's reaction, such as at this point in the session, that brings us to reflect on such contradictions. Things were, however, quite different in the theories discussed above about the true or reflexive self, whose differing emphases were able successfully to focus the various facets of the patient's themes of self. The theories interfered with each other without coming into conflict.

I will conclude my observations here, but would like to end by again pointing out that in order for such a deductive analysis to distinguish the theoretical elements and clinical concepts that arise in a session, it has to proceed within a relatively rough framework. It is therefore unable to grasp fully the subtlety of cognitive processes taking place within the analyst in the analytic session.

5
The failure of practice to inform theory and the role of implicit theory in bridging the transmission gap

PETER FONAGY

Introduction

Over recent decades, psychoanalytic theory has become increasingly fragmented. The decline in citations of recent psychoanalytic articles in all journals, including psychoanalytic ones, provides evidence of this (Fonagy, 1996). Not only are contributors to the social science and medical literature increasingly disinterested in psychoanalytic journal publications, but analysts themselves are apparently less interested in the ideas of other, currently active, analytic groups. Arguably, the major psychoanalytic schools that emerged following Freud's death, and that organized the discipline over the second half of the twentieth century, are fragmenting in the twenty-first. This process, euphemistically characterized in the literature as pluralism, could potentially be fatal to psychoanalysis. If present trends for theoretical schism continue, and psychoanalytic writers come to share no more than history and terminology, the discipline ultimately faces theoretical entropy, with all writers

Psychoanalysis: From Practice to Theory. Edited by J. Canestri. © 2006 Whurr Publishers Ltd (a subsidiary of John Wiley & Sons Ltd).

jealously protecting their ever-diminishing psychoanalytic patch. As the possibility of consensus recedes further and further, it will become increasingly difficult to claim a general application for any particular theory, and thus even the theoretical potential of psychoanalytic theories interfacing with clinical practice could disappear.

This chapter aims to make a contribution to halting or even reversing this process by offering an analysis of how the current fragmentation of theory might have come about through the apparently close association of practice and theory. We will argue that the fragmentation of psychoanalytic theory can, in part, be understood in terms of the problematic relationship that has evolved between psychoanalytic theory and clinical practice. Psychoanalytic theory is intended to help practitioners make sense of clinical phenomena and guide interpretative and other interventions. However, the theories that practitioners actually rely on are contaminated by theory-driven expectation, specified beyond available data and weakened by their extensive reliance on induction. Uncritical faith in the scientific nature of psychoanalytic theory may lead to the petrification of psychoanalytic practice and the reification of constructs essential to clinical work. Because of the current diversity of theories, particular, arguably arbitrary, features of clinical practice have become the sole means of retaining the identity of the theory and the profession. Yet in the absence of clear injunctions about the aspects of practice that are genuinely theory-driven, it becomes difficult to know what features of practice may be altered without threatening the entire theoretical edifice. The politically motivated illusion of a direct connection of practice to theory, coupled with the weak links that actually exist between theory and practice, may lead practitioners to be overly cautious about experimenting with new techniques guided by their accumulated implicit understanding of the mind. A rigidly enforced code of practice serves to create an illusion of integrity and unity in a theory inductively elaborated almost beyond the possibility of useful connections to practice being made.

This chapter argues that practice should be liberated from theory, permitting theory to evolve in the context of radically modified patterns of practice. If theory were decoupled from practice, technique might progress on purely pragmatic grounds, on the basis of what is seen to work. Psychoanalytic theory of mental function could then follow practice, integrating what is newly discovered through innovative methods of clinical work. We believe that the database for this enterprise is already there in an implicit (as opposed to publicly recognized) psychoanalytic knowledge base that is already being mined, but chiefly by clinical theoreticians who end up contributing to orientations that rival our own. This pragmatic, principally action-oriented use of theory would bring psychoanalysis more in line with modern, post-empirical views of science.

The epistemological status of clinical theory

Psychoanalytic theory is drawn from clinical practice. Freud described the relationship between treatment and theoretical development as an inseparable bond:

> In psycho-analysis there has existed from the very first an inseparable bond between cure and research. Knowledge brought therapeutic success. It was impossible to treat a patient without learning something new; it was impossible to gain fresh insight without perceiving its beneficial results. Our analytic procedure is the only one in which this precious conjunction is assured. It is only by carrying on our analytic pastoral work that we can deepen our dawning comprehension of the human mind. This prospect of scientific gain has been the proudest and happiest feature of analytic work. (Freud, 1926, p. 256)

The marriage of theoretical development to clinical observations creates a major epistemological problem for psychoanalysis that has been extensively reviewed and discussed (e.g. Edelson, 1989; Meissner, 1989) and here will be considered only in abstract terms. In making clinical judgements and decisions we use arguments that may give us good reasons for believing in certain conclusions, but they do not compel acceptance in the manner that deductive arguments might.

All clinicians work with inductive inferences. Generally speaking, induction refers to any form of inference in which a move is made from a finite set of observations to a conclusion about how things generally behave. Although there are several forms of inductive inference, here we are concerned with simple enumerative inductions, which start from the premise that as one phenomenon has always followed another thus far, we may conclude that these phenomena will always co-occur. By contrast, a deductively valid inference is marked by the fact that if what we infer from is true, it is quite impossible for what we infer to be false. If we know that all poor children are unhappy and Joshua is a poor child, we can deduce that Joshua is unhappy. By contrast, from knowing that Joshua has been sexually abused by his foster carer we can induce that his precocious sexuality is due to experience of maltreatment, but we cannot make a deduction to this effect.

In therapeutic work we are confronted with a finite set of observations, based on formal or informal assessments, as well as the evolving treatment process. From such a sample, the clinician draws conclusions about how the person generally behaves and formulations about why he or she does so. In practice, induction is made not simply on the accumulation of past observations about a particular individual, but formalizations of past cases by other clinicians in so-called 'clinical theories'. We consider theories to lend support to inductive observations because we assume that theories imply that the number of observations on which an inductive inference is based is very considerable and this somehow lends weight to the conclusions. In so doing, however, we are merely applying inductive arguments for induction. Arguing that inductions are generally acceptable because our experience has shown them to work so far is itself an inductive argument. As Bertrand Russell (1967) argued, it can hardly help to observe that past futures have conformed to past pasts. What we want to know is if future futures will conform to future pasts. The argument that past co-occurrence has probative value is merely rhetorical; it proves nothing and can have little credibility.

Clinical technique is not entailed in psychoanalytic theory

It is our impression that psychoanalytic clinical practice is not logically deducible from currently available theory. There are several reasons for this. First, psychoanalytic technique is known to have originally developed on a trial-and-error basis. Freud willingly acknowledged this when he wrote: 'the technical rules which I am putting forward have been arrived at from my own experience in the course of many years, after unfortunate results had led me to abandon other methods' (1912b, p. 111). For example, free association is acknowledged by Laplanche and Pontalis (1973, p. 227) to have been 'found' (reached empirically) rather than deduced. Similarly, Melanie Klein's (1927) and Anna Freud's (1926) discovery of play therapy could hardly be considered to have been driven by theory. More recently, Kernberg made the case for his modified technique with borderline patients by referring to what 'clinical experience has repeatedly demonstrated' (1975, p. 91) and the incidental findings of the Menninger Foundation Psychotherapy Research Project (1975, p. 82). Most technical developments are based on ordinary daily experience. For example, Kleinian analysts have learned to emphasize the interpretation of defence and to be a great deal more cautious in how and when they interpret envy or destructiveness. Most British analysts have come to give priority to the interpretation of affect and mental state in the here-and-now relationship (Sandler and Dreher, 1995), etc.[1]

---

[1] We mention these technical changes with approval for both the specific technical advances referred to and the process by which they came to benefit practice. The negative tone of the argument is entirely addressed at the claims, rival to ours, that changes in technique have been driven by increased psychoanalytic understanding of the mind or improved understanding of the process of therapeutic change (e.g. Terman, 1989).

Second, innovative clinical procedures may, of course, be theoretically guided. If this were so, we would expect practices to have been logically derivable from theory, at least in some instances. Such claims are commonly made (Freud, 1904, p. 252; Kohut, 1971, p. 264). A single example will have to suffice here. Gedo boldly stated that: 'principles of psychoanalytic practice . . . [are] . . . based on rational deductions from our most current conception of psychic functioning' (1979, p. 16). In fact, his book made the claim that the unfavourable outcomes of developmental problems can be reversed 'only by dealing with those results of all antecedent developmental vicissitudes that later gave rise to maladaptation' (1979, p. 21). What sounds like, and is claimed to be, 'a rational deduction' is in fact a hypothesis, emphatically stated to disguise the absence of logical argument supporting it. It is one thing to assume that development follows an epigenetic scheme, but quite another to claim that in therapy all earlier vicissitudes must be dealt with. There is no evidence for Gedo's claim, even from within the self-psychological theoretical camp from which the suggestion emanates (Kohut, 1984; Terman, 1989). In fact, the differences between Kohut's and Gedo's therapeutic approaches illustrate the absence of a deductive tie between the epigenetic model to which self-psychologists subscribe and the technical propositions which are claimed to relate to these. For example, Kohut (1984, pp. 42-6) explicitly recommends that, under certain circumstances, developmental vicissitudes, such as narcissistic traumata, should be left alone.

Third, psychoanalysts do not understand why or how their treatment works, nor do they claim to (see, for example, Fenichel, 1941, p. 111; Fairbairn, 1958, p. 385; Matte-Blanco, 1975, p. 386; Modell, 1976, p. 285; Kohut, 1977, p. 105).[2] Is it conceivable that such a state of affairs could arise if practice were logically entailed in theory? Surely, if this were the case, a clear theoretical explanation for curative action would be readily forthcoming. The state of epistemic affairs is well summarized in Matte-Blanco's words: 'The fact is that nobody has, so far, succeeded in establishing with great precision what the factors are and how they combine with our understanding to produce the cure' (1975, p. 386). If practice were logically entailed in theory, we would undoubtedly have a clear, or at least clearer, theoretical explanation for therapeutic action.

Fourth, psychoanalytic practice has changed in essence little, if at all, since Freud's original description in a few brief papers written before

---

[2] One of the most intelligent commentators on the field of psychoanalysis, Arnold Cooper, concluded his review of the field by pointing to 'a change of view from the earliest days of analysis, when a single therapeutic element was sought to explain the effects of analysis, to the present, when we see the therapeutic effect depending upon multiple interacting processes, none of which can be assigned clear priority in our present state of ignorance' (1989, p. 24).

the First World War (Freud, 1912a; 1912b; 1913a). The extensive supervision based on reported psychotherapeutic process, which forms the core part of psychoanalytic training, serves to ensure that psychoanalysts, at least in the course of training, adhere relatively closely to so-called 'traditional' technique. This is not to say that there have been no stylistic changes in psychoanalytic technique, but these have left the fundamentals (free association, interpretation, insight, transference and countertransference focus) largely unaffected. Over the same century, such enormous theoretical advances have taken place that it is hardly practical to attempt to provide integrative summaries of psychoanalytic theories. The discrepancy in the rates of progress between theory and practice is quite remarkable and would be hard to understand were it not for the relative independence of these two activities.

Technique has, of course, changed somewhat, but current technique is far more recognizably Freudian than current theory. Technical changes that are suggested are relatively minor (e.g. the value of early transference interpretation or self-disclosure) and not radical (e.g. using psychodrama in place of free association to reveal unconscious representational systems). Radical technical innovations are seen as taking the proposer 'beyond the pale', as though such modes of intervention could no longer be considered to fall within the domain of psychoanalytic theoretical explanations. But, of course, psychic change needs to be explained whatever its cause (Fonagy, 1989). If the current argument is sound, change brought about through the application of classical psychoanalytic technique is no easier to account for than change following behaviour therapy or religious conversion, and the 'inseparable bond' between theory and practice can be maintained only through powerful rhetorical claims. The tendency to disguise the loose coupling of theory to practice behind rhetoric closes the door on imaginative clinical exploration by fostering the illusion of theory-based technical certainty. The converse is also true. New theoretical ideas can claim acceptance and legitimacy in public theory through tracing their origins to relatively unmodified therapeutic technique and in this process reinforce the immutability of the latter. The slow development of psychoanalytic technique is, we believe, partly attributable to the tendency of inventors of new theories to seek validation for these hypotheses via the congruence of new ideas with accepted clinical practices. The practices are claimed as uniquely effective and unchangeable, at least until a new theory evolves.

Fifth, the thorny issue of therapeutic effectiveness might also imply the independence of theory and practice. There is relatively little evidence to support the clinical claims of psychoanalysis as a viable treatment for psychological disorder (Fonagy and Target, 1996; Roth and

Fonagy, 1996; Fonagy *et al.*, 2002; Gabbard, Gunderson and Fonagy, 2002). There is much stronger support for many of its theoretical claims (e.g. Fonagy, Steele *et al.*, 1993; Bucci, 1997; Westen, 1999), including those related to treatment process (e.g. Luborsky and Luborsky, 1995). While accepting that lack of evidence for effectiveness does not imply lack of effectiveness, the discrepancy may also be explained by the assumption that practice is not entailed within theory. The evidence that exists is for a theory of mind that contains unconscious dynamic elements. Evidence for the translation of psychological theory to clinical practice is lacking.

For example, work from our, and other, laboratories has provided good evidence for the psychoanalytic notion (e.g. Fraiberg, Adelson and Shapiro, 1975) that the parent's experience of having been parented is transmitted to the next generation, determining aspects of the nature of the child's relationship to that caretaker (Fonagy, Steele *et al.*, 1993). There is far less evidence to suggest that addressing the parent's past conflicts in a psychotherapeutic context might help to establish secure attachment relationships with their child (van IJzendoorn, Juffer and Duyvesteyn, 1995). Actually, the theory says little about how knowledge concerning transgenerational relational links may be most effectively used in a clinical context. Does it necessarily follow from psychoanalytic theory that insight by the parents into their own childhood experience would be the best way of preventing transgenerational transmission of maladaptive patterns of relating? Or is the closest analogue to insight-oriented psychotherapy chosen almost automatically by psychoanalytic clinicians as this is what actually serves to define their theoretical identity?

Sixth, as has been implied, it has been impossible to achieve any kind of one-to-one mapping between therapeutic technique and theoretical frameworks. It is as easy to illustrate how the same theory can generate different techniques, as how the same technique is justified by different theories. Campbell (1982), for example, demonstrated how clinicians with broadly similar theoretical orientations differed in the extent to which they adopted a position of technical neutrality, shared their thoughts and feelings with their patients or gratified their patients' primitive developmental needs. By contrast, clinicians using very different theoretical frameworks can arrive at very similar treatment approaches. Kernberg's (1989) work with borderline patients has much in common with those who practise using a Kleinian frame of reference (Steiner, 1993), for example. Both these observations imply that practice is not logically entailed within theory.

Seventh, one may legitimately ask: What is psychoanalytic theory about if it is not about psychoanalytic practice? The answer is that it is predominantly about the elaboration of a psychological model and the way that this might be applied to the understanding of mental disorder, and to a lesser extent to other aspects of human behaviour (literature, the arts, history, etc.). Freud's corpus may be an eloquent example. His technical papers take up far less than a single one of the 23 volumes of his collected psychological writings. The value of theory for the psychoanalytic practitioner is in elaborating the meaning of behaviour in mental state terms, which can then be communicated to the patient. How such elaboration is done, or indeed whether it is helpful to do it, is not readily deducible from the theory.

Practice as inspiration for theory and the over-specification of psychoanalytic theory

Having claimed that, in psychoanalytic work, practice is not logically entailed in theory as is generally claimed, we would like briefly to review some ideas concerning the actual nature of the relationship between these two domains. Naturally, we recognize that it is inconceivable that no relationship between theory and practice exists. Theory orients clinicians in their observation, description and explanation of clinical phenomena. These will inevitably influence technique even though no logical relationship exists between the two. This relationship is particularly clear in psychoanalytic attempts to provide nosologies, or classification systems for psychological disorders (e.g. A. Freud, 1965; Kernberg, 1989). Such categories are evidently theory-driven and are commonly used to construct 'models' or analogies either to suggest or to rationalize therapeutic principles. Models are also used to draw likely inferences to therapeutic interventions. Models of development, models of the mind and models of disorder have all been used in this way. It should be clearly stated that these are common-sense inductive arguments rather than formal deductions. They may have 'face validity', but are not compelling.

As psychoanalysts we have often made the mistake of assuming that we were doing more than model construction – that our practice is theory-based. The price to pay for such an assumption may be the petrification of practice. In the absence of clear injunctions about the aspects of practice that are genuinely theory-driven, it becomes difficult to know which aspects of practice are grounded in valid theories, and which may be dispensed with. For example, if on the basis of Freud's structural model of the mind (Freud, 1923) it is suggested that psychic change may be attained only by changes in the patient's defences or their strengthening (Fenichel, 1945), then all interventions which do not entail one of these two modalities must be ruled out of the psychoanalytic clinical armamentarium. This was the classical Anna Freudian position taken in relation to Melanie Klein's so-called 'deep' or 'direct' interpretations of unconscious wishes (King and Steiner, 1991). Yet the rationale for this technical stricture rests in the hydraulic metaphor of early Freudian thought (what French psychoanalysis labelled the First Topography) and is not truly entailed by the structural theory (the Second Topography). This is not to say that the recommendation itself – 'avoid deep interpretations' – was not a sensible one. In fact, it is our impression that Kleinian clinicians have tended to move away from the direct interpretations of unconscious desires (see Bott Spillius, 1994). The burden of this argument is that the illusion of direct connection to theory, coupled with the weakness of the links between theory and practice, may lead practitioners to be unduly cautious about experimenting with new techniques since they cannot know what the theory does or does not permit.

There are obvious problems in the evidential base of many psychoanalytic theories that might preclude a direct relationship to technique. Currently, few standards other than plausibility and coherence serve as gatekeeper criteria to the body of public theory in psychoanalysis. Clinical work is infinitely rich and can thus be an inexhaustible source of inspiration. A concerted attempt to design more stringent conditions for permitting speculations (however inspired) to enter the body of theory may serve to impede creativity in the short term, but may enhance productivity in the long run. For example, what would have happened if clinically-based theoretical papers were required to describe at least 20 treatment cases, homogeneous from a particular standpoint, rather than one, in order to be considered acceptable support for a particular theoretical innovation? Would the introduction of this criterion have precluded important theoretical advances? We cannot imagine that it would be hard to gather 20 cases that clearly illustrate projective identification at work. Some, more specific claims, such as 'projective identification is a behavioural re-enactment in which the patient unconsciously "identifies with the aggressor", a parent, while the analyst experiences the feeling of the child being acted upon' (Porder, 1987, p. 350), might be harder to establish. Surely, one consequence would be fewer psychoanalytic papers, fewer journals and perhaps more multi-authored articles. Perhaps even more importantly, there might be fewer theories, but a stronger link between the theories that exist and the clinical practice that is followed.

The argument that theory and practice are not interdependent appears to fly in the face of the common observation of the valuing (perhaps even idealizing) of theory by practitioners. The relatively healthy state of psychoanalytic book publishing over the past century speaks directly to this. Yet, nothing that has been said so far negates the existence of a close relationship between technique and theory. While there is little to suggest that a direct or explicit relationship (such as theory dictates technique) currently pertains or is likely to be attained in the near future, more subtle, but more profound relationships between theory and practice are possible, and it is to one of these that we shall now turn. In brief, we suggest that the break of relationship is not between theory and practice, but between 'scientific theory' and practice. The break between practice and theory has occurred precisely as a result of the overly close link between theory and practice, because in psychoanalysis theory fulfils an important clinical function. To elaborate this point we have to explore an aspect of the failure of psychoanalytic theory as a scientific theory.

As philosophers have relatively recently concluded, one facet of Freud's brilliant insights was to have extended common sense or folk psychology to non-conscious mental functioning (Hopkins, 1992; Wollheim, 1995). Cognitive neuroscience has revealed that most of the work of the brain is non-conscious (Kihlstrom, 1987). Freud (1900; 1923b), having recognized the importance of this fact in the development of psychopathology, advanced two radical propositions. First, mental health problems (by which he probably meant behaviours or phenomenological experiences which either the person or those in his immediate social surroundings complain about) may be understood in terms of non-consciously experienced mental states (beliefs and desires) (Breuer and Freud, 1895). Second, the effective treatment of mental health problems can be undertaken if (and only if) the individual suffering from mental disorder is made aware of these non-conscious, and by definition maladaptive, beliefs or desires in an interpersonal context of considerable emotional intensity (Freud, 1909; 1916). The two key principles of mentalization for Freud are that intentionality is not restricted to consciousness and that the expansion of the capacity to think about desires, feelings and thoughts of which the patient is unaware is therapeutic when undertaken in the context of an attachment relationship.

Freud's argument turned out to have an intellectual potency which is arguably hardly equalled in the history of human ideas. From it followed the discovery of meaning in madness, the revolutionization of psychiatry, the emergence of a civilization where unreason and disorder could no longer automatically be disclaimed and discarded, the recognition of the importance of early childhood and a developmental approach to the study of mind and the possibility to envisage human creation (art, music, literature, even science) in its greatest complexity. But Freud 'over-specified' his theory. He linked his discovery of pathogenic unconscious influence to specific contents that commonly created non-conscious conflicts of ideas and thus created and sustained problems of adaptation (e.g. unconscious conflicts concerning toilet training) (Freud, 1905; 1920; 1927). Anna Freud (1974) went further when she attempted to establish specific links between types of childhood mental health problems and categories of troublesome, non-conscious mental contents. This simplistic implementation of a good theory was inevitably counterproductive. The range of psychosocial experiences that reach a common symptomatic end-point is probably limitless (equi-finality). Similarly, the same experience may antedate a variety of clinical manifestations (Cicchetti and Cohen, 1995). Unfortunately, by over-specifying the theory, Freud laid psychoanalysis open to endless revisions and updating of aspects of theory that were never fundamental to his ideas (Fonagy and Target, 2003). For example, Melanie Klein, focusing on infancy, was struck by the apparent destructiveness and cruelty manifested by normal (her own) children (Klein et al., 1946). As the scientific methodology offering relatively firm data on infant mental states was not yet available (e.g. Stern, 1994), she felt free to attribute extraordinarily complex ideation to the young infant without a genuine risk of contradiction (envy, projective identification and the depressive position). Other psychoanalytic clinicians, whose interest was focused on somewhat later developmental periods (e.g. Margaret Mahler – see Mahler, Pine and Bergman, 1975), specified quite different central psychological conflicts (in this case, symbiosis, separation-individuation, etc.).

We are not claiming that either of these, or the many hundreds of other (Kazdin, 2000), ideas concerning unconscious causes of conflict was 'wrong'. It is very likely that both conflicts over destructive jealousy (envy) of a loved object and the conflict between a desire for separateness and the wish to retain an illusion of union with a caregiver are important assumptions about mental states in understanding minds in distress. The problem is one of trying to claim exclusivity for any or all of these ideas. As such specificity in relating theories to clinical work is rarely attained, new psychoanalytic theories are developed without systematic reference to the old as 'supplemental' to the original theory. Thus, new ideas overlap with, but do not replace, the original formulation. Psychoanalysts found a way around the empirical problems created by partially incompatible formulations that nevertheless needed to be employed concurrently. They loosened the definition of all the categories under consideration. The potential embarrassment of negative instances where, for example, signs of unconscious hostility were not observed to lead to mood disorder, could be avoided if both the putative antecedent (hostility) and consequent (mood disorder) were only to be loosely defined (Sandler, 1983). Disappointingly, yet also inevitably, this has led psychoanalysts to embrace an antagonism towards operationalization and an explicit preference for ambiguity. Equally predictable has been the multiplication of theories, rejection of parsimony as a criterion for eliminating competing ideas, the geographical specificity of particular theoretical traditions, the over-valuation of spoken and written rhetoric as criteria of validity, the polymorphous use of concepts and ultimately a theoretical edifice which is beyond the power of any individual to summarize and integrate.

Here we are not pleading for an integrationist model (Goldfried, 1995; 2001). Rather, we are suggesting that Freud's original rich theorization is to blame for later psychoanalytic clinicians conflating the framework of psychological mechanisms implied by the theory with the specific mental contents that populate this structural framework. Unconscious conflict is core theory,[3] and as such could probably be linked with recommendations about technique. Envy, oedipal rivalry, separation-individuation conflicts, narcissistic traumata are elaborations at a different level – one of clinical observation – and are, therefore, too confounded with practice to permit deductive inferences to clinical method. That one person (the analyst) thinks about what appear to be gaps in the other person's (the patient's) understanding of a life situation, making the unconscious conscious, is core theory. What that situation is – whether it is the therapy situation itself (the transference) or life outside (the external world) – may be less intrinsically relevant. There are basic structures of personhood that define the clinical enterprise. That this is over-specified in most psychoanalytic theoretical accounts is clear from the happy coexistence of the many hundreds of apparently equally efficacious alternatives that have little in common beyond the dual principles of the focused elaboration on non-conscious intentionality and the intensity of the interpersonal context within which this happens.

In Peter Schaffer's play *Amadeus*, about the life of Mozart, King Joseph II explains his dislike of Mozart's production by saying: 'There were too many notes!' Many philosophers have felt similarly about psychoanalytic ideas. Ludwig Wittgenstein writes in his preface to the *Tractatus*: 'What can be said at all can be said clearly, and what we cannot

---

[3] Some propositions within any scientific theory are likely to be protected from refutation, to be in this sense treated as unfalsifiable (Lakatos, 1970). Such propositions are considered to constitute the core of a scientific theory. The theory refers to 'unobservables' and the principles that govern their causal interaction. The principle of methodology that justifies protecting core theory from refutation is the central role that such aspect of theory plays in making predictions. The refutation of core theory would paralyse the theory, experiments could not be constructed because there would be nothing to put to a test. Core aspects of theory cannot be given up because they are needed to organize action and therefore appropriately will not be given up to anomalies alone, only to alternative theories good enough to put in their place. Arguably, core psychoanalytic theory was not given up by social scientists throughout the twentieth century, despite numerous anomalous observations, because nothing existed to replace it. The emergence of cognitive theory and therapy, together with neuroscience at the end of the century, began to threaten the core theory because it could provide a viable alternative that could be seen to occupy a similar position within the understanding of human behaviour.

talk about we must pass over in silence.' No wonder, then, that subjective experience has largely eluded psychological disciplines other than psychoanalysis. No wonder that psychoanalysts fear that the introduction of research methods from this barren world risks the destruction of the phenomena they cherish. Friedrich Nietzsche talks of unpretentious truths that have been discovered by means of rigorous method and opposes this method to metaphysics that blind us and make us happy. Nietzsche here distinguishes boring empirical fact from evocative narrative. Holding on to unpretentious truths demonstrates courage of a different sort from that shown by psychoanalytic investigations of the unconscious. It is a turning away from what is appealing. Whittle (2000) called it 'cognitive asceticism'.

The over-specification of psychoanalytic theory might be considered the primary cause of its current problem of fragmentation. Core theory is re-specified by each generation of theoreticians, leading to a kind of uncontainable exuberance of ideas that we learn, teach and use as formal psychoanalytic theory. Luxuriating in an absence of parsimony is not an end in itself for the psychoanalytic scholar. Her or his determination to create new distinctions and elaborations is driven by the wishes of the consumers of theoretical ideas, the practising clinicians.[4] The clinician's daily task is to address the individual's self-narrative and create (co-construct) a fuller, richer, more satisfying account than the patient has been capable of creating in isolation (e.g. Holmes, 1998). Cognitive asceticism is of little relevance to the clinician, whose principal task is to create a narrative that can fill the gaps in a person's experience of life. Thus theory has profound heuristic value for the clinician. Theories support understanding. Psychoanalytic theories are inherently and irretrievably inductive. They are derived precisely to elaborate a specific human conundrum. They cannot be bound by the minimalist principles that are the residues of positivism because they would be of little value if they did. They are adventurous; they dig deep. They are acts of imagination about how our minds function, which are judged principally according to how well they fit our own and our patients' subjective experience (see Whittle, 2000). Theory has to be over-specified in order to work, in order to capture one or other subtle aspect of an infinitely complex system: human subjectivity.[5] This is not to say that over-

---

[4] As the theoretician is also most often a clinician within the context of psychoanalytic theorization, the former has firsthand knowledge of the latter's unquenchable desire for new formulations, closer-fitting models and increasingly convincing explanations.

[5] There is, of course, a built-in process of new theory creation in this dynamic. Theories will capture an aspect of subjectivity only while that subjectivity is unchanged. The act of capturing it, however, inevitably changes subjectivity creating a need now to capture it in a new way. The process is complicated by occurring simultaneously at an intersubjective (patient–analyst) and cultural level. Thus renewal, or at least change, might be required by change of subjectivity at an individual or social level with complex patterns of interaction between them.

specified theories are not true, but the indication of their value rests in the subjective reaction of the clinician in the process of attempting to fathom the subjectivity of his client.

The role of the implicit knowledge base and implications for the development of innovative techniques

To sum up what has been claimed so far. We have argued that because of the limitations under which psychoanalysts work and the massive burden of their historical tradition, direct links between theory and research have been hard to establish. Specifically, that the claims that have been made about the existence of these links are poorly grounded in fact and have, in part, caused the loose use of theoretical constructs and led to the ossification of those aspects of practice which inappropriately carry the burden of defining the clinical discipline of psychoanalysis. While theory does not define practice, the fact that practitioners find theory useful has been used as validation of the extremely diverse set of ideas that currently constitute public psychoanalytic theory. The value of over-specifying the ideas at the core of psychoanalysis probably rests in their intuitive appeal to both analyst and analysand as the two are jointly engaged in the task of elaborating the life-narrative of the patient so as to make it more coherent and comprehensible.

So, why would a theory 'feel right', 'be of value', 'be felt to be useful' at least for a limited historical period? We suggest that this might be because they are metaphoric approximations, at a subjective level for both analyst and patient, of certain types of deeply unconscious internal experience that pertain not to an idea, but rather to a mode of mental function, a mental process (Fonagy, 1982; Fonagy, Moran et al., 1993). Aspects of psychoanalytic theory may be thought of as theorists' attempts to use metaphors to grasp the nature of the mental processes and mechanisms of which they have no conscious knowledge and which are not available to direct introspection. We should not accept simplistic critiques of metaphoric thought in psychoanalysis. Science uses metaphor in the absence of detailed knowledge of the underlying process. Provided that metaphor is not confused with a full understanding, or to use Freud's metaphor, the scaffolding is not mistaken for the building, heuristic considerations might outweigh any disadvantages of their use. Thus, while there is wisdom and truth in our theories, they will not behave like theories in modern sciences. Psychoanalytic theories also impact on us at an unconscious level. The particular configuration of ideas fits with an inner experience. We are rich in theory because theory sustains clinical activity and it is hard to imagine how this richness can ever be reduced by research or by other methods without also compromising the quality of the fit between a psychoanalytic model of mind and subjective experience. This formulation of the role of theory fits surprisingly well with currently popular, post-empiricist views of science and knowledge.

In post-empiricist epistemology it is accepted that empirical beliefs constitute a theory within which no exact mapping is possible between specific beliefs and particular experiences (Bolton, 1999). There can be no sharp distinction between theory and empirical data. In the empiricism of John Locke and David Hume, knowledge was assumed to be derived from sense experience, where the latter is an unconditional given (Quine, 1953). Sense experience was assumed to entail no activity on the part of the self. In modern post-empiricism, by contrast, the self is seen as an active agent processing sense data into information *relevant to action*. Sense experience involves cognitive activity. Perception is assumed to be organized in the service of action to yield hypotheses that might aid the planning of action. An example of this would be generating expectations about the outcome of action. Such hypotheses ultimately aggregate to generate theory. But theory always betrays its origins as subserving action, never 'immaculate' in its conception. Theory is systemic in relation to experience, and sense experience is always in the service of action. Psychoanalytic theory, like any theory, unconsciously serves to organize action. The truth of a theory is thus no longer seen as something absolutely entailed within the relation of the theory to an external reality. Rather, validity of a theory rests in its capacity to enable action. Knowledge is not an awareness of absolute facts, but the capacity to attain a goal within a specific context or setting. The North American tradition of pragmatism lies at the root of this postmodern, action-based epistemology.

Our views of scientific theories have changed from generalized, absolute, grand, omnibus accounts to more local, differentiated, specific rules used to guide action. Theory becomes a working, living, tightly organized but flexible set of assumptions that is not sharply separated from other bodies of knowledge. Basically, whatever works, whatever is needed to explain, can be integrated into the theory. We suggest that this post-empiricist reconstruction of theory has not yet taken place within the public theory of psychoanalysis. It is held in a somewhat mysterious, unexplored container of knowledge that one might call *the implicit psychoanalytic knowledge base*. Joseph Sandler drew attention to this almost 20 years ago (Sandler, 1983; Sandler and Dreher, 1995). Sandler, anticipating many of these epistemological developments, explicitly suggested that public theory grew out of this implicit, non-conscious understanding of interpersonal and intrapsychic processes that clinicians normally gain through engaging in intensive psychotherapeutic work with the background of core psychoanalytic theory behind them.

A number of assumptions are implied by the current formulation of theory–practice links. First, a non-conscious psychoanalytic knowledge base exists, probably built or superimposed on the cognitive structures provided by a common-sense or lay psychology (Churchland, Ramachandran and Sejnowski, 1994). This all-important system for understanding the mind guides all of us (analysts, patients, children and adults) through the great complexities of interpersonal interaction and provides knowledge of minds essential for self-awareness. Second, for psychoanalysts, this knowledge base is massively deepened by clinical experience. Proximity to another mind afforded by psychoanalytic treatment will inevitably deepen an implicit, non-conscious, procedural, action-focused understanding of mental function. Third, formal theory is essential in a number of ways, but the least important of these may be its traditionally desired function, that of organizing clinical observations. Core theory may be crucial in creating a foundation for interpersonal and inter-subjective experience. Thus Freud's assumption concerning non-conscious intentionality is undoubtedly essential if feelings and ideas outside of conscious awareness are to be brought into the realm of that which the analyst can explore. Perhaps an even more important facet of core theory may be to enable the analytic observer to stay 'within range' of another subjectivity. We have understood much about inter-subjective interactions and the interdependence of subjectivities – enough to appreciate that the close proximity of another subjectivity can potentially undermine the robustness of the observer's self-understanding and self-awareness (Fonagy, 2003). Core theory provides the scaffolding to withstand these pressures.

Thus the psychoanalytic knowledge base has been and remains a vastly valuable reservoir for producing understanding of people with the power to guide action in the clinical context (technique). However, the epistemological tradition of psychoanalysis and its grand failure to eliminate aspects of theory that were not helpful, its absolutist tendencies, have led to a situation where this implicit rich knowledge base could not be regularly and systematically mined to guide therapy, unless the action generated was consistent with some grand and slowly changing public theory. The separation of the public from the implicit theory created somewhat arbitrary restrictions on theoretical development together with a petrification of clinical practice.

This is not to say that the implicit, action-oriented knowledge base remained unexploited within psychoanalysis. Elsewhere, we have explored the ways in which implicit theory is used by clinicians to guide their daily work with patients (Canestri *et al.*, 2002). Most extensive use of this body of knowledge has not been by psychoanalysts. In fact, arguably, the knowledge base actually generated many, if not all, the major advances of psychological therapeutic technique of the twentieth century. It is not an exaggeration to claim that approaches such as gestalt, client-centred, some kinds of family therapy, most brief psychotherapies and some especially more recent forms of cognitive therapy all originated from within the psychoanalytic knowledge base. Schema theory (Young, 1999) is object relations theory by another name and it is nothing short of a travesty that an effective therapy closely based on these ideas is not termed psychoanalytic. The way past relationship patterns impact on current relationships is an integral part of our knowledge base. Yet our epistemology limits the exploitation of this understanding to very specific therapeutic contexts. The knowledge base is mined, often by psychoanalysts, but as this happens the name psychoanalysis is withdrawn as if it has to be retained for something in principle circumscribed, but in practice not defined at all. We need to be cautious over the matter of criteria of identity. What truly matters are general and specific features of content and not names. Theory and technique must be made open to elaboration. The priority is the derivation of effective and efficient procedures for implementing change rooted in our understanding of mental function. We use an implicit source of knowledge, but our politically-driven epistemology forces us to deny its relevance and sometimes even existence.

Conclusions

Let us return to Freud's basic discoveries. Fundamental to the psychoanalytic orientation is the notion that becoming aware of patterns of thinking or behaving that were previously outside of consciousness has therapeutic value. The task of therapy is both to enhance the patient's capacity to think about the mental processes that underlie his or her feelings, thoughts and behaviour, and also to use such enhanced capacities to reflect on patterns of interactions that are maladaptive and cause distress. The assumption of psychoanalytic technique is that making latent meaning manifest can initiate a process of change in understanding. Freud's theories about what this meant and how to do it were modified. Much can be said about the specific contexts in which an individual's problems emerge, but these have no necessary causal relationship to the patient's current functioning. It is the capacity to reflect and arrive at meaning about conscious experience which is inherently therapeutic according to core Freudian theory. The specific understandings appear to be far more open to variation. There is a skeleton of theory about the way new meanings are created by two human minds trying to fit together ideas and meanings about subjectivity, but it is the 'how' rather than the 'what' of this interpersonal process that our growing understanding of therapy leads us towards. The theory that psychoanalysts work with is a combination of public and private (implicit) constructions. It is the contention of the present chapter that both these are valuable, but not necessarily for their 'truth value'. The former, public theory, may be an over-specification of core ideas that conflict with other formulations with equal claim to prompting therapeutically effective action, but is likely to contain within it a metaphoric approximation to how the mind functions which has intuitive appeal to both clinician and patient. The latter, the implicit or private theory of the clinician, which we can only discern by observing the clinician at work, constitutes a particularly powerful reservoir of insights about the mind, but one that is inadequately exploited by formal psychoanalytic theorization. We believe that much progress in psychotherapy outside of psychoanalysis has made use of the intuitive understanding of the mind in therapeutic interpersonal relationships to develop effective intervention strategies which now compete directly with our own.

Perhaps we have been too generous with our insights. Perhaps it is high time that we delved into our reservoir of psychological understanding ourselves and took up the challenge of generating creative and efficacious new forms of intervention which are not modelled on classical psychoanalysis, do not represent dilutions of a clinical model which might be outmoded, was perhaps never particularly effective and in any case has uncertain links with our understanding of mental function, and focus on providing innovative effective (and cost effective) treatment models for treatment-resistant conditions. If psychoanalytic theory is to have an influence on the psychiatric treatment approaches of the twenty-first century, it will do so only if the constraining influence of attempting to tie clinical intervention to a public theory is fully recognized. It must be widely appreciated that accumulated psychoanalytic knowledge is far broader than we commonly appreciate, that we know both much more and much less about the mind than is codified in psychoanalytic texts and that we should approach creative modifications of technique not from the point of view of a Freudian superego-ish father tut-tutting at the breaking of imagined barriers and taboos, but from the perspective of a benevolent figure encouraging playful engagement with ideas in both the sphere of individual therapy and the sphere of protocol development.

6
Some perspectives on relationships of theory and technique

WILLIAM I. GROSSMAN

Introduction

The relationships between theory and technique have been the focus of attention and controversy among psychoanalysts since the beginning of the collaboration and disagreements between Breuer and Freud (1895). Although there has been a great deal of illuminating discussion on the subject, technique has not yet been deducible from the theories of mind and theories of interaction derived from clinical experience, nor from the theoretical formulations based on thoughtful considerations derived from philosophical reflection and interdisciplinary study. One important reason for this is that we do not have a systematic statement of psychoanalytic theory or systematic expositions of the many current theoretical orientations. We do have many theoretical ideas derived from various sources, as I shall discuss in this chapter. Explanations of clinical experiences based on such ideas may be offered as rationales even when significant aspects of the experiences are only indirectly related to them. The lack of systematic expositions obscures the fact that one of the problems in talking about the relationship of theory and practice has to do with there being a number of different kinds of theoretical concerns related to practice. A major division is one between conceptions of process and conceptions of interpretation. In addition, even with a sys-

Psychoanalysis: From Practice to Theory. Edited by J. Canestri. © 2006 Whurr Publishers Ltd (a subsidiary of John Wiley & Sons Ltd).

tematized theory, some intermediate ideas are required to link theory and technique, as Hartmann (1951) remarked.

In the absence of systematic theoretical expositions, the synthesis and application of the available theoretical orientations and related ideas is the concern and the task of all analysts. The wealth of examples and discussion in the clinical literature provides assistance for ongoing reflection on one's own experience as a therapist. In addition to the literature, other sources of knowledge and more personal discussions contribute to the development of clinical understanding and judgement as an ongoing process in any therapist's professional life. Theoretical ideas play a role in this reflection.

From the point of view of this chapter, that ongoing reflection is at the heart of psychoanalysis. For this reason, the problem of the relationship of theory and technique is best seen from the perspective that the therapist is the connection between theory and technique. It is the working therapist whose conscious and unconscious commitments to ideas about theory and technique provide links between the two that logic alone cannot. Learning analytic theory and technique is training in how to link theory and technique. This process also joins the analyst to a community of analysts, a thought community addressing these problems from particular perspectives. Among these perspectives is attention to unconscious fantasies of therapist and patient, as well as their conscious and unconscious conjoint fantasies. The role of conscious constructions and conceptualizations, as well as the shared frameworks and orientations of therapist and patient, need to be considered too.

The idea of a thought community and its associated thought style are important in understanding both the origins of and the guides to and supports for the way a psychoanalyst thinks about theory in relationship to practice. The thought community is important, too, for the processes of change in thinking about psychoanalysis and psychotherapy.

My goal in this chapter is to locate the place of *ideas about theory* and *theoretical ideas* themselves in the thinking of therapists in relation to their patients and to their colleagues. In doing this, I shall try to consider the roles of conscious and unconscious theorizing. This goal requires the exploration of the subject from a number of perspectives rather than presenting a grand synthesis. This means covering a number of ideas briefly, offering, in effect, a map of the terrain. In doing this, I shall necessarily repeat many familiar ideas in order to place them in a somewhat different context.

On some current points of view

Writing on the relationships between theory and technique today poses a number of dilemmas in addition to the lack of systematization that I have mentioned. There is the question of which theory and technique we are referring to. At the present time, there are a number of prominent schools considered to be psychoanalysis in the United States whose techniques have yet to be clearly articulated with their stated theoretical commitments. These must be compared with British, European-continental and South American views. It is clear that the theoretical systems of all these points of view are considerably different in their terminology, conceptualization and usage. Although some authors suggest that there is more similarity in the clinical approaches of all schools and similarity in their successes, this belief remains to be convincingly demonstrated. Of course, there is similarity in so far as there is currently a widespread attention to transference, countertransference and their management, though often with differing conceptions of these terms and divergent clinical approaches.

It is possible to point to some aspects of current thinking about the clinical situation that are generally recognized by the adherents of many points of view, along with their shared interest in countertransference. Among these is the idea that the therapist's subjectivity is inevitable. I prefer this expression to the term 'irreducible subjectivity' since the latter seems to miss the point that we are interested in the way subjectivity and objectivity are both inevitable, though distributed or organized in various ways. Subjectivity is inevitable since whatever we say is subjective in some way, even when we choose to express ideas that are regarded as objective. In that case, subjectivity resides in part of what is said and the reasons for saying it. The important issue is the awareness of one's own subjectivity and the recognition that this is subjective too.

There appears to be general agreement that we are concerned with the role of inevitable unconscious fantasies associated with the therapist's attitude to patients and the likelihood of unconscious 'enactments' as a consequence. The idea that all observation is theory-laden and that publicly asserted theory might not be the same as the theory that can be inferred from a therapist's work are also widely held (Abend, 1979; Arlow, 1981; Sandler, 1983; Grossman, 1995). The publicly asserted theories are likely to be the formulations learned in the course of training or from some admired teacher or writings. As is well known, such statements of theoretical commitment are likely to be assertions of allegiance based, at least in part, on unconscious attachment and identification. As a result, the connection to the thinking involved in specific clinical problems or laboratory research may be uncertain.

Conscious and unconscious in current views

I shall now address some of the consequences and paradoxes of these current views, among which is the *inescapable objectivity* of theorizers and formulators who may be either analysts or commentators, or both. Anticipating my conclusion, I suggest that as psychoanalysis deals with greater complexities, it becomes increasingly difficult to balance the necessary multiple viewpoints. There is no end to this process occurring in theory and technique. The normal development of what we call objectivity is what creates for us our versions of material and social reality and how we define them. Objectivity has its own rules, even though subjectivity and the unconscious processes play their roles in it. A balanced consideration of these issues is necessary and includes a consideration of the *relatively* autonomous aspects, as well as the dynamic mutual involvement of subjectivity and objectivity, both conscious and unconscious.

Current thinking emphasizes the idea of unconscious participation of psychoanalyst and analysand and their efforts to arrive at a shared understanding. The undermining of the relevance and place of conscious judgement furthers Freud's project of showing that many apparently reasonable ideas had unconscious meanings and motives that might belie their conscious intentions. His systematic attention to this problem occurred at a time when rationality and positivism were desirable goals for a scientific psychiatry that took 'mature sciences' like physics as a model. In that climate of thought, the idea of an unconscious in a number of forms came on the scene from a number of sources to challenge the security that objectivity and faith seemed to offer. It was in this atmosphere that one of the most striking aspects of Freud's ideas was the discovery everywhere of the irrational unconscious concealed by consciousness. The more or less systematic concentration on this point of view was the main path taken by Freudian psychoanalysis through the twentieth century. A number of Freud's observations are especially relevant here. These deal with the double meaning of any conscious judgement (1912-13), the reading of one person's unconscious by other people and especially by paranoids (1901), the unconscious meanings of any systems, like theories, religions, works of literature, and so on. Freud noted that it is the task of the psychoanalyst to find unconscious meanings in his or her way of thinking, in their personal systems of thought.

More recently, the general agreement that enactments are inevitable, that every interpretation of the therapist has and expresses some unconscious intention, brings this point of view to its logical conclusion. There is, however, a tendency to overlook the way that this point of view, and judgements based on it, are presented as objectively true, even obvious, and thus are examples of a way of thinking about facts, reality and certainty that they are intended to undermine and dismiss. Of course, assuming this objective stance is necessary as one step in continuous reflection.

Self-observation, too, requires an objective stance in introspection and self-understanding, although it is a compromise too.

The idea of the ubiquity of unconscious influence in the formulation of clinical material and in clinical interaction has been used to minimize the role of conscious and rational points of view in the establishment of subjectivity. Points of view that are said to be subjective are compromises between emotional attitudes and some form of judgement. When those judgements are psychoanalytic and therapeutic, psychoanalytic ideas form a part of the therapist's subjective views. As such, these views refer to both fantasy and the system of theory of which the therapist's ideas are subjective versions.

Current views emphasizing the unconscious aspect of subjectivity tend to ignore the fact that the importance of the 'discovery' of the unconscious was that it involved a modification of an established and accepted point of view that rational and realistic consciousness dealt with some kind of ultimately knowable reality. The idea of unconscious mental activity did not displace that view. The existence and functioning of consciousness was accepted, and its contents had to be better understood. This was the significance of Chapter 7 of the *Interpretation of Dreams* (1900) and Freud's paper on the 'Unconscious' (1915), both of which describe consciousness as constructed dynamically, a compromise between conscious and unconscious thinking. This picture was more complete than other views that consciousness was purely logical and realistic. Other psychiatric and philosophical works recognized some kind of unconscious or subconscious mental activity. Psychoanalysis stressed that unconscious desires deflected, disrupted or distorted realistic conscious purposes and left gaps in realistic conscious thought and the flow of thoughts. The gaps might be closed by symptoms and symptomatic acts.

Now, with the valuable extension of our understanding of the complexity of our interpretive systems and of the treatment situation in which we find the unconscious everywhere, we must rediscover the role of consciousness and of reasoning. The view that finds only the unconscious of the therapist and the patient's knowledge of the therapist's unconscious everywhere is a conscious, objective and positivistic point of view. This is one point of view of experience among others. The other points of view include perspectives that look for meaning in various actions and expressions, meanings that are implicit and unconscious in a different sense. These actions, attitudes and expressions reflect the systems and conventions of social attitudes and views of relationships and reality that may be shared and understood by both therapist and patient within a particular culture. These shared views may also become unconscious and involved in conflict. What patients and therapists say and do can be interpreted according to various points of view, of course. They may also be intended in some unconscious way as a communication by patient or therapist, and/or an expression of something emotional, whether formulated or not. This is *one* possible point of view. It is, for our analytic purposes, a *necessary* point of view. Freud's emphasis on the similarity of the minds of patients and analysts, and the requirement for both to be able to follow the 'fundamental rule', ought to bring us to this point of view.

This is the basis for our thinking about 'psychic reality', a concept that is distinguished from some other reality whose knowability has long been in question. However the philosophical questions may be answered, psychoanalysis needs a counterpoise to the closed-in subjectivity of psychic reality. Various current concepts can be viewed as attempts at solutions to this problem. Among these concepts are 'consensual validation', 'intersubjectivity' and 'thirdness', all of which suggest a sharing of reality, jointly acknowledged truth, mutual agreement, as well as mutual understanding and recognition. In this way, a kind of provisional *objectivity with regard to the subjectivity* of the therapeutic couple is established on the basis of shared conscious judgement and emotional response. A kind of negotiation can occur in this way. But now we come to another turn of the wheel since a shared agreement can, from another perspective, be shared subjectivity as well. These agreements have unconscious meanings that must be sought as well. Shared agreement about understanding also reflects other kinds of more rational but unconscious shared points of view, some kind of common ground and background. This background includes such things as meta-theories, worldviews, social outlooks and other sources of mutually accepted and often unquestioned assumptions and 'truths'.

These considerations point to what seems to be the fact that we cannot do without some idea of objectivity and the idea that in some way our shared points of view point to some kind of objective reality. Even those of us who believe in the inevitability of subjective viewpoints believe that this is some kind of fact, even though we may keep in mind that this truth may be transient with the advent of some other point of view. It has been said that 'truth is the daughter of time, not of authority'.

So, the idea of *conjoint objectivity about subjectivity* is one instance of a broader principle that plays a role in clinical process, judgement and the development of theories. This principle holds that the objectivity of a point of view depends on the place it has in the thinking of a group subscribing to the point of view. Facts are facts within some system of thought. Facts never speak for themselves. That is, oversimplifying somewhat, those that share common theories that say how things are to be discussed and explained form a community of thought and have a common style of thought. Ours is what Freud called 'the psychoanalytic mode of thought'.

At this point in the discussion, it is useful to note that the way theories are worked out from clinical observation is, as Freud often noted, similar to the process of scientific discovery. That process involves multiple viewpoints, trial and error, wandering and serendipity, chance, inspiration and perspiration. From the disorderliness of process, the order of a logical theoretical system is distilled and the impurities of methodological vagaries removed. What remains is the logical and objective system of thought, which is often presented as derived from or leading to the observations (Fleck, [1935] 1979; Rapaport, 1960). At times, chance observations or observations based on faulty reasoning or theory, or following technological inventions based on practical manipulations, are taken as supporting a theory with which they are loosely connected. All of these possibilities are easily found in the history of science. The history of medicine has a wealth of stories of medicinal discoveries by herbal healers and shamans whose conceptions of disease were regarded as proved by their empirical successes.

In psychoanalysis, changes in theory may be called on to explain or rationalize technical modifications based on pragmatic considerations. Of course, at other times observations are deliberately or unconsciously sought to confirm some theoretical ideas. Again, all of these possibilities can be found.

For the clinician, the theories provide an implicit or explicit framework for expectations of how things work and what things mean while observations are opening the way to many possible explanations. Everyone takes this for granted and knows that, without our placing some value on conscious judgement, there would be no point in theoretical and clinical arguments. So, systematic formulations of theory, technique, principles and process are necessary, even though they are necessarily modified for purposes of research and personalized for treatment (Hartmann, 1951; Sandler, 1983; Stein, 1991; Grossman, 1995; and others). Clinical concepts draw on, constitute and imply general conceptions of mind and behaviour, no less than meta-psychology does (Klein, 1976). However, any person's clinical 'theories', or formulations, have multiple sources, and not simply psychoanalytic ideas.

I have been describing a shifting and balancing of our understanding of the roles of consciousness and unconsciousness in object relations. For the therapist, balancing clinical and theoretical understanding is a preconscious creative process *informed by* theory. Therefore, how the relationship of conscious and unconscious knowledge and the meaning of theory and technique are learned requires some further consideration.

Learning to link theory and technique

This section describes how learning to be an analyst establishes an emotional relationship with teachers, the literature and its authors. This means considering some factors affecting the way ideas about the connection between theory and technique become the individual psychoanalyst's way of thinking and framing experience within a community of thought. This process establishes a link between the individual's development as a psychoanalyst and the thinking of the group to which the analyst belongs. To this end, teaching provides precepts, examples and interactions by means of which learning occurs and various kinds of experience are acquired. The present discussion focuses on the experience of learning. According to my view, learning about psychoanalysis and about psychotherapy in general is a special case of learning about other people that occupies a person's entire life – if so desired.

Two aspects of learning about technique will be considered. One is gaining experience in finding theoretical ideas in observed clinical events and finding clinical instances for theoretical ideas. The other aspect to be considered is that learning promotes thinking about treatment as other members of the group think, although the outcome may at times be opposition to the group. That is, the process of learning psychoanalysis is a process of interchanges with the psychoanalytic group and of intergenerational transmission. As such, it engages the issues of affiliation and separation. Learning to think like an analyst involves dialogues on theory, literature and clinical problems.

We could say, in a general way, that theory is the dialogue of theoreticians, while technique refers to the dialogues of analysts and patients. In the clinical situation, the theory is in the background as the narrative framework for the discussion of events defined as events by the theory. That is one of the functions of theories. It is a guideline for a perspective-reducing experience to some version of subjective and interactive terms communicable in the clinical situation.

Clinically, one problem is how to use interpretive understanding with patients. It is a question of formulating understanding, stating that understanding, acting on its implications, and acting on the understanding by saying something that addresses the roles of patients and therapists, for instance, by addressing transference and how the patient treats the analyst's interventions and the analyst. The point is that psychoanalytic understanding may lead to a choice among a number of therapeutic actions ranging from interpretation to advice. The possibility of these choices may be used to distinguish between psychoanalysis and psychotherapies.

The literature of psychoanalysis is what people have to say to each other in the context of publication. That is one version of what they have to say about their theories, their practices, their patients and themselves. What they say to their colleagues is another matter and what they say to their friends yet another. Public theories are the theories that psychoanalysts are willing or feel compelled to communicate to colleagues in the context of discussion. These are often statements of theory more or less as learned or opposition to what has been taught. These are now generally recognized as being different from private 'theories' and implicit 'theories' that guide therapeutic activity (Sandler, 1983; Brierley, [1943] 1991). The latter are perhaps better designated as private and implicit explanations since 'theory' implies something more systematic than is generally warranted. (The explanations may be systematic, but the system may be that of characteristic thinking, which includes other belief systems.) Moreover, what is called 'implicit theory' is often an interpretation by the observer, something inferred and formulated from what a therapist does, says or writes by way of description or explanation of a case.

Finally, training as a mode of transmission of psychoanalytic knowledge includes modelling and provides model solutions to conflict through interpretation. The student's experiences of modelling are complex since they involve not only imitation and identification, but also the quasi-therapeutic aspects of the supervision process. That is, the interaction with teachers is an emotional experience in which the possibility of conflict, its resolution and broadened self-perception are possible, as are less desirable consequences. Of course, we expect some kind of fluctuating transference to occur as well as transient identification with patients.

The pedagogy of psychoanalysis and psychotherapy shares features with the ways people have always learned to understand others through experiences with their elders and through the literature of wisdom, consisting of aphorisms, admonitions and advice to the would-be wise. Exemplary narratives, stories, fables and more elaborate literary and philosophical creations with overt or covert religious, moral, ethical and philosophical implications are also important, emotionally laden kinds of instruction. Psychoanalytic training is ostensibly more systematic and has a theoretical and technical framework. That framework is more, or perhaps differently, specific than the ordinary conventional frameworks. These other ordinary orientations acquired during development form a *Weltanschauung* or social orientation underlying the experience of psychoanalytic training, giving a personal cast to learning. These emotional aspects of the learning process influence the therapist's creation of and belief in a subjective version of what is taught.

As a literature of examples and sometimes exhortations, the psychoanalytic literature relies on case presentations that cannot possibly serve as proof for the conceptualizations offered. These presentations are important because they present narratives of treatment, development, understanding and models of thinking about relationships with patients and mental functioning. These models in relation to particular problems supplement the models found in supervision of the therapist's own experiences with patients and offer a basis for comparison with their own subjectively perceived interactions.

The supervisory situation is also an opportunity to test the supervisor's and student's understanding of the material and the consequences they expect in response to appropriate interpretations. In group supervision or case presentations, multiple formulations of process and predictions can be compared. From another point of view, the individual supervisory situation is a group of three among whom some mutual understanding is a desirable outcome.

Experiences of supervision and reading supplement the personal analysis in providing the possibility of learning self-observation through the eyes of the other, learning by interaction. This is part of the psychoanalyst's developing story of personal experience with patients as well as being part of normal development. In this learning process, an important subjective component lies in blending analytic narratives of understanding self and other with those similar narratives learned through the special interests of the therapist – a kind of interdisciplinary thinking (Grossman, 2000; 2002).

Another way of looking at this is to say that the psychoanalytic point of view looks at patients' histories as human dramas, as patients themselves may do. The scenarios of these dramas may be viewed as comparable to literary dramas, as Freud did when he saw the relationship of a son and his parents as an oedipal scenario. Many people with deep interests in literature have a special facility in recognizing such models in patients' narratives. It is then possible to recognize similar scenarios in the transference. At times, one can recognize in a patient's associations or dreams a personal version of a familiar fairy tale (Freud, 1913b).

Other special interests, such as history, philosophy, biology and the arts, give their own particular imprints and metaphors to psychoanalytic formulations and interpretations. Scientific narratives of psychology offer a link to the community of science, while perhaps suggesting a somewhat more distant, certain and authoritative view of relationships. Oversimplifying, perhaps, we might say, too, that those interested in politics are sensitive to the dramas of power, aggression and control.

Similarly, the mutual shaping of such interests and psychoanalytic thinking can be seen in supervision and in the psychoanalytic literature.

Supervisors and authors are likely to blend their own, suitably modified versions of theory and technique expressed in suitable metaphors derived from these other interests in the process of discussing clinical presentations. These influences may be found in the selection of material to interpret and in the way the material is interpreted. Taken together, the combination of interests and the sharing of points of view help to promote the development of multiple perspectives.

So far, I have been viewing the processes of learning how to link theory and technique from the perspective of learning through emotionally invested interchanges with colleagues and teachers in a manner analogous to other experiences of learning to understand other people. I have noted the development of a personal point of view that shapes the understanding of theory and its expression in technique by assimilating theory and practice to other personal interests.

One of the ways that the emotional ties in learning exert their effects is through their impact on self-observation. Like the experience of being in analysis, supervision and reading about psychotherapy stimulate self-observation, that is, an attempt to have a more or less objective view of one's self which is none the less emotionally evocative. It might be said that psychoanalysis and supervision are a kind of training in self-observation that promotes the possibility of developing a capacity for new experience. In a sense, these situations involve seeing oneself in the mirror of another person. This metaphor was used by Freud (1912b) to describe the psychoanalyst's helping the analysand to observe him- or herself. Winnicott (1971) and Kohut (1971) described the mother's and analyst's mirroring function. To these I add the idea that the therapist must learn to use the patient as the mirror and interpreter of the therapist's interventions. Case presentations are a kind of training for that experience. However, this does not necessarily mean that the patient gives a clear reflection. No doubt patients know a great deal about their therapists' responses and even some aspects of the motives for them. For instance, patients are likely to recognize their therapists' affective reactions. While some current literature sometimes sounds as though a patient's perceptions are freer of transference than the therapist's, this seems at times to suggest the fantasy of the 'clever baby'. However, the patient's reflection provides material for the analyst's self-reflection through an understanding of how the patient understands and uses interventions.

Whether or not supervision involves direct discussion of countertransference, discussions of process are necessarily reflections on the thinking and responses of the supervisee. As everyone knows, the anticipation of this experience influences how material is presented. However, this influence is not only conscious but also unconscious. The presence of another person has been recognized as influencing the way one thinks and associates freely in the presence of another person, and even how a person can think about oneself when engaged with another (Loewenstein, 1963; Grossman, 1967; Schafer, 1997).

In the course of learning to link theory and technique, a relationship develops with the ideas about both theory and technique that retains something of the emotional context. The resulting emotional relation with ideas accompanies the expected evaluation of psychoanalytic concepts as part of a theoretical and clinical system. This complex set of processes inevitably entails unconscious conflict in which ideas about treatment and theory are involved.

Conflicts arise in connection with transferences to and identifications with the teachers, and the imagined great figures of the field who have written the authoritative works or works critical of those works. Conflicts arise too in response to ideas and feelings stirred up by the subject matter which inevitably touches on fantasies, both conscious and unconscious, and on their associated conflicts as well. Finally, for this discussion, the gradual acquisition of clinical experience plays its part since the clinical situation evokes responses that potentially require support and clarification by teachers and colleagues and some kind of resolution of a personal kind.

In case discussions with colleagues, in supervision and other discussion groups, the experiences of the dialogues become part of the therapist's associative responses to patients, sometimes in supportive ways. Positive reflection on the therapist's understanding fosters the development of a clinically oriented version of the theoretical framework that becomes a part of the therapist's way of thinking which can exert its influence in the background.

At other times, these associations may involve another person's formulation of clinical reports. If those comments have made a strong impression, they may be taken as commands to interpret in a particular way. When parallel processes are active in case discussion, the therapist who feels intimidated or humiliated in the mirror of those whose comments arouse painful self-reflection may enact an identification with the hurtful interlocutor in response to the patient. The conflicts evoked by the supervisory relationship may in this and other ways contribute to countertransference issues.

The psychoanalytic thought community

In thinking about the relationship of the individual's thought to the thought of the group, the perspective of Ludwik Fleck ([1935] 1979) provides a useful framework. He used the development of the Wasserman test for syphilis to explore the processes of scientific discovery. He showed the role of the thought community's ideas about science and disease in shaping the research and its exposition. By considering the problems from this angle, he was able to demonstrate the way erroneous theories can lead to useful discoveries.

Fleck's perspective on theorization and research has been important for understanding science as process and for considering the development of thinking in medicine and science in general. It is to him that we owe acknowledgement for the ideas of 'thought collectives' and 'thought styles'. His ideas provided one stimulus for Kuhn's (1962) conception of paradigms. At the present time, various ideas about group ways of thinking have become a commonplace. They comprise our contemporary thought style. Concepts like paradigms (Kuhn, 1962), styles of reasoning (Davidson, 2001) and others have become familiar in current studies in the history and philosophy of science. In fact, they have recently been employed in critical discussions of medical thinking and research (Rose, 2000; Weiss, 2003). These ideas are important for our reflections on our own work and our concepts.

In the present work, I am attempting to consider the relationships between theory and technique from that perspective, emphasizing the way that psychoanalytic training leads to the acquisition of the psychoanalytic thought style. Freud's views (1921) on the ties of identification and idealization in groups and Rapaport's (1951) ideas on the 'socialization of thinking' and the 'psychosocial point of view' in analytic theory address some of the intricate relationships between the thought of the individual and the group.

Considering the relationships fostered by training leads to the idea that learning and teaching involve the transmission of knowledge concerning the application of a thought system. The system deals with theory and treatment as it is contextualized in the thought style of a group, the thought community. The therapist's ideas are *subjective versions of some kinds of shared systems of ideas referring to theory and technique.* The relationships in which this occurs gives the ideas an emotional significance, and this gives what is learned its personal meaning and conviction. Necessary connections to one or a number of thought communities lead to the sense of inevitability and objectivity of beliefs. These play a role in shaping the 'inevitable subjectivity' that is the individual version of the thought style. One function of the psychoanalytic literature is to promote discussion and to foster the creation and maintenance of a community of thought.

Thought communities are recognizable by their commonly accepted and unquestioned assumptions, premises, common-sense quality and taken-for-granted ideological framework and beliefs. The group affiliation has great narcissistic value. One consequence is that in this way the group supports, without question, formulations involving connections that are only apparent and not logically related. This should be distinguished from the politics of the profession and its institutions.

Everyone belongs to more than one thought community. However, during any period, there are commonalities unifying different thought communities. These are seen dramatically in the mutual relationships between sciences and arts at various periods, as well as in popular models for formulating ideas.

Concluding remarks

Clinical behaviour is guided by ideas about and rules of conduct which may or may not be tied to theory as distinguished from tradition, as it is gathered in training and may be explained, however, as though it is theory. That is, in the course of training, traditions of treatment are explained or justified by reference to theory, but may in fact be working concepts based on a teacher's experience or tradition. These ideas may, for example, be generalizations about how sessions should go or what constitutes a good process. Also included might be ideas about timing and tact, the way to phrase interpretations, aphorisms about the order of interpretations, recommendations on self-revelation, and so on. They may be thought of as applications of theory since they may have some connection with theory to the extent that they can exemplify theory, although they are not necessarily derived from it. These precepts can be stated in theoretical language which may obscure the use of theoretical expression for description. However, the decision as to what aspects of theory are applicable in generating the rules guiding behaviour involves judgement, which is an individual matter involving other factors in thinking about the choice.

The question then remains whether there can be more systematic and theoretical understanding of the systems and processes of interpretation. The topic is complex and cannot be explored in this narrow arena. My own view is that systems of interpretation can be formalized to a considerable extent and can be related to other considerations of process. The issue is complicated since it has long been well known that any narratives to be interpreted can be interpreted according to a number of systems. Therefore, the integration of interpretation and process needs to be multiple, corresponding to the multiple systems of interpretation and their relevance.

For these reasons, there are probably limitations on the degree to which a theory of technique may be systematized and formalized. In any case, such a theory would have to take into account the role of the therapist in the process as the translator of principles, derived from more general theoretical ideas, into practice. In a certain sense, my chapter is an effort in that direction or perhaps a component of such a formulation. I have tried to explore the kind of activities theorizing and technique involve.

The conclusion of these reflections is that psychotherapy is much like other clinical disciplines. Clinical medicine relies on both research findings and practical experience transmitted by study, precepts, examples and practical training supervised by knowledgeable authorities. Much that is learned has been empirically demonstrated to be useful without reliance on prior theoretical justification. Even when these procedures are based on experimental findings, their implementation may be a matter of judgement and skill. Of course, this is equally true when it is a matter of finding the means to implement theoretical knowledge in practical experiments (see, e.g., Dyson, 1998) as well as in some engineering applications.

As I have suggested earlier, our grand visions of how a science ought to develop is based on the idea that knowledge should evolve as Newton is supposed to have made it happen. This ideal is now generally regarded as unrealizable and not particularly desirable. We do better to try to understand the way knowledge evolves, increases and is constantly revised. Psychoanalytic ideas, observations, experiences and judgements have something to offer in this direction, even though all such conclusions must be provisional.

Acknowledgement

The valuable suggestions and criticism offered by Dr Roy Schafer and Dr Arnold Wilson are gratefully acknowledged.

7
Theory as transition: spatial metaphors of the mind and the analytic space[1]

GAIL S. REED

As Professor G lay down on the couch for his first analytic session, he gestured towards my desk with its somewhat disorderly evidence of work in progress and, in an imperious and dismissive tone, said: 'You really ought to put up a screen there.' Not too much later in the analysis, Professor G mentioned that he had slept in an alcove next to his parents' bedroom. As evidence accumulated, it was not surprising to find that looking away was a prominent defence and not difficult to suppose that Professor G had prescribed a reproduction of the very doors which had closed out everything and yet nothing.

Professor G's transference was characterized by acute but unacknowledged depressive reactions to cancellations, weekend separations and vacations. He gradually became aware of resentment and vindictiveness towards me, but never of any underlying positive attachment that might have provided an underpinning for his feeling of betrayal. He described rescue fantasies from childhood in which a woman, ill-treated by men, picked him out of a crowd and recognized his devotion. He

---

[1] *The Psychoanalytic Quarterly* has kindly granted use of copyright of this chapter, first published in *The Psychoanalytic Quarterly*, LXXII (2003), 1: 97–129.

Psychoanalysis: From Practice to Theory. Edited by J. Canestri. © 2006 Whurr Publishers Ltd (a subsidiary of John Wiley & Sons Ltd).

resented that I did not respond adequately to his attempts to get me to admire him. Nevertheless, he felt intense jealousy when he read that I was giving a course with a male colleague. He rationalized and isolated this reaction and was embarrassed to feel its accuracy when I made the connection. He feared his father and covered over the fear with contempt and loathing. Eventually, he produced some very direct primal scene material related to both the transference and his childhood.

Professor G's associations were quite productive. Together with occasional enactments, they encouraged formulations on an oedipal level which included a wish to be his analyst's/mother's one and only, a sense of her betrayal by being with his father (my work, family or a colleague), the narcissistic injury of being excluded from the parental couple, murderous wishes for vengeance towards both parents, envy of his father for being stronger and better equipped, longing for his father to lend him strength, hatred of his analyst/mother and of all women because they always disappointed him by proving to be impure. His verbal responses to these and other related interpretations enlarged their scope and seemed to confirm them. Relevant primal scene reactions occurred in the transference and led to explicit, previously repressed, confirmatory childhood memories. His shock, castration anxiety, rage and feeling of betrayal by his mother/analyst, wish for vengeance, sense of his inadequacy as a male, envy of and longing to acquire power from his father/analyst all emerged feelingly.

Something fundamental remained immovable, however. Professor G continued to react with painful symptoms to changes in the schedule which he took as slights, to be unaware of any positive attachment to me, to enjoy subtly this failure as a vengeance. Insights into the past and his relationship with primary objects were used more as a means of diminishing my importance than as a pathway to insight and change. Although his work, which he had at best performed *pro forma*, became a significant source of accomplishment, pleasure and satisfaction to him, his object relationships remained unrewarding. He played a significant, caring and considerate paternal role with three young nieces, the daughters of his widowed younger sister. Otherwise he stayed in a bleak, unsatisfying, mutually vengeful relationship, continued to behave in unacknowledged, often quite subtly vindictive ways towards me, and was generally isolated. If his associations to my interventions seemed to carry the work further in individual sessions, he remained passive in his attitude towards the material he provided and more often than not completely forgot the insights arrived at.

Realizing the need to re-examine my understanding of Professor G and of the work we were doing together, I began to scrutinize my subjective states when with him. Although routine, a reassessment of this nature is, in fact, complex. The literature has emphasized the sequence through which self-analysis leads to new insight and results in changes in one's understanding of a patient. Such a sequence appropriately privileges the analyst's conflicted contribution to stalemate. Indeed, it would be quite possible to identify equivalent countertransferential forces in me. However, there is a less recognized aspect of the process of reassessment, one certainly also connected to countertransference but in a far less direct fashion. It is this aspect that I wish to discuss in this chapter.

What I have in mind is the analyst's change, during the process of reassessment, in what I shall call metaphors of transition. In paying attention to what I was feeling, I was *imaginatively reorienting my position as analyst vis-à-vis the patient in space from a position where I was an outside interpreter of a transference involving me to one where I was the recipient of a communication inside me.* That is, *I was changing the metaphor which provided the imagery not only for our places in relation to each other in space, but in the form and manner of Professor G's communication with me.* Through it, I sought to gain better imaginative access to that aspect of Professor G's inner life unknown to him, as well as to the unknown aspect of my own inner life that was responding to what I could not see in his.

Spatial metaphors of the mind of this nature are often distillations of theories of mental functioning that directly affect technique. It makes a difference in both how one listens and talks to a patient whether one imagines oneself to be the outside observer of a transference fantasy involving oneself, or a participant in it, for instance. Although we often think about the kind of shift I have described as a change in theoretical orientation, sometimes a shift in the use of metaphor may represent an expansion of one's use of the original theory beyond its metaphorical constraints. Thus while the type of opening up I refer to may well represent a working through of a countertransference that had allowed the analyst to become imaginatively imprisoned by the dominant metaphors of a particular theory, it may just as well represent a working through of a transference to a particular teacher who stands for a way of thinking clinically and who has consequently become invested with the mantle of authority.

In either case, metaphors are crucial to the way theories function in the clinical setting. They play a central role because of the nature of psychoanalytic theories of the functioning of the mind. Despite our tendency to think of these theories as relatively objective constructs, psychoanalytic theories are best conceived of as transitions between inner, or what is lived, and outer, or what can be observed and expressed.

Theory, transition and metaphor

The idea of a psychoanalytic theory of the mind having a transitional function will seem alien to most of us despite the knowledge that the subjectivity that theories of the mind's functioning attempt to account for cannot be arrived at by exclusive reliance on externally observable phenomena, that there exists a divide between what is observable and therefore capable of being described and what is lived and thus only very partially and approximately observable and communicable. That divide must be crossed by the conjectures that comprise a particular theory. Analogously, psychoanalysis, as a treatment method, requires its practitioners to cross the divide within themselves between inner and outer, known and unknown, with regularity and to encourage patients to become adept in the same way. Analysts imagine not only that part of ourselves that is only vaguely apprehended, but that aspect of the patient's mind that we need help grasping, as well. We use imagination, together with a method of listening, to put ourselves in the place of our patients in order to understand what the latter experience, and sometimes also to articulate that experience.

If the result of imagination in clinical psychoanalysis is the analyst's and patient's halting and piecemeal articulation of a difficult-to-apprehend part of the latter's experience and the complex reasons that comprise it, the distillation of analogous imagination in articulated theory is the metaphor. Although related to analogy, metaphor does not explicitly recognize its analogical origin. Instead, it crosses over disparate categories and combines them in ways that surprise. Love is not *like* a red rose, it *is* one and the mind *is* deep, a space to be plumbed. Metaphor creates, in language, that illusory space between two categories analogous to transitional space in which the categories are neither one nor the other, but both and neither. It thus becomes the vehicle that links what we intuit but can barely verbalize with what we can perceive and know. It is essential for the work of the mind that studies itself, given the limitations and paradox that the fact of the mind studying itself entails, to posit and to have this transitional space for imagination that metaphor provides.

Frequently, the poetic affinities of metaphor have made it an unpopular vehicle for the expression of theory. Far from disappearing, however, metaphor has generally become implicit. Here is a passage from a paper by Winnicott on primitive emotional development:

> There are long stretches of time in a normal infant's life in which a baby does not mind whether he is in many bits or one whole being, or whether he lives in his mother's face or in his whole body, provided that from time to time he comes together and feels something. (Winnicott, 1945, p. 150)

Despite Winnicott's writing as though he had access to the inner experience of an infant, most people who read this passage in context do not seem to care that the author cannot possibly ascertain what the infant external to himself experiences (Ogden, 2001). Winnicott has just been discussing the patient who fills his first session of the week with details of every hour of the time spent without the analyst at the weekend and concluding that the patient may need 'to be known in all his bits and pieces by one person, the analyst' (1945, p. 150). At this point in his text, Winnicott invokes 'The ordinary stuff of infant life' (1945, p. 150) and describes the unintegrated state in the way it appears above. As Ogden (2001) argues in discussing this passage at length, the analyst of the patient who recites his weekend activities may be tempted out of impotence and anger to make a resistance interpretation even if his clinical sense is that the patient is doing something adaptive. Winnicott's accomplishment is to link the patient's behaviour with the object's role in providing an integrating experience so that the analyst has a theoretical reason to continue to listen rather than to act on his frustration.

But it is how Winnicott makes this link that is of particular interest. In his general explication of his conception of an infantile unintegrated state that is a basis for later regressive disintegration, he moves back and forth between his imaginative recreation of infantile development and his clinical experience so that the two become fused in our consciousness and it is difficult to say which informs which. At the moment in his text of imaginative encounter with the frustrating patient, it appears natural that Winnicott reaches out for a baby. The authoritative statements about the infant's subjective state that follow do not strike us as impossible to know *because we read them as metaphors for the patient who spends his hour describing his time spent without the analyst.*

To be sure, there is a double direction in Winnicott's paper: on one side it points to the metaphorical, experiential view I am emphasizing; on the other, to the more concrete developmental perspective (albeit with a minimalist timetable and a focus on inner process, not external event) that is manifestly asserted. But this very double direction exemplifies and illuminates the transitional function of psychoanalytic theory in the subtle encompassing without denomination of metaphorical/subjective and developmental/objective positions.

Thinking of theory as a transition between outer and inner inevitably brings up transitional objects and phenomena (Winnicott, 1951; 1971) to which I have already indirectly referred. Winnicott's contribution is a theory about the psychological coming into being of the mind (Roussillon, 1999). To focus on how the mind uses theory in clinical work is to focus on an analogous process: how our understanding of what has heretofore been inner and unknown, in ourselves and/or in another, comes into being as something conscious. Of course, there is an inherent circularity in a theory about the mind's functioning being used to characterize the way our minds use a theory about the way our minds function, but this circularity is inevitable, a variation on the paradox of which Freud made us aware by articulating the existence of the unconscious: since the mental functioning we attempt to explain occurs partly beyond our conscious awareness, we study the unknown dimensions of the mind with the very instrument composed of unknown dimensions beyond our knowledge.

Although we are more familiar with psychoanalytic theories that are presented as though 'obliged to maintain a "scientific" distance from their object of analysis' (Roussillon, 1999, p. 11; my translation), it is more accurate to think of them as transitions between outer and inner and more useful to assess their value partly by the way they help us to cross a similar divide in ourselves in the process of doing clinical work. Writing theory as though it were objective truth limits it, as well as obscuring its transitional function. For example, in a seminal paper by Isaacs (1948), which set out the Kleinian position on fantasy during the controversial discussions at the British Society (Reed and Baudry, 1997, p. 245), the role of transition is shifted away from theory through equivocation. Fantasy, Isaacs said, was both 'the psychic representative of instinct' and 'the subjective interpretation of experience'. Fantasy as the mental embodiment of instinct is fantasy conceived as a wholly inner event, which is then objectified as structure. Fantasy as the interpretation of experience is fantasy as subjective transformation of external reality. Although the definitions are different, Isaacs treats them as equivalent, and in that way the concept of fantasy, with its two *different* definitions which are treated as equivalents, becomes the vehicle of transition. Theory then mistakenly appears not to be transition, but as definitively *describing* an inner transition.

Brenner (2000), to name a psychoanalytic theoretician whose careful argumentation more closely reflects contemporary concerns with the methodology of evidence, names the sources of his data, labels the conclusions resulting in his clearly articulated version of conflict theory as conjectures, proceeds to reason according to the laws of logic and insists that his inferences do not contradict established facts in neighbouring fields. However, he presents data from religious myths to support conclusions (originally based on adult psychoanalyses) concerning early childhood sexual and aggressive impulses. Although these data may have undergone significant transformations from their childhood origins, he does not take into account the possibility or nature of these transformations, nor does he acknowledge that those transformations might undermine the data he uses to establish the nature of early childhood conflict.

The transitionality of the theory is buried in the neglected transformations that the data have undergone.

There is a direct correspondence between the objective vision of theory shared by Brenner and Isaacs and the content of the theories they formulate. Following Freud and Klein, both hypothesize theory that minimizes the variable contribution of specific material reality to individual psychic reality and emphasizes universal psychodynamic, intrapsychic processes (Green, 2000b).[2] This emphasis leads to formulations of self-sustaining systems. For instance, in Freud, the drive is towards the object representation of the drive cathexis, that is, towards something already represented within and then re-found. In Klein, the object representation is governed by pre-wired phantasy which includes internal objects so that the relation to the primary object is already a transference. Both theories thus assume that what is unconscious can be retrieved because it is already represented, whether it is buried within the mind or projected into another. A theory that takes more explicitly into account the intersubjective, circumstantial quality of the object relation as well as its intrapsychic consequences may also take into account the possibility that qualities of the object, a psychotic mother, to take an extreme instance, could lead to a failure of representation, to an intrapsychic state in which an object is either eternally and intrusively present or decathected and missing (Green, 1975). That is, such a theory reorients the analyst towards thinking about the potential relation of subject to object as that relation is shaped but not dominated by the drive derivatives. A reorientation of this nature encourages us to focus substantively on the process of symbolization, the many gradations between the presence of the object and its ultimate representation and the pathology associated with different outcomes of the process. That is, it leads us to focus on the processes of *transition from presence to symbolized absence*. It is these very processes that are required of a body of theory that must bridge what is lived and what can be expressed. I will return to this issue when I discuss the concept of analytic space. The point here is that the insistence on theory as objective entity rather than as transitional function may restrict the potential scope and complexity of theoretical formulations that ought to account for fragmentation, faulty symbolization and experiences of nothingness as well as of hidden presence.

No matter how careful our conjectural process or how certain our theory, theory ultimately traverses a chasm from that which is observed

---

[2] I am here emphasizing the focus of the theories. Practice is another matter. Because patients teach us to look beyond the blinders that theories might impose, we learn to take into account what is crucial, and in so doing collectively correct theoretical emphases. Practitioners of either theory would surely argue that specific circumstances of material reality are not overlooked in practice and indeed that theoretical provision for them exists.

to that which is inferred about the inner life of a subject who is other than we, or other than the part of us that is conscious. Evaluations of the basis on which the leap from observation to inference occurs aside, the vehicle of choice to carry us over a chasm not unlike Pascal's void is metaphor. Moreover, one might say that for a practising clinician who must hourly bridge the gap between abstract theory and the challenges and mysteries of work with a (not the) patient, the imaginative transition afforded by metaphor is a necessity.

Although I have concentrated on how theories restrict the metaphors available to us, theories also provide us with the means to make transitions through the richness of the metaphors they do provide. The metaphor links disparate worlds, conscious expression and unconscious fantasy (Arlow, 1979), lived and verbalized experience, the states of different subjects. Through it, the patient may become an infant for us in the very way love becomes a rose. That is, our experience, real or imagined, of holding a squalling baby and trying to calm him has to do with our hope that he will recognize a state of protection and calm connected to us, and it is this experience we summon both to the metaphor and to the clinical situation it attempts to clarify. Metaphor, visible or invisible, is the transitional mechanism *par excellence*.

Spatial metaphor

Metaphors inherent in specific theories exert a powerful influence on the way we use theories, as well as on the way we think about how we use them. For the sake of this chapter I shall restrict myself to metaphors of space that evoke a concept of both the psyche and of the relationship possible between analyst and analysand and limit myself to a consideration of spatial metaphor associated with (a) the classical or conflict model, (b) the Kleinian or the paranoid/schizoid position, and (c) that elaborated by Green (1975). Depending partly on the theory, mental space can be imagined:

- As largely contained within the borders of the mind of the individual and including a buried portion that the analysis uncovers through the transference. The boundary between analyst and patient is established and largely intact and there is an equivalent boundary between the analyst as transference fantasy inside the mind of the patient and the analyst as materially real without.
- As dispersed among self and object and within parts of self and parts of objects, so that parts of self and object are rearranged and reassigned in terms of what is unwanted and what is desired. A boundary providing function is required of the analyst because the mental space

of the patient and the space in which the relation between analyst and patient takes place may become congruent and fused and may need to be separated.
- As dispersed in relation to a maternal/analyst surround that is seen as belonging to neither one nor the other, but as a mutual space of facilitation, potential and creativity. This transitional space comes into being as an analytic space in which communication occurs and representation, if it has been heretofore compromised, is possible.

The analyst imaginatively saturated with spatial metaphors, both implied and explicit, will conceive of him- or herself, the patient and their role in arriving at a cure congruently with what the metaphors evoke. My work with Professor G is telling in this regard.

Once I began to focus on my reactions to incidents like the opening instructions on decorating, I realized that I always felt taken aback, invaded, dispossessed, inadequate and sometimes righteously angry. Contemplating retrospectively the incident I have described, for instance, it struck me that I was experiencing Professor G as asserting a dictatorship of design, wiping me out as a separate person with a taste of my own. This realization freed me from being so like Professor G that I was sharing his tendency to look away and refuse to see things that led to painful feelings. I was able to see clearly for the first time that there had been no room for difference between him and me. *I began to imagine that he had collapsed the space between us.*

To speak of the space collapsed between us is actually to invoke the absence of two kinds of space. One is that needed to maintain the 'as if-ness' of the transference, where the image of the analyst saturated with, say, negative feeling may be held at the same time as the different image of the analyst as analyst. The other is the space that allowed a difference between us as individual subjects. In recognizing the absence of a space for difference between us, I was re-establishing it in my own mind. The transference, I began to see, was not one Professor G could join me in observing from without. Moreover, it was much less triadic than dyadic. That is, if one were to think from my new perspective about the primal scene that had been such a focus of our work, it would be in terms of the existence of only an omnipotent subject and a degraded object, the two being undifferentiated. Each figure was, through his narcissistic identifications, an unintegrated aspect of Professor G.

What I had seen as a well-delineated, structured oedipal triangle in which my work represented an object of more value to me than he was reorganizing itself in my understanding to become a condensed scene of projected and introjected 'bits and pieces' of himself. In it, once he found himself thwarted in his wish for a narcissistic union with me, his mother/analyst, he took on a sadistic and omniscient omnipotence, a parody of the paternal authority he did not genuinely have, and evoked in me (or projected into me) that part of himself identified with the helplessness and inadequacy of the child-onlooker as it was condensed with the victimhood, powerlessness and degradation of the mother/whore. I had unwittingly been joining him in the actualization of this scene.

As a result of my imagining a different spatial relationship between us, I also saw that Professor G's words at these charged moments could not be treated as associations. Rather, they were acts asserting his omnipotent control of me. My feeling invaded also became a significant piece of data, an immediate affective communication from him to me that signalled his attempt to control me. It existed on a plane different from that of word patterns we could contemplate together. In avoiding cognizance of this invasion, I had been identified with Professor G's omnipotent cancelling out the difference between us. In assuming his capacity to join me in deducing the unconscious content concealed and presented by his associations, I was overestimating his capacity for differentiated functioning in a way that complemented his inflating of himself. Now, instead of assuming that he possessed this capacity reliably, I began to recognize the subtle way in which his use of free association was a successful attempt at getting me to admire him by creating in me a good feeling about my ability to interpret his unconscious fantasies.

Emphasis on the data of what I was feeling with Professor G led me further to recognize that Professor G could not always be spoken to as if he had an integrated ego. His collapsing the difference between us, so that I felt taken over, invaded and possessed, meant that he was destroying the contact between us as separate individuals and evoking in me feelings that corresponded with aspects of himself that he wished either to incorporate or to get rid of. I was not the neutral observer of his transference to me. I was a receptacle for denied or wished for aspects of himself and unconscious aspects of myself were facilitating these introjective and projective processes.

I began also to see that his tender feelings for his nieces were a central expression of a disavowed part of himself. These feelings could be expressed towards them only because he could expel his frightening dependence on me by locating it outside of himself and in these children in a relationship where his little nieces were dependent on him. At the same time he could be helpful and understanding to them in a way he experienced that I was to him without acknowledging in any way that he experienced me as helpful or understanding, let alone that he needed me to be that way. Care-giving and being taken care of was another way besides being admired by an admired object that he could secretly recreate a state that was without boundary between us.

These new perceptions enabled me to change my interpretative tack and focus on Professor G's lack of differentiation from me, first as it appeared in the mental state where he achieved admiration. His feeling admired by me and his lack of differentiation were both aspects of himself, in the normal course of our psychoanalytic work together, that were silent and successfully masked, but that emerged in moments such as his first hour on the couch with a suddenness I always experienced as shocking. I gradually learned that the moments in which he reacted like this were moments in which he experienced a shock that undermined a persistent defensive fantasy. In it he and I were an amalgamated and omnipotent unit. Either he was my admired part or I was his. No wonder, then, that unanticipated cancellations on my part led to massive hostile reactions. These reactions occurred when he experienced me to be acting independently and elicited in response the devastated other side of his grandiosity. He then attempted to get even by some often subtle manoeuvre, a request for a change of appointment, for instance, which, if I agreed, reassured him about his special status and ability to control me because of it.

After much focus on his wish to be one powerful entity with me, he began to recognize and talk about his shame and sense of inadequacy. He discovered how he used women whom he perceived as powerful. By making them into extensions of himself, he protected himself from paralysing anxiety. He began to see that he felt this anxiety when he had to do something on his own. He forgot the work we did less and less often.

Work on a dream during this period illustrates some of this new psychic movement. The context was his receipt of my bill reflecting a larger, previously agreed fee. He began by mentioning that he had become exhausted and, unable to face paying his bills the night before, awoke with a painful physical symptom. Although he gave no indication of realizing it, this symptom usually accompanied unrecognized depressive states connected to the transference. The dream he had, he remarked, had 'nothing to do with' his eagerness to pay me the new fee and his inability to stay awake long enough to write the cheque. I intervened to say that he might be asserting this irrelevance to protect himself from painful feelings connected to my having asked for an increased fee. He continued by describing his dream. In it, he had to fix the silencer on his car. The silencer was unusually constructed: 'There was a small screw, shaped like a V, like a set screw. It screwed into the larger screw in a very beautiful way. When screwed in, it was completely flush. A very nice piece of engineering, but the small screw had been lost.' In the associations, he noted the sexual references, waiting for me to pick up on them, then when I did not, began to speak about the 'pleasure and excitement' of observing how 'this tiny screw goes into the larger screw, perfectly flush'. The silencer and a big engine had fallen down under the car. 'They were all held in place by this little screw.' As he spoke, his exaggerated wonder, pleasure in the beauty and engineering of this device and admiration for it were palpable. I could feel his intense, almost manic excitement. I became aware of momentarily sharing it, not as admiration for the engineering, but as admiration for a dream image exactly representing his wished for union with me. I suggested that the little screw perfectly flush inside the bigger screw, controlling everything, holding everything together, depicted the relationship he sought with me, indeed was seeking with me now where I would be so carried away by admiration for him that we would both feel enhanced and together.

He returned to his having 'shut down' the night before. He had not then connected his mood to his feelings about my bill, but did so now. He then remembered a dream in which he could not be forceful in a group of adolescent girls because his voice was weak. Some of these girls were very excitable and excited. Something about very emotional women frightened him. I connected his feeling of helplessness and his inhibition to his disappointment in me. He believed my raising the fee showed that I was indifferent to him. I might get excited, but then I dropped him, and he felt frightened by his disappointment in and consequent rage towards me. Being dropped was the opposite of the feeling he had imagining the two flush screws together. If he were together with me in the way he wanted, he would not feel anxious about being with excitable and exciting women.

He was just thinking about his difficulty being alone, he said. The previous night he had been alone when paying his bills. It was like something he had recently talked about with me, his not wanting to go alone after the session to a new place to meet someone he did not know: 'I wanted to be with someone to take away my anxiety, to take care of me. . . . It sounds strange, being angry because someone doesn't do these things for me.' He talked about how, as a child, he felt the women in the house were his servants and how he still wanted to be treated in that way. I suggested that he wanted me to be an extension of him so that he could be sure that I would do whatever he needed me to do so that he would not feel anxious and on his own. He acknowledged: 'There's a lot of evidence for that in how I have run my life.' He continued that he felt the pain from his symptom, but not the resentment he must be harbouring for not getting his way. He would feel protected if he could control me in the way he wants to. I said it would spare him the anxiety he felt when he was on his own, but that he had always needed to wear a mask with people because he was ashamed that he felt so anxious. After a brief pause, he reported that the pain had disappeared. He said the fact that the silencer fell off means it was defective. There was some confusion about the car and there was something wrong with him; he could not hold it up. The previous day he realized that he had avoided taking the initiative with a woman in whom he was interested. He hoped he would have another opportunity.

To return to the metaphors that initially influenced my understanding of and technical approach to Professor G, without being aware of it, I at first imagined Professor G and myself inhabiting separate spheres that intersected at the point of communication. To facilitate that communication, I might cross briefly into Professor G's sphere, but only enough to make a trial identification, that is, to sample his subjective state (Beres and Arlow, 1974). I imagined Professor G's mind as a self-contained, more or less accessible, whole in which the least accessible unconscious parts could be understood by virtue of his associations and affective reactions, particularly as they involved fantasies about me.

In the second version, however, I imagined the space between us as collapsed so that we were each inside the other's minds. Minds in this image were not self-contained but dispersed, unintegrated and intermingled so that parts of each could be interchanged. That is, in a more abstract formulation, contact between us as differentiated individuals had been replaced by narcissistic exchanges of unintegrated internalizations and externalizations. This second version, clearly closer to the explicit spatial metaphors that make up a Kleinian description of the paranoid schizoid position (Klein, 1946), was more conscious than the first.

Classical theory is expressed more extensively by abstract concepts. Thus, although metaphors function as transitions to the patient's inner state, channelling aspects of the analyst's imagination, they tend to go unnoticed. In these metaphors the mind is evoked imaginatively in the way I first imagined Professor G's, as self-contained and as concealing significant elements buried in its depths.[3] The neurotic model at the base of this theorizing emphasizes intactness. One 'speaks to *the* ego' in interpreting anxiety before impulse. If there is a flaw in the functioning of the superego, it is not that the superego is in pieces, but that there are lacunae in an agency otherwise assumed to be whole. Intactness brings with it the idea of delineated boundaries among spaces, and thus

---

[3] The analyst's work, Freud wrote in a famous analogy, 'resembles . . . an archaeologist's excavation of some dwelling place that has been destroyed and buried' (Freud, 1937, p. 259).

between the minds of selves and objects.[4] There is a clear distinction between the transferential analyst *within* the transference neurosis (that is, within the patient's mind) whose presence is to be interpreted and the materially real analyst *without* who does the interpreting (Reed, 1994).

This spatial conception gives rise to ideas of a therapeutic split and therapeutic alliance and influenced my initial assumptions about Professor G's capacity reliably and consistently to observe himself. Both the therapeutic split and alliance are based on the capacity to be connected to and differentiated from the object and are very different from a defensive split in a narcissistic organization, the state of affairs I came to understand was the case with Professor G.

The primacy afforded the drives draws attention to their exigencies in the space between their matrix in the subject[5] and their revelation by objects. This emphasis minimizes the subject/object poles where the interface with material reality occurs, and thus channels attention away from the quality of a particular object's interactions with a particular subject. In addition, any potential fragmentation or lack of integration in the related agencies or objects tends to be relegated to a place of secondary importance. As Arlow points out, the concept of part-object makes no sense because the object is whatever the drive seeks out for its satisfaction, whether a whole person or a part of a person (Arlow, 1980) since the object is always the object representation of the drive cathexis, whatever its quality. I tended to concentrate on conflict, beginning with the drive derivative, and my attention was in this way diverted from the divided state of Professor G's ego.

Given the power of unrecognized metaphor to influence our thinking, the psyche that emerges as our imaginative default is thus a space extending in depth and containing significant content to be uncovered, only unrecognized traces of which are initially available. In the version more connected to the structural theory than the topographic, integrated, discernibly whole agencies, id, ego and superego, interact and

---

[4] The transference neurosis, Freud wrote, was 'an intermediate region between fantasy and real life', something enclosed, a 'playground', accessible from outside itself to interpretation by the materially real analyst. The analyst within its boundaries was a version of the patient's fantasy to be dissolved along with the transference neurosis by interpretation of the contained fantasies (Reed, 1994). Despite a similarity of lexicon, this intermediate region with its definite boundaries between fantasy and reality, self and other is very different from Winnicott's transitional space of indistinct ownership, its me/not me fluidity, its material and purposefully metaphoric fuzziness.

[5] I use the term subject, following Green (2000), to denote that which is the opposite of object, at once the source and executor of the drives. It is a composite denoting the series comprising terms such as self and ego, in both their conscious or unconscious dimensions. Just as there is no one object, but rather objects, there is no one subject.

conflict with each other by means of drives arising from the depth of the id and executed and/or defended against by aspects of the ego. This rather closed, intrapsychic space also contains a deep unconscious to be uncovered, though it is parcelled out between the id (the drives) and the ego (the seat of memory and fantasy). In both versions, the conflicts that occur within it are capable of being observed from without. Indeed, the analyst as archaeologist is first and foremost an observer/detective expected to remain separate from that version of him- or herself that is located within the patient's transference as fantasy. Because there is an assumption that the patient has an intact ego, the data used for interpretation are the verbal derivatives of the drives (or their equivalents in action) as these have combined with ego activities, memory, wish, defence and childhood understanding or distortion, into a network of unconscious fantasy/memory constellations. With this image of a closed, integrated and delineated mental space in our minds, we listen to the derivatives as products of that mind and seek to make its workings intelligible to that aspect of the patient's ego allied with the working analyst and that is able to grasp its own incongruities.[6] I assumed a degree of differentiation in line with these expectations. The power of these metaphors works against distinguishing between an effective mask (Kernberg, 1984) and a healthy adaptation.

To be sure, this image of the mind is not required by the theory. Nor, therefore, were my assumptions dictated by it. Formulations such as the splitting that forms part of perverse conflict solution (Freud, 1927; 1938; Reed, 1997; 2001), or of inter-systemic conflict, for example (Rangell, 1963), Jacobson's formulations on the self and the object world (e.g. 1954), and Kernberg's synthesis and expansion of conflict theory to encompass object relations theory expand our imaginative horizons. These formulations include the potential for conflict solutions that differ in their power to create structural *discontinuity* from compromise formations of a neurotic nature. Laplanche and Pontalis (1973) emphasize the phenomenon of discontinuity by describing the splitting of the ego as comprised of two separate defensive solutions, one based on neurotic mechanisms utilizing repression, the other on psychotic mechanisms utilizing denial. Such a formulation brings us to a universe in which the patient is indeed divided and individual agencies are not intact.

However, such formulations tend to run counter to the dominant metaphors we, as members of an analytic group (Reed, 1994; Grossman,

---

[6] Given a patient more obviously compromised in his or her integration, I suspect that these metaphors of space lead to a clinical tendency that Nasir Ilahi (personal communication) has noticed: to wait silently, or to make only supportive interventions, in the expectation that the patient will be 'reborn' as an integrated individual in the oedipal phase.

1995), ascribe to an authoritative theory and that then influence the technique we employ. At the imaginative visual level, the metaphoric undertow pulls our imagination towards the conceptualizing of integrated entities that interact by virtue of the predominant drive energies. Operating within the imaginative universe provided by this theory and reinforced by the authority we unconsciously ascribe to it, we tend to speak to a patient in conflict in a way that assumes that he or she is capable of experiencing both sides of the conflict at the same time and of containing it. This idea is not the totality of the theory so much as *the intuitive and unrecognized byproduct of the way we imagine the theory working through specific metaphor to create the necessary transition between inner and outer*. Such a metaphorical level may function together with countertransference to narrow existing options when creative divergence is most necessary. In the case of Professor G, my overestimation of his capacity to be separate and connected was an aspect of the admiration he sought so that there was a fit between his defensive needs and the way my countertransference availed itself of theory.

Far different from the space of classical analysis is that metaphorical space in which the multiple processes of projective identification occur, that is, in Klein's paranoid-schizoid universe. There, space tends to extend horizontally; as parts of the self cross into the other, parts of the idealized other are assimilated into the self. The unit of delineation here is also the individual psyche, but a psyche in 'bits and pieces', to use Winnicott's (1945) phrase. The theory posits a potential whole self and a whole other, but treats them as readily dispersible, its parts interchangeable. It assumes a partial self that utilizes an other it distorts. Space must, therefore, include this distorted and cannibalized self, or parts of selves, and complementary other, or parts of other.

Moreover, given this imaginative rendering, the analyst occupies the space with the patient, is the recipient of projected and introjected aspects of the patient's self. This movement of parts of the self into the other and vice versa becomes a major, non-verbal means of communication that either supplements or replaces the verbal derivatives of drives that are free associations. This communication can take place because of the greater fluidity and lack of separation between working and transferential analyst, analyst and patient. The therapeutic analyst contains the projections of the analysand and in so doing helps the patient to integrate split-off parts of him- or herself.

Three major differences from classical evocation result from the differences in images, implied or described. First, there is an emphasis on the state of the executor and recipient of the drives. Subject and object are seen as interacting through the agency of the drives, with the latter in the background and the former in the foreground. Thus, whether the ego and its object(s) are in an integrated or unintegrated state at any given moment becomes an important and immediate clinical concern. The object, however, remains a product of pre-existing fantasy so that every relation to a materially real object is a transference. Second, there is a change in how the spatial relationship between analyst and patient is conceived. Just as the ego and object can be integrated or unintegrated, so the object and subject of analysis and therefore also the transference and countertransference are potentially less separate and separable. That is, the emphasis is less on the boundaries between the analyst and the patient than on the frequency with which those boundaries may be crossed and on the therapeutic need to sort out parts of self and object in order to re-establish boundaries through the containing function of the analyst. One might say, in spatial terms, that the analyst and patient are situated differently *vis-à-vis* each other than is the case in a classical or conflict model. Rather than the materially real analyst observing the fate of a fantasy about himself within the patient's transference, we must account for a materially real analyst discovering elements of the patient within himself and possibly losing elements of himself within the patient. Third, there is a concomitant change in the conception of what constitutes analytic data because the image of parts of the self crossing over into the other and influencing that other leads directly to the valorizing of non-verbal subjective states in the analyst. Verbal derivatives are no longer a sufficient, or even the primary, source of information about the patient. When they are used, they are taken to refer to mental states of the subject in relation to the transference object.

The analytic space

The shift of working metaphor I have described accompanies psychic reorganization in the analyst and helps foster it by enlarging the metaphoric universe through which transitions from the analyst's understanding of the more remote reaches of himself to those of the patient are effected. This process of subjective transformation in the analyst seems best expressed not by speaking of a change of theory, but by a third set of spatial metaphors that unifies the two previous approaches. These can be found in Andre Green's concept of analytic space that draws on Freud, Winnicott and Bion. Winnicott's phrase about the baby not minding for long stretches of time 'whether he is in many bits or whether he lives in his mother's face or in his own body' (1945, p. 150) evokes the ambiguity of the interplay between an unintegrated self and maternal surround. The conjunction, assuming adequate mothering, creates a space of potential and facilitation.

Similarly, the effort of the analyst to understand himself with the patient and, by understanding what is alien in himself to understand what is other in the patient, and the effort by the patient to put as much of what he or she experiences into words that convey both the known and unknown portions of him- or herself, create a complex intertwining of doubles, consisting of what each party 'lives and what they communicate', that is a 'potential space', the analytic session, where shared metaphor becomes possible (Green, 1975, p. 12). This entwining set of doubles has been called the analytic third (Ogden, 1994).[7]

This metaphorical space belongs to neither analyst nor patient, but is the creation of both. It is a space analogous to the transitional object of the infant which '*is not an internal object* (which is a mental concept) – it is a possession. Yet it is not (for the infant) an external object either' (Winnicott, 1973, p. 237). There is in Winnicott already a complex interaction between inner and outer. For the transitional object to exist for the infant, adequate provision of care from the external object is required. Otherwise, the internal object becomes too persecutory, 'fails to have meaning for the infant . . . and the transitional object becomes meaningless too' (Winnicott, 1973, p. 237). That is, the structure and integration of the inner world depends on the interrelation between external care and internal dynamics.

The analytic space is also a place of intersection, but in Green's conceptualization, what comprises that intersection is a complex interaction between intersubjective and intrapsychic for both patient and analyst. The particularities of the patient's objects and his or her ensuing degree of representation of them intersect with and influence the dynamic internal interplay among drives and subject in a way that affects the analyst not only intersubjectively but also intrapsychically. It is here that the patient's ability or inability to symbolize the object as absent becomes a crucial issue of treatment because the degree of representation of which the patient is capable affects the patient's thinking and the degree of integration of the ego and the object representations. If an object is too intrusive, it is impossible to represent it and thus to conceive of absence, if too idealized, it remains impossible to connect with (Green, 1975). In either case, a persecutory object may be held on to, to ward off the threat of nothingness and emptiness (Green, 1993) and the analyst kept excluded in a position of impotence and empty-headedness.

The analytic space has a frame, analogous to the mother's arms (Green, 1997). Mutable and living, it is created by the gradual articula-

---

[7] Ogden's (1994) reading emphasizes intersubjectivity at the expense of the intrapsychic. My reading of Green, particularly a more recent clarification of the topic (Green, 2000b), is that he emphasizes a continuing dialectic between the intersubjective and the intrapsychic.

tion of the affects and conflicts that arise within the setting for analyst and patient and that they pursue together. The relationship between them provides the context out of which meaning evolves. The movement is towards a discrimination of what is inner and alien in oneself and what belongs to the other.

The metaphorical space between analyst and patient here is one in which a gap between them (between what is lived in the patient and communicated, and what is lived with the patient in the analyst and communicated as understanding) is transformed into a space of communication that is neither that of one mind nor the other. Rather, it is a space that provides the context in which meaning between analyst and patient can exist. The analyst must be able to use his capacity for understanding himself and the patient to reach the communication in the material given him by the patient 'as well as gauging the possible effect, across this gap, of what he, in return, can communicate to the patient' (Green, 1975, p. 5). To create this space and transform the gap, the analyst has to offer himself first as a narcissistic object, what Green calls a 'similar other'. 'I subordinate all access to the otherness of the other, as other, to the existence of . . . another person who is similar enough to be able to identify with him or her and thus be of assistance to that person in his or her . . . helplessness' (2000, p. 19). That is, one does not assume a degree of separation (difference) of self from object, either in the sense of the self as alienated from its unconscious or as it is capable of enough integration to symbolize the absence of the object.

> Difference of the other as different (either intrapsychically the other in so far as he or she is unconscious; or intersubjectively the other in so far as he or she is an ego outside of oneself) is both a development of the similar other or an opening towards a new destination: that which is similar is no longer so. It is other. I can imagine it, for I no longer need the support provided by my similitude. Consciousness of being separated from the other no longer threatens my position as an ego. (Green, 2000, p. 19)

With a growing sense of communication and understanding about what is alien in the self and in the other comes a growing delineation of boundaries between self and other. The intrapsychic here duplicates the intersubjective. One gets to know the alienated parts of the self through the similar other.

Where early development has not been severely impaired, the construction of an analytic space may be barely discernible and attention quickly focused instead on the neurotic conflicts that deploy themselves within it. Where early development has been impaired, the construction of the analytic space takes primacy of place because it is a space the very construction of which facilitates new structure. Given Green's conception of non-neurotic patients as suffering the dual and competing anxieties of separation from and intrusion of the primary object that makes it impossible to symbolize the object in its absence, this idea of a mutual space allows also for an intermediate relation that is neither intrusive nor separate. Data derive from both internal subjective states in the analyst and the patient's associations. The analysis of non-neurotic patients will depend more on the former, because it depends on the hazardous enterprise of induction, as Green remarks (1975, p. 5), and that implies the scrutiny by the analyst of his or her subjective state and his or her contributions to the patient's reaction. The analysis of neurosis, on the other hand, requires primarily that one listen to the associations and deduce from them the unconscious fantasies.

Discussion

It is possible in these terms to understand the shift in metaphors that allowed me to make the transition between Professor G's subjectivity and my own not as a shift from one theory to another arising from a recognition of error, as I have provisionally described it, but *as part of a larger inductive analytic process. In this process the transition from outer to inner and from conscious to unconscious, as well as the establishment of the space in which these transitions occur, take place very gradually.* For Professor G and myself, this process included as a first stage the enactment between us, given who we each were and what we were trying to do together.

At the beginning of this process, Professor G did not admit the need for treatment, but characteristically availed himself of outside circumstances. Nevertheless, he also let me know indirectly quite early on about his problems in relationships, his anxieties, his difficulty in taking initiatives, his proclivity for being hurt. He was both unconsciously communicating his inner pain to me and working very hard at pretending it did not exist. Moreover, this need to conceal who he thought he was and what he felt went to the most profound roots of his character. Charming and personable, he used these gifts to stay distant without at all seeming to. His was not a performance in the usual sense of the term. His life was a performance: to seem normal when he did not feel himself to be so.

I was both taken in by his performance and, by the very nature of the analytic compact, not taken in, since I was attempting to hear what he indirectly told me about his inner pain. From the start, then, there was a division in me that reflected the division in him and prevented me from seeing that the apparently collaborating, reasonable person on the couch was not someone reasonably willing to work on identified 'problems'. His division was such that one side disavowed his awareness of difficulties while the other was painfully aware of them. Although I began to interpret early his tendency to look away, and gradually became aware of his forgetting previous work, particularly that in which we established conflicts that caused him pain, I tended to think about him as someone who used disavowal as a defence against certain conflicts, but otherwise was fairly consistently aware of his difficulties. I tended to treat the side that was aware as all of him.

If my doing so led me unwittingly to participate in a mutually admiring narcissistic enactment, that participation can also be seen as necessary to the analytic work. It respected Professor G's fragile adaptation, sparing him premature mortification and alleviating his anxiety over being different from me by the temporary reinforcement of his illusory omnipotence. At the same time, it established the preconditions for the creation of an analytic space. That is, despite my theory-syntonic efforts to do otherwise, I began by participating in an enactment in which I was similar to Professor G. My inner work would be gradually to become similarly *other*, to differentiate myself enough to communicate my understanding of what was happening and had happened between us and why.

From this point of view, and from a point of view that excludes my unconscious intuition, quite ironically, the implied metaphors dominant in the conflict model influenced my technique in a way that facilitated Professor G's staging of a performance and my participating in it. The performance both prevented either of us from discovering too quickly what lay beneath and provided us with a baseline of experiences that could ultimately be transformed from the manifest performance into what it concealed. For example, when breaches in the hidden strength he derived from me became occasionally apparent – with the appearance of his unacknowledged depressions and the painful symptom around separations, for instance – the contempt with which he met my interpretations about his loss of me allowed the subject to be broached while he both 'saved face' and revealed important genetic data by reversing roles. It gradually emerged that he was showing me the contempt he felt for himself for having feelings (only girls have feelings) and that he had originally experienced from his parents and siblings towards himself.

I do not mean to imply that the metaphors inherent in the conflict model directly influenced my technique so as to create the performance. Rather, they influenced my technique in an unintended manner that served both Professor G's intrapsychic and our intersubjective needs. Without them, and given a different analyst, some other way would have been needed and found to do the same thing.

In retrospect, from the perspective of the creation of an analytic space, my reassessment of my approach to Professor G was a step in an already ongoing process. I had become conscious of a slight frustration that gradually metamorphosed into a sense of a block inside myself, the affective representation of the split-off part of Professor G to which I was not listening and that undermined the work which led to his owning his inner difficulties. The attempt to reassess, shift of working metaphors, ensuing reorientation and change of interpretative tack seem to me as best seen as ways I had of integrating this new awareness in myself. They were all part of my growing comprehension of Professor G that emerged as the analytic space became gradually more established and elaborated, and that in turn facilitated its establishment and elaboration.

Conclusion

The view of theory as transitional is directly related to the idea of a transitional analytic space where what the patient lives but cannot directly articulate can gradually be put into words through the analyst's communication of his or her understanding and where the analyst's simultaneous inner transitional work allows this understanding to occur. Theory which helps the analyst make the transition between what he or she experiences and what he or she begins to grasp consciously in him- or herself and then in the patient interacts with the analyst as though it were the analyst's benign surround. Just as the analyst's articulated understanding functions to contain or hold the more disturbed, fragmented patient, so well-functioning metaphors of transition work to hold the analyst at difficult or obscure junctures of the analytic work, uniting disparate clinical experiences with a patient and unarticulated intuitions arising from these and other life experiences (real and imagined) with an apparently more abstract explanation. The new understanding then enables the clinician to feel support for a strong intuition instead of being caught in a conflict where what feels right clinically seems to involve going against the tenets of the theory. Metaphor embedded in theory thus facilitates the creation of the analytic space. I do not mean, of course, that any idea makes a valid theory, only that how we use theory in the clinical situation and what the theory provides for us as clinicians both go beyond the manifest content of a given theory to its form and what that form evokes in us and that evaluation of a theory needs to include an assessment of the way and degree it facilitates our ability to make the transition between inner and outer.

Psychoanalytic theory has not generally been considered from the perspective of its transitionality. Rather, it has been taken as a 'consensually validated view of reality, shared by a number of people, having an independent status *so far as the individual is concerned*' (Grossman, 1995). This only partly conscious way of viewing theory allows free rein for the more insidious unconscious meaning of theory as authority and to the act of applying it as a submission to authority (Reed, 1994;

Grossman, 1995), a meaning which influences the form of many current controversies and often overshadows the specific clinical context. In contrast, the concept of a transitional analytic space created through the subjective interactions and understanding of patient and analyst provides a larger and more inclusive context for what happens between them. Because it is mutable and evolving, it emphasizes process and is far less likely to encourage the turning of technical guideline into behavioural rule.

By virtue of this greater integration, the type of 'error' in which I engaged, a transient misapplication of theory that was an adaptive enactment, may be seen as the very stuff of the analysis of transference. Thus, 'error' becomes data. Indeed, there is a refocusing from 'error' to the particular clinical context in which it occurs so that what is important is the meaning of the action in the context of a particular analyst and patient interrelationship. Although the mode through which analyst and patient at first communicate (or better still, miscommunicate), undoubtedly serves the latter's adaptation as well as the former's conflicts, that mode is also the material out of which the analytic space is forged.

Especially with more disturbed patients, the concept of the analytic space has technical consequences. Interventions may be chosen to foster the transitional process and thus the construction of the analytic space. For example, where there is a lack of differentiation, interpretative interventions ought to introduce difference between self and object, but only gradually, through the mediation of the inevitably already established narcissistic transference object, whether one calls this transference object a part-object, a self-object or a 'similar other'. On the one hand, such a technique avoids the intrusion that occurs with many interpretations which assume the patient is differentiated when he or she is not, or which proceed to interpret the lack of differentiation from the point of view of the differentiated analyst rather than the undifferentiated patient. On the other, the treatment does not stop with the establishment of a narcissistic transference, but proceeds to the analysis of this transference. Differentiation and the exploration of the intrapsychic that differentiation makes possible remain the treatment goals.

8
The analytic mind at work: counterinductive knowledge and the blunders of so-called 'theory of science'[1]

JORGE L. AHUMADA

The kind invitation of Dr Jorge Canestri to revisit my 'Counterinduction in psychoanalytic practice: epistemic and technical aspects' (1997a), published in Dr Horacio Etchegoyen's *Festschrift*, has prompted me to reassess how the psychoanalytic mind works, the debate on its epistemic place and the wider issues of 'theory of science'. In the empirical tradition of Aristotle and Charles Darwin, what follows builds on Freud's conviction of the link between everyday thought and scientific thinking, clinical analytic work being part and parcel of scientific work. Indeed, as he puts it in the *New Introductory Lectures*, 'Scientific thinking does not differ in its nature from the normal activity of thought' (1933, p. 170); furthermore, 'Progress in scientific work is just as it is in an analysis' (1933, p. 174). Building on this idea of the coincidence of therapy and enquiry, my approach focuses on the clinical situation as a double work on the evidence (2004), the analyst and analysand being involved in a

---

[1] Partly based on a panel presentation at the Argentine Psychoanalytic Association, 18 November 2003, under the title 'Discoverer's induction'.

Psychoanalysis: From Practice to Theory. Edited by J. Canestri. © 2006 Whurr Publishers Ltd (a subsidiary of John Wiley & Sons Ltd).

logic of disclosures and refutations where both gain knowledge from the experience.

In the process of accessing the evidences of his unconscious lifestream, the analysand traverses contradictory anxieties and wishes resulting from his diverse levels of mind and his ego-splits and relational splits. This contradictoriness, as studied earlier (1991), adopts the form of paradox, the analysand's conscious 'theories' about himself being at the core of his *un*knowing. The interaction, then, involves the enacted, mainly unconscious pragmatics (Freud's thing-presentations), and what is verbalized, which has a neat if often skewed and tendentious link to reality. And while Winnicott (1953) found that the clinical process must sustain the paradox, this is but an indispensable technical first step, it being a main goal of psychoanalysis eventually to resolve paradoxes through insight.

The clinical exposition presents a two-pronged unconscious dilemma, pre-oedipal and oedipal, posed to the patient's observing ego, which being itself part of the conflict is centrally involved in *un*knowing. Evolutions come from gaining what Bertrand Russell (1911) called 'knowledge by acquaintance' from various sources: memories, dreams, instances in and out of session; these evidences impinge counterinductively on the patient's pre-existent 'theories', both the unconscious and conscious. Much – though by no means all – evidential mapping is mediated by the analyst's interpretations; however, it falls on the analysand to sort out what is pertinent and what is not.

This approach is true to Freud along several dimensions:

1. That thought is primarily unconscious, as held from the *Studies on Hysteria* (Freud 1895) onward.
2. His statement in a letter to Sandor Ferenczi of August 1915: 'I consider that one should not make theories. They should arrive unexpectedly in your house, like a stranger one hasn't invited' (Gribinski, 1994, p. 1019). Thus, the weight of the evidences, which are always multiple (the 'knowledge by acquaintance', in Russell's terms), impacts on thinking, allowing us to revise our 'theories'. This counterinductive epistemic posture is located at the opposite pole of deducticisms, which are the postures deriving knowledge deductively from premises.
3. The limit drawn between *psychoanalysis* as the analyst's task and the analysand's evolving *psycho-synthesis*, the refurbishing of his personal meanings coming about 'without our intervention' (Freud, 1919, pp. 160–1).
4. His overall idea that 'it is in fact only through *his own* experience and mishaps that a person learns sense' (Freud, 1914, p. 153, emphasis

added): our epistemic focus rests on a careful mapping of disanalogies and errors, not on overblown notions of truth.
5. His idea of analytic neutrality, which includes our interventions: as he puts it, the analysand's 'conflicts will only be successfully solved and his resistances overcome if the anticipatory ideas [i.e. the interpretations] tally with what is real in him. Whatever in the doctor's conjectures is inaccurate drops out in the course of the analysis; it has to be withdrawn and replaced by something more correct' (Freud, 1916, p. 452). Therefore, analytic interpretations are *conjectures in search of evidential disclosures*, rather than truth-injections.

Counterinduction must be shown rather than explained or defined. My example is that of a boy just over a year old as he 'dialogues' with a building's lift in front of its doors, shouting: *col, miní* (Spanish baby-talk for 'lift, come'). Calmly at first, then imperiously, he would finally be shocked and angry that the lift did not respond to his call. Summoning the lift just as he does his carers discloses an *iconic equation* whereby he assimilates it in the felt *class* of his carers, and deals with it as he does with them, by voicing his wishes. Given that the lift does *not* respond to his enacted wish-driven requests, the boy will – counterinductively – modify his personalistic 'theory' about lifts.

As Freud knew well, children's thinking proceeds from the animate to the inanimate: the child sets apart from himself a world of wish-driven animate objects, and only later comes to recognize the attributes pertaining to those objects. Psyche evolves from an action-intentional universe of *self-attributed* ways of relating and meanings, to a later delineation of conscious understandings of attributes as pertaining to the objects themselves.

In the case of our baby boy we depend on context and observation to grasp what went on, including what his words mean. His ongoing experience with a lift perceived as animated will eventually lead him to differentiate animated objects (which he evidently believes the lift to be) from inanimate ones. As his mounting imperiousness shows, corrections of error must from an early stage traverse emotional barriers of active *un*knowing. Similarly, the analysand's unconscious 'theories' will 'deductively' assimilate a world of emotional and relational attributes addressed mostly to personal objects, himself included.

I will now turn to the clinical exposition.

Clinical illustration

Let me expand on the course of a patient, now in his forties, accessing the interplay of oral and genital anxieties.

The patient had consulted in his early twenties due to apathy, being stuck in his studies, dire social difficulties, indecisiveness and an inability to approach women; he didn't even masturbate. Lack of enthusiasm and personal agency was the unifying theme: he felt that whatever he did was forced. He had no assurance that he was doing anything properly, and in any case it gave him no pleasure. He attributed his general apathy, and his apathy towards women, to inherent lack, but we recognized during his drawn-out treatment that it responded to deep-seated terrors: here his conscious 'theories' about himself were part of the *un*knowing.

It soon emerged that his motivation for seeking a consultation had arisen months before when, on stopping at a red traffic light, a transvestite had opened the door of his car, jumped in and kissed him on the mouth. The ensuing fright gave him no relief. A strong attraction to transvestites intertwined with his terrors, prompting his fear that he was a homosexual. In the analysis of what I considered a severe obsessional state and, at two decades' distance, I now take as an obsessional restitution of an autistic state, progress was slow, due to the blocks to insight, but none the less steady.

A childhood memory that emerged in the first year of analysis illustrates the phallic anxieties that formed one prong of the unconscious pincers deadening his psychic space. At elementary school he was poor at sports but a fast runner. On one occasion he was in the lead in a race almost as far as the finishing line when he realized he was going to win; at this he panicked, slowed his pace and came second. (Needless to say, confronting rivals has never been his forte.) He also recalled anxieties about his parents: when they went out together he was terrified that they would die.

In this initial stage of analysis, sexuality evolved in encounters with transvestite prostitutes who masturbated or fellated him, then in a short liaison with a girl, and from then on in long affairs. His first amorous 'crush' in the analysis and his first sexual relation ever was with a companion at work he felt fascinated by and who seduced him; a beautiful, fleeting girl who moved from one place to another. He pursued for over a year until she left the country. Being in pursuit of her spared him from fully confronting his anxieties of entrapment. His next relationship, with a troubled if lively divorcée a decade older than him, lasted a couple of years. In this relationship he took the initiative, as the age difference mitigated his fears of engulfment, while allowing him to gain some insight into them.

As to the pre-oedipal prong of his dilemma, fusional impulses governed his links to women on amorous or physical contact, leading to entrapment and to excruciating feelings when threatened by loss of their approval, not to say their anger or actual demise. Thus he was up in the air, externally and internally. At times he verged on mimetic robotization in his attempts to anticipate and fulfil the women's wishes, which became all-powerful; their expectations that he deliver on his 'commitment' had a torpedo-like impact, and self-recrimination on these grounds was ever-present.

Phantasies of being masturbated by feminized, cross-dressing inmates while in jail emerged as soon as he started to masturbate, early in treatment. Images of transvestites helped him attain an erection when approaching and during vaginal penetration. Consequently, he often thought of himself as homosexual, and at times homosexuality seemed to offer a way out of his lack of zest and apathy to women. He lost his erection and excitement when the woman was sexually aroused; his terror when the woman fellated him evinces the oral impetus of these genitally expressed anxieties.[2] An unexpected erection when talking on the phone with a girl came as a counterinduction to his conscious theory about his 'apathy': this experience, mentioned in passing, allowed me to show him that what he saw as sexual apathy appeared, on the contrary, as over-excitability he cannot contain.

Five years into analysis he stopped, having graduated, gained some degree of professional efficacy and an ongoing if not really satisfactory sexual relationship. That his father paid my fees also played a role. He returned more than a decade later, at first consulting sporadically over practical decisions, such as an offer of a full-time appointment as a technical adviser that was incompatible with his freelance work. He had turned the post down because of the responsibilities involved and because it would have meant giving up his independence, but thereafter he was troubled by the thought that he had made a serious mistake. In those consultations he mentioned in passing a terrifying phantasy on nearing orgasm in an intensely felt relationship: the door opened and a man came in to attack him. At the point when he resumed analysis he vaguely remembered this phantasy, but it sounded alien.

All in all, he claimed that he had been satisfied with his progress: now, though, his work and his love life were stagnating. He was more aware of losing his independence in sexual relations where he played the role of fiancé whether he liked it or not, and he felt stuck in a long-term relationship that he experienced as an emotional and sexual wasteland. In fact, what brought him back to treatment was that his fiancée, who was working overseas, had asked him to join her for a week. He was torn

---

[2] See Busch de Ahumada (2003) for a detailed clinical exposition of the process of analysis in a case of transvestism in a five-year-old child in which projection of oral anxieties into the female genitals was central to the dynamics.

between feeling that that would delay his ending an engagement that was going nowhere, and an urge to join her in order to avoid losing her. Besides, he feared jeopardizing a new affair he had started which was intended in good measure to get him out of his present relationship; but again he was afraid that this affair would entrap him. Though he had been thinking about starting analysis again for some years, it was this dilemma that brought him back to the analyst's couch.

This decisional stalemate was an example of his never being confident of acting appropriately and in tune with his own wishes, as opposed to doing what he felt he ought to do. The longstanding fiancée he was separating from was an amiable, but rather remote girl a few years older than him. Initially, he had felt relieved and proud of her autonomy and lack of emotional demands. Their sexual relationship was poor; the woman ideologized her frigidity, holding that clitoral stimulation is essential for women. While resentful at her lack of response, consciously he colluded with her ideology and largely blamed his own lack of passion. Years earlier they had considered having a child, which she urged and he postponed, then an early menopause ended her ability to have a child. He blamed himself for this, which made his difficulties in leaving her worse. That he felt women as unwaveringly justified in their requests, expectations, complaints and gripes, as well as in their personal ideologies, built up an unconditional realm amounting, in Ferenczi's (1909) terms, to maternal hypnosis. Though initially he felt no anger and thought my questions about his anger were irrelevant, and it was still difficult for him to access his anger, submissiveness was most notable in relation to women. Being possessed by what we called the 'Krypton effect' (named after the meteorites coming from Superman's planet which deprived him of his strength) was the greater the more emotionally involved he was, a process that emptied him of personal agency.

On the other hand, increased pleasure in coitus heightened his homosexual fantasies and anxieties, as happened during an enjoyable coitus where he found himself, in a kind of psychic somersault, taking the position of an attractive woman in coitus (passing under the brunt of his anxieties, in Ferenczi's term (1914), to subject-homoerotism). This in turn prompted a nightmare. He was in his childhood sandpit playing with a little girl, when a car ran her over. He spent the rest of the dream desperately searching for her in desolate and dirty places and sewers where he finally found her, mangled, at which point he woke up terrified (on enquiry the dream's car turned out to be the same make as his father's at the time). Relevantly, while working on the dream, he recalled having had an intense coitus while half-asleep the night before, and then, much to his surprise, manifested explosively a wish to be 'a sexual and working stallion'. However, in the next session he had forgotten this virile outburst, and I was able to point to this amnesia.

His link to his parents was appreciative but emotionally numb, and he saw them rather as a unit. Although they are both in good shape, he is somewhat apprehensive about their health. He has no overt conflicts with his mother, but he is aware of being exceedingly careful to keep his distance from her. His father is a reliable, stable and successful professional who knows how to avoid conflicts; notably, my patient has never clashed with him. The dream about the father's car may depict a major unconscious clash with his father, which has led to damage and the feminization of a part of himself. How this issue was to come alive in the transference in order to be worked through was, of course, another matter.

At the time of the session to be discussed, some five years into the second course of analysis, progress was considerable in his ability to work, and for the first time he felt he was living a life of his own, which happened initially, and still mainly, when he was playing golf. He had attempted to learn to play golf in childhood, with his father, but without success. In fact, in adolescence he strongly equated his inability to play golf with his incapacity to form relationships with girls and his conviction that he would never have a viable erection. As already described, during this second stage of his analysis he had two long-term relationships with women: he now knows he is quite attractive, but feels women choose him instead of his choosing them (he does not approach women unless given obvious signals). He lost all sense of initiative as the relationship settled and felt more and more trapped in the woman's demands for affective long-term commitment. This set up a vicious circle of parasitic possessiveness whereby closeness and enthusiasm led to entrapment.

As the relationship turned into a prison, he finally made the woman feel so frustrated that she ended the affair. This brought on strong feelings of loss as well as notable relief at getting out of the bind. However, with each break feelings of loss were less cataclysmic, while relief at freeing himself became acceptable, and he came to grasp that the intensity, and at times the persecutory character, of the loss resulted from an unbearable guilt at killing both the amorous relationship and the woman involved. On that basis he was very concerned about how his former partners came out of the break-up, and was relieved when they eventually found new partners. His most recent relationship, which lasted a couple of years, was fairly satisfactory for over a year and at that time he had his best sexual encounters ever, as he grudgingly admitted. This, though, heightened his sense of entrapment and he gradually lost his drive. The mounting and often ill-humoured demands of his fiancée for him to marry her led to their break-up which she initiated, but which in the final stages he consciously encouraged.

He came to the session, lay on the couch, and said he had got up that morning with no energy – as routinely happened on Mondays. I mentioned that he seemed to ignore, as he usually does, his anger at getting up and starting the working week, and perhaps in coming to the session. Smiling, he said this might be true, and that in fact it had been an unusually busy weekend. (Such a comment was itself unusual, given his huge difficulty in admitting to enthusiasm, partly due to a feeling that this elicits my rivalry.) Also, following the weekend he had a series of dreams he does not recall, except his being enticed by cross-dressers in jail, with the difference, he noticed, that now it was the prison wardens who were the transvestites.

During the weekend he went to the cinema with a former fiancée he hadn't seen for some time. He was thrilled at the idea of sexual contact; knowing she would resist the emotional impact of resuming a sexual relationship allowed him, he came to realize, to feel the thrill as his own and not a response to her demands. This theme was to the fore the next night on going out with a woman, M, he had met shortly before, and with whom he had had some half-hearted sexual encounters.

He had doubted whether he wanted to see her again, but somehow this came about. After a week with no contact, she called round in an undemanding way and he found himself inviting her out for dinner. So they went, and on taking her home he felt tired and pressured to go to bed with her again. To his relief she said her sister was visiting her and was sleeping there; he then felt obliged to invite her to his apartment, but found the idea that she would stay the night unbearable. Rejecting the idea made him feel much better. He told her he would call round the next evening after he had played a round of golf, which she took well. He was glad at having had the date on his own terms, and not on her felt demands.

The following evening he had a good erection and ejaculated inside her – something he is usually anxious about and has trouble with. They stayed in bed relaxed, and an hour later rather to his surprise he tried coitus again; this time he did not manage to ejaculate inside her and had masturbated with her help, but nevertheless felt good about it. Then they went out for dinner and he took her home. They made no plans to meet again. While happy about the weekend, this pleasure soon soured with regard to the girl and his link to me. He said he felt that, based on his enjoyable weekend, I would start pushing him for a deeper 'commitment' to the woman – which we both knew telescoped into marrying her and having children.

I told him he condensed a double system of meanings in his language: thus, the term 'commitment', while seemingly coming up in terms of a *felt* link to the woman, turns into a command. Although first saying he enjoyed the weekend because he had been able to feel that he was acting on his own initiative, this gave way to a feeling of slavish 'commitment': enjoyment thus reverted to an obligation and I was perceived as railroading him into a 'commitment'. His agreement reinstated the problem. He said that if he were to go out with another girl, he would feel – and feel that I felt – that he was not doing so because he wished it and liked the other girl more but, on the contrary, that he was avoiding emotional 'commitment' to M.

Thus interpretations turned into my mandates on what he was supposed to do – not to fail in his 'duties' to the woman, or alternatively not to let his own pleasure slip away. In this way his decisions or wishes simply vanished. What may seem a semantic issue, an idiolect condensing a double system of meanings for the term 'commitment', amounts – internally and transferentially – to an enacted iconic equation akin in its dynamics to the dream about his father's car: interpretations were felt as enactments that hit on and sidelined his agency.

Concerning the dream mentioned in passing, I told him some changes might be going on. While he saw me as a sort of analytic prison warden whom he submitted to by transcoding interpretations into mandates, the dream hinted at pushing the prison wardens into the feminine role, which might mean his wish to display a masculine one.

Perhaps as a result of these interpretations, over the weekend at the golf course he played at par three times in a row, which had never occurred before. Characteristically, he dismissed his pleasure at this; however, this coexisted with an underlying, overblown thrust to play every hole at par from now on, as evinced by his disappointment at achieving a bogey in the following round. That he played badly in the next brought – predictably enough – myriad self-recriminations. However, the following session brought the first definite virile phantasy impersonation in his long treatment: a daydream of being Robert Capa, the famous war cameraman who lived his life fully in action, fearlessly at the brink and who – he mentioned – enjoyed lots of affairs with beautiful women, Ingrid Bergman among them, and had resisted her desire to marry him.

I shall now consider a Monday session that took place a few weeks later. It had been a rather unusual weekend, and he had a dream just before waking. He was with L (his last long-term fiancée) at an ice cream parlour which a famous academic ran. He asked for a long drink made of ice cream and a blend of liquors, but felt that this famous academic was not attending to him as he should. He wanted to go on the road with the girl, and though worried about drink driving, decided to go. He had had two other short dreams. In one he tenderly embraced his last fiancée while feeling sexual excitement. The second dream made him ashamed, and he said he had never had one like it. This was an erotic dream involving his mother: it was just an image, she was younger than she is now, and he stroked her leg.

This weekend was also unusual. On Sunday it rained and his golf tournament was cancelled. On Friday night he went with an ex-fiancée, S, to see a classic film he liked very much. Though tired, he had enjoyed himself; at the cinema they had embraced tenderly and pleasurably, rather as friends. He noticed he was having an erection but it was very relaxed and pleasurable, and he was happy when he got home. However, he found it symptomatic that the next morning, on finding a message from S asking him to call her back, he panicked and fantasized all kinds of reproaches and claims from her, foremost that he marry her. So it was quite a relief when he phoned her to discover that having run out of cash, all she wanted was a small loan. I told him then that his enjoyment is manifest only while free enough in a personal space undisturbed by possessive claims, and these claims are felt explosively as a result of minor incidents.

What he brought up next throws more light on his problems with his masculinity. Before going to the cinema with S, he found a cross-dressers' contact number on the Internet. On calling he was told of a meeting that would take place that week, and that despite not being a cross-dresser he would be welcome. He found the idea of being the only man among feminized, submissive cross-dressers exciting. He felt much more of a man in that situation than he managed with women. As far as can be gathered, he felt the submissiveness of feminized men as a reassurance against his not easily recognizable fear that his masculine sexual pleasure and activity were a sort of hubris that would expose him to annihilating warfare on the side of his unconscious oedipal rival.

After the weekend he said he missed many putts in the Saturday golf tournament but winning the long drive had made him happy. The day had been spent with no pressure – he had played golf and then gone to an experimental cinema show. That night he had an erotic dream, which was unusual and puzzled him. It was a dream about Aurora, the middle-aged Indian maid who cleans his apartment – in his eyes as unattractive a woman as they come. She undressed and he had a big, hard erection, while her body became that of an attractive girl, quite different from her own. At the point when he was expecting her to grab his penis, he woke up. He linked the dream with winning the long drive, especially since two people had made sexual innuendoes at the time: an older player said that after his big drive all the girls would be after him, and somebody's wife wryly said that winning the long drive sounded very masculine.

I commented that Aurora's presence in the dream might depend on her submissive attitude; that following what came up about the cross-dressers' meeting, which had been sexually unarousing as they had behaved like girls fooling around with each other rather than submitting to him, might mean that winning the long drive was seen as a form of masculinity, and the woman's submissiveness created the context for his big erection in the erotic dream, as he felt his relation with women to be more strongly asymmetrical the more attractive he found them. When asymmetry is mitigated by Aurora's submissiveness and unattractiveness, he can feel masculine and excited.

My analysand's inhibitions about pleasure can be grasped in terms of Matte-Blanco's (1975; 1988) conceptions of the unconscious functioning in terms of classes, as an infinitization of both phallic and oral dynamics. I reported a huge infinitization elsewhere (1997) in a post-autistic adolescent boy whose sole waking phantasy was being the only boy in the universe, partner to the only girl with whom he was the sole possessor of every car, plane, boat and gun in the world. As Ferraro (2001) stressed, phallic logic tends to absolutize, which in my analysand led to an either/or psychic dilemma with no possible place for both his oedipal rival and himself. That he got no thrill from the transvestites' meeting, where the girlie display was to one another instead of to his masculinity, supports this idea.

Here we find the dynamic primacy of a traumatic background: contact with cross-dressers and closely delimited erotic intimacy with his longtime fiancée, S, are bearable and thus enjoyable because they involve what Hardin and Hardin (2000, p. 1249) call a 'leavable' object – in the case of the cross-dressers, because they are only mimetic womanly forms; in the case of contacts with S, because they respect a contract of non-possession, having renounced each other. In such fashion the traumatic conflation and infinitization of the genital and the oral is controlled.

On theory-realism and pattern-realism

The conceptual aspects of my enterprise impinge on the distortions brought about by what in unified terms is known as the 'theory of science'. I shall build my case in Freud's wake, showing how our clinical work employs what to Popper's theory-realism is the worst of all possible epistemic scenarios – 'the method of having no theory at all' (1979, p. 365). It goes without saying that Freud's method of free association, and of free-floating attention on the analyst's part, puts to work in the realm of the psyche the 'method of having no theory at all'.

Now, the term 'theory' covers a host of meanings ranging from 'a system of ideas or statements explaining something, especially one based on general principles independent of the things to be explained; a hypothesis that has been confirmed or established by observation or experiment and is accepted as accounting for known facts'; to 'the formulation of abstract knowledge or speculative thought; systematic conception of some thing. Freq. opp. to *practice*'; and, loosely, 'an unsubstantiated hypothesis' (The New Shorter OED, 1995, p. 3274). To Popper 'theory' means *formal* theory, positing as mandatory the use of formal theories in realms where no formal theories are extant. The same goes for his use of the term logic.

Since Aristotle it has been known that *formal* logic requires that its component elements be identical, which is definitely not the case in many realms of empirical enquiry, least of all the psychic. This makes it necessary to distinguish between *informal*, 'background knowledge' or informal 'theories', on the one hand, and *formal* theory operating as a 'logic' on the other.

Informal logic, which examines the complexities and contrariness of arguments in natural languages and traces the main ingredients in our patterns of inference, lacks the precision and elegance of a formal theory (Tully, 1995). Moreover, as Reichenbach (1947) notes, formal logic studies purely cognitive statements, while those given in the flesh to someone are instrumental and pertain to pragmatics, not logic. Besides, in the actual process of knowledge abstract statements must be verified in terms of directly observable states of affairs. As Ayer (1956, p. 17) puts it, what verifies the statement that I have a headache is my feeling a headache, not my having a feeling of confidence that the statement that I have a headache is true. The process of knowledge as it happens in clinical psychoanalysis deals not just with statements addressed to someone but also, and centrally, with the ongoing, emotional difficulties which distort statements or preclude them and, importantly, with how statements come about.

Theory-realisms subordinate the idea of objectivity to reduction to variables and predictability. The seemingly opposed brands of theory-realism Popper spearheads as falsificationism and Grünbaum as strict inductivism are mirror images: by different routes they put up as requisite the formalization of the conceptual apparatus, they forward reductionistic definitions of what is deemed empirical and, crucially, they define scientific objectivity as reduction to well-behaved variables and predictability.[3]

---

[3] Popper's stance retains mainstream status in the public mind, despite being discredited in specialist quarters following Kuhn's (1962) and Lakatos's (1970) critiques. To his attempt to present his notions as a logic defining what is scientific and what is not, Lakatos counters that Popper's stance amounts less to a logic than to an ideology.

Popper's top-down theory-realism and Grünbaum's bottom-up theory-realism share the assumption of the mechanical nature of the mind in relation to psychic processes. They do not make it explicit, but it underlies, to give a prime example, Grünbaum's demand that the causal groundings of notions of the mind comply with the sort of baseline that the law of inertia provides in physics (see Ahumada, 1997b). The premise that for the study of the mind to be deemed scientific it must be thought of as mechanical is expressed by Wittgenstein (who was first an engineer, then a logician and later philosopher of language) in his *Lectures and Conversations on Aesthetics, Psychology and Religious Belief*: 'Paradigm of the sciences is mechanics. If people imagine a psychology, their ideal is a mechanics of the soul' (1938, pp. 28-9). Thus, from what Charles Peirce (1883, p. 215) saw as the two and only two kinds of thought – mechanical (formal) and anthropomorphic – Popper and Grünbaum admit as science only what is framed in formal-mechanical ways.

Popper states in *Objective Knowledge* that his *objectivism* purports to avoid the psychological problems of induction, and that it operates on *strictly logical grounds* (1979, p. 26). But logic is a highly heterogeneous field and offers no clues as to which sort of logic is to be used. This is true of all fields of empirical enquiry and also of formal sciences, mathematics included.

The unitary label 'theory of science' deriving from Auguste Comte and the Vienna Circle, which characterizes Popper's unremitting logicism, disregards the dissimilar nature of the scientific endeavours. It was clear to Aristotle more than 2,000 years ago that misguided attempts to force the precision of a given research beyond what the phenomena explored allow, will backfire and introduce distortion.

Popper follows Aristotle in that first, '*all science, and all philosophy, are enlightened common sense*' (1979, p. 34; Popper's emphasis); second, that '*the growth of all knowledge consists in the modification of previous knowledge*' – either its alteration or its large-scale rejection; and third, that 'knowledge never begins from nothing, but always comes from *some* background knowledge' (1979, p. 71; Popper's emphasis). Freud would no doubt agree.

But Popper parts company with Aristotle, Darwin and Freud when, after acknowledging that science is enlightened common sense, he decries as particularly misleading for the theory of knowledge the primacy accorded to observation (1979, p. 34): his scientific mind is a theoreticist mind operating in the classical physics from which he draws his examples on how all science supposedly works. Newtonian celestial mechanics models Popperian science, built on the belief that, as Hacking crucially quotes him, 'science has a pretty tight *deductive structure*' and that 'all sciences should employ the same methods, so that the human sciences have the same methodology as physics' (Hacking, 1983, p. 5; Popper's emphasis). However, says Hacking, such deductivist postulation gets scant support from the history of science; even in the history of physics there are many instances in which surprising observations preceded and provided the impetus for the formulation of theory. In a later paper Hacking (1992) distinguishes, on the one hand, our background knowledge and expectations – unsystematic and mostly taken for granted – framing any possible observation, and, on the other, the high-level theories which most often play no direct role in experiment.

Popper's deductivist-formalist premises amount to what Quine (1957, pp. 118–19) calls a *legislative postulation* which institutes truth by convention unencumbered by attempts at justification concerning its viability for the realm of the mind. In so doing he overlooks the fact that postulates, 'though they are postulates always by fiat, are not *therefore* true by fiat' (Quine, 1957 p. 131). Much of what goes by the name of 'theory' is postulation; however, as Quine pertinently quotes from Bertrand Russell, 'the method of "postulating" what we want has many advantages; they are the same as the advantages of theft over honest toil' (1964, p. 133). Let me add that over 60 years ago, in a letter of 22 December 1942, Otto Neurath wrote to Rudolf Carnap: 'I read Popper again ... how empty all that stuff is. ... No feeling for scientific research' (quoted by Feyerabend, 1987, p. 191n).

Elsewhere (1997c) I have argued that in the empirical disciplines, the term 'theory' is broad-ranging, from '*formula-theories*' used in mathematical formulae of which the prime example is Newton's formula for gravity (so-called 'Newtonian mechanics'), to '*frame-theories*' exemplified by Darwin's theory of the evolution of species. Frame-theories are not formalized, do not sustain strict deduction and serve as general settings for thought, to be amplified, detailed and accommodated by further observations. Gooding (1992) underlines that philosophers of science streamline scientists' activities into logically transparent structures, *normative reconstructions*, highlighting non-situational and theoretical goals at the expense of contextual and practical ones. What I call frame-theories correspond to the explicit parts of our ever-present background knowledge. For clinical purposes, we must deal with the ever-present background *un*knowing, the analysand's 'unconscious theories' (Money-Kyrle, 1965), both enacted and emotional, which organize his experience in unknown 'deductive' ways.

The priority Popper accords to tightly formalized deduction as the unitary method for all sciences disregards the enormous differences between the inanimate and the animate. That all science is universalistic and non-contextual is a solidly Platonic-Cartesian notion: it was Plato who, in the *Republic*, argued from the geometrical theorem that only

Forms – abstract entities outside space and time – are fully real, while our commonplace realities are not: whereby the theorem becomes paradigmatic and infallibility as *necessary* truth demarcates knowledge from mere opinion, entailing that knowledge demands a world of changeless objects (Williams, 2000).

To counter Popper's and Grünbaum's *theory-realisms*, a quite different stance needs to be taken: a *pattern-realism* which harks back to Aristotle and Darwin, encompassing the huge and varied field of the observational sciences – the human sciences included. The view that all sciences employ the same methodology effaces what distinguishes, say, ethology from physics. Gregory Bateson illustrates this with his observation that when I kick a stone I give energy to it and it moves with that energy, but when I kick a dog its response comes from its own energy (1979, p. 108); a dog is not a predictable, well-behaved Newtonian variable, so we might find to our cost that while one dog may flee or whimper, another may just as easily turn round and bite us!

Bateson's dog helps approach the issue of causes and motives. No doubt the kick is Newtonianly causal as far as the stone's movement is concerned, being repeatable under similar initial conditions. Kicking the dog would not be deemed 'causal' in a physicalistic sense because it does not entail 'an invariable connection' (Bouveresse, 1991, p. 73). The motive (cause or reason) is that a dog is not mechanical; being animate, its response to a kick will be strongly context-dependent: results will depend on its being your own dog or not, and even if it is your dog, on what type of dog it is. There is nothing teleological about this, it just evinces that work in these domains requires a *logica situs*, a situational logic allowing for Complexity of Causes, in Mill's (1852) hallowed terms. So it happens that this is *not* a nomological domain fitting Popper–Hempel mechanical-like 'covering laws': even our simplest of examples, Bateson kicking the dog, shows that historical factors (being or not being the dog's owner, among others) can hardly be ignored and must be assessed in each case.

For Popper, as for Wittgenstein, only a *formalized* theory is truly a *theory*: hence Copernicus and Darwin did not discover true theories, only a fertile point of view (Wittgenstein, 1980, p. 18e). In such formalist vein Bouveresse argues after Wittgenstein that 'Freud's theory – like Darwin's – is related more to what we can call the 'morphological' approach than to causal explanation properly speaking' (1991, p. 131), namely causal in mechanical terms.

John Searle considers this an egregious mistake: the evidently false assumption that unless there is a type-reduction to the theories of physics of whatever entities are at stake, these entities do not exist (1992, p. 47). What is decried as a 'morphological' approach is the sort of *logica situs* befitting observational sciences: thus, the demand that ethology be reducible to physics is preposterous, and it is just as preposterous to assume that a science of the psyche should be. A *logica situs*, a situational logic, must rely on ostensiveness. Moreover, the tension between passivity and agency intrinsic to many psychic happenstances does not permit dichotomies between 'cause' and 'reason'.

While in the case of observational sciences Mill hit the nail on the head better than Popper's 'theory-realism', avowing in *On Liberty* that 'the truth depends on a balance to be struck between two sets of conflicting reasons . . . and it has to be shown why that other theory cannot be the true one' (1859, p. 98), it is Mill's inspiration and arch-adversary, William Whewell, who provides an elastic enough inductivist frame fit for the sort of scientific thought that, far from formal logic and formalized theory, makes due place for Darwin's and Freud's ways of enquiry and concept-building:

> Induction *is* inconclusive *as reasoning*. It is not reasoning: it is another way of getting at truth. . . . It is known from observation, but it is not *demonstrated*. . . . Induction is, as Aristotle says, opposed to syllogistic reasoning, and yet it is a means of discovering truth: not only so, but a means of discovery of primary truths, immediately derived from observation. . . . I have elsewhere taught that all induction involved a *Conception* of the mind applied to facts. (1850, p. 317)

In induction, says Whewell, 'there is always a *new conception*, a principle of connection and unity, supplied by the mind, and superimposed upon the particulars' (1858, p. 163). That scientific induction involves the joint evolution of conceptions and facts means that 'Conception must be formed before it can be defined' (1849, p. 284). Man, he holds, 'is the Interpreter of nature; not the Spectator merely, but the Interpreter' (1849, p. 281), and he expounds 'the difficulty of getting hold of the right conception, as a proof that induction is not a mere juxtaposition of facts' (1849, p. 282). He does not mince his words about the obstacles involved in arriving at a conception apt for binding together the observed facts: 'the process of obtaining new conceptions is, to most minds, far more unwelcome than any labour in exploring old ideas. The effort is indeed painful and oppressive; *it is feeling in the dark for an object that we cannot find*' (1858, pp. 181–2; emphasis added).

It is noteworthy that although Whewell explicitly leaves out of his enquiry the 'emotions, thoughts and mental conditions' (1858, p. 159) in thus describing the scientist's struggle at finding the right conception, none the less he might as well be describing every analyst's and every analysand's struggle to attain the right conceptions for insight and psychic growth.

Darwin and Freud found counterfactuals essential in building their scientific concepts (Ernest Jones (1953) rightly called Freud the 'Darwin of the mind'). Relevantly, Wittgenstein's associate and editor, the Finnish logician Georg-Henrik von Wright, pursued a logical concept of counterinduction, though here it might be argued that counterinduction functions outside and against ratiocinations, and as such cannot be defined in properly logical terms.

Against the Popperian demarcation argument, Blackburn, following Lakatos, highlights that a nineteenth-century Newtonian would have been quite unable to conceive of circumstances which would lead him to declare the general principles of mechanics false. This being so, he asks: 'Why demand higher standards from psychoanalysts or social scientists than from physicists?' (1984, p. 256). As explained above, the case of Bateson's dog requires a *logica situs*, a situational logic making room for Complexity of Causes, accountable to local and historical factors. When historical factors are involved, says von Wright (1971), causal events create new situations requiring practical inferences which could not have been made before; Bateson's kicking the dog a second time would be influenced by the result of his first kick, both participants having been modified by its outcomes. This involves an *inferential* method where, as specified by Whewell in 1858 for all empirical enquiry, induction means *inference to the best available explanation*, rather than formal deduction.

On background knowledge, unconscious theories, pattern-realism and counterinduction

Psychic concepts attempt to grasp a relational realm. Relational concepts in the domain of the psyche are vague: they intend to cover vague objects, which must be enquired into and discerned in depth in each case. Aren't what we call love, anger or, in the case of my analysand, apathy, vague objects in the sense of being complex, changing and unfolding over time, and of having no predeterminable limits? As they approach vague objects, our psychic notions are perforce open concepts, which come to life as unfolded and redefined anew on being put to use in each singular instance.

Pattern-realism entails both analysand and analyst undertaking a mapping of the various unfoldings of the repetition compulsion (the analysand's unconscious theories), at the crossroads of an unconscious logic operating in the main in terms of classes, and a conscious logic drawn in terms of individuals. Such multiple unfoldings need to traverse a variety of ongoing paradoxes on the road to psychic evolution and growth. Centrally, as against the mechanical objects ruling the Popperian conception for all scientific endeavours, *the 'object' that clinical psychoanalysis deals with is at the same time a subject and an object* (both dimensions are present in the Freudian understanding of *Selbst*): a *historical, evidence-seeking subject/object*, and what is more, she or he is both an *unknowing* and a *knowing subject*.

This peculiar scientific endeavour, clinical psychoanalysis, *amounts to a huge observational, counterinductive extension of everyday practical logic*. Thus my approach to objectivity centres less on testing my own interpretations or theories and more on how the analysand gathers and tests (and modifies or refutes) *his or her* 'unconscious theories': in other words, my focus is on helping the analysand to gain reliable 'evidences-realism', mainly by way of his current experiences.

Amplifying my argument (1997a, p. 186), my idea about the counterinductive use of the psychoanalytic method needs to distinguish four psychic levels on the part of the analysand: (1) an underlying quasi-tautological level of *mis*-conceptual unconscious 'frames' or 'theories' about relationships, at a time misconceived and misconceiving, which rule the analysand's failed inductions; (2) those enacted and verbal derivatives of such mis-conceptual 'frames' which attain some representability; (3) perceptual and mnemic levels that are partly, but it must be hoped just partly, under the sway of his mis-conceptual unconscious meaning 'frames'; and (4) a capacity to grasp the verbal descriptions and conjectures (i.e. the interpretations) advanced by the analyst, as well as their relevance for the evidential interchanges that take place in and out of session.

Thus we find two quite different quasi-tautologies for both analysand and analyst, though in dissimilar manner: psychic reality, the *unknown* 'deductive' matrix of unconscious 'theories' about relationships, and conscious inferential thought, itself under the partial sway of the unconscious. Interpretations may operate on two levels: as markers for the ostensible, and as 'meta-theoretical' conjectures posed by the analyst about the analysand's 'unconscious theories' that happen to be modelling the session.

Having argued that core psychic evolutions require that the analysand traverses counterinductively an enacted pragmatic paradox (1991; 1994; 1997a; 2004), I mention that to von Wright the dynamics of the psychoanalytic process are best grasped logically in terms of counterinduction (personal communication 1995). Far from deductive Popperian-Hempelian 'covering laws', here receptivity to the *un*expected in new events permits that they operate as counterfactuals impinging on and modifying our unconscious and conscious conceptual frames, which opens the way to *new* findings and allows the analyst's (and the analysand's) realism to operate, in Hanly's (1992) terms, as *critical realism*.

Last but not least, only psychoanalysis seems to take into account the daunting topic of the never fully accomplished psychic differentiations and the confusions between self and object. In order not to complicate the exposition further, this topic was alluded to in the material only in passing, but differentiations between self and object are a concomitant of every step in psychic evolutions, and here the working out of the relevant evidences in attaining evolved conceptions is hardy indeed. As we cited above, 'The effort is indeed painful and oppressive; it is feeling in the dark for an object that we cannot find' (Whewell, 1858, pp. 181-2).

In conclusion, let me recall that a few years ago, in a presentation at the British Society, I (2001b) brought a roar of friendly laughter when, asked about evidence, I responded that the trouble with evidence is that it is not evident. To stitch things together, I added that evidence not being evident is why we as psychoanalysts need the method. Which is, I gather, valid for both analyst and analysand in our double work on the evidence.

9
Infantile sexual theories and cognitive development: psychoanalysis and theoretical production[1]

SAMUEL ZYSMAN

Introduction

The aim of this chapter is to examine from a psychoanalytic perspective the types of relationship that presumably exist between the acquisition of knowledge in general, the formulation of theories based on the generalization of such knowledge and the existence of infantile sexual theories (IST) considered by psychoanalysis, whose relevance with respect to this process I shall try to establish.

What we already know is that the clinical practice of our discipline is sustained by various theories (not always mutually compatible), and that both the clinical material supplied by patients and analytic inter-

---

[1] The first time I contributed to this subject was in 1997, when I participated in a panel at the Barcelona, IPA Congress, whose main subject was human sexuality. On that occasion, my participation was titled 'Infantile sexual theories and infantile sexuality'. In that paper, emphasis was laid on the importance of making the distinction between infantile and adult sexuality, in the context of contemporary culture and in that of the psychoanalytic session. An abbreviated version of my presentation was published in *La Psychiatrie de l'Enfant*, XLI, 2 (1998).

Psychoanalysis: From Practice to Theory. Edited by J. Canestri. © 2006 Whurr Publishers Ltd (a subsidiary of John Wiley & Sons Ltd).

pretations may be considered as the vehicles of 'theories' basically dealing with these patients' problems. If we assume that this is so, it would be meaningful to carry out a psychoanalytic enquiry into theories in general, not only as such but also as products of human minds. Moreover, we should not forget to take into account the conditions in which theories are produced, as well as the possible relationships between these conditions and theoretical statements themselves. Since I consider myself to be, first and foremost, a clinical psychoanalyst (with experience in child psychoanalysis) and only secondly an epistemological enthusiast, I am aware that my proposal may be seen as risky because it involves using psychoanalytic theoretical notions, whose scientific status is still in debate, to deal with the issue of the construction of theories in general. Though attractive and necessary, this proposal, which I shall put forward briefly, is a difficult task; therefore I request the benevolent attention of those who may examine my ideas. I also hope to be able to show in this context that infantile sexual theories not only constitute an excellent field of research, but that, in fact, they are an integral part of the subject involved in this exposition as well.

Even if I shall immediately deal in detail with the Freudian concepts on IST, let us recall that in his 1908 paper on 'The Sexual Theories of Children' (SE 9: 210-11), not only does Freud describe them as 'theories', but also that he states that 'They are indispensable, moreover, for an understanding of the neuroses themselves; for in them these childish theories are still operative and acquire a determining influence upon the form taken by the symptoms.' Thus, by constructing a 'general theory of neurosis', in which sexuality was the main unconscious source of psychical conflict, Freud makes use of his clinical findings (perhaps it would be more accurate to speak of the findings of the 'Little Hans' case history) to expand that theory with a new one: a theory that puts forward that there are imperfect 'theories' about sexuality which are, however, instrumental to symptom-formation in both children and adults. On the one hand, this widening of what we may define as a 'family of theories' (Klimovsky, 1994, p. 170) supports the assertion that there is an infantile neurosis lying behind every adult neurosis. As Freud holds, both types of neurosis express the existence of 'infantile sexual theories' (which manifest themselves through symptoms and become an integral part of the phenomenon of transference, in terms of the above-mentioned 'patient's theories about himself'). On the other hand, *this extension of the theory turns into a knot of epistemological problems raised by the existence of relationships between psychical conflicts and the construction of theories.* It is true that in classical literature IST are mainly considered from the viewpoint of their defensive function. This was the Freudian approach in the context of his first topographic theory and of his psychopathology at the time. In fact, Freud had to corroborate empirically not only the presence of neuroses in children but also, in particular, their sexual aetiology. However, we should always bear in mind that he found it convenient to include an explicit remark addressed to a hypothetical methodological objection concerning the reliability of the conclusions drawn from the analogy between the reports of both healthy and neurotic children, as well as to underline the relevance of IST for the elucidation of myths and fairy tales.

Thus the threefold significance of IST can clearly be seen: as the expression of infantile sexuality; as fantasies inherent to the transference phenomenon; and as a revealing aspect of creative activity. The relatively restricted space assigned to them in psychoanalytic literature must have some sort of explanation, and I shall try to expand on this subject.

Humanity has travelled a difficult path to learn to understand and accept that the child is a human being from birth, with feelings and needs that have to be understood and assisted, with a capacity to develop some ideas about their surrounding world – no matter how provisional they may be. This is well known to child analysts, and historians of culture as well as writers have painted revealing pictures of the neglect and suffering to which children were subjected in the course of past centuries. The status of childhood was very often humiliating, even abject. One of the most sophisticated and stupid ways of abusing children has been the deeply rooted habit of considering them as incapable of making any kind of judgement, as beings who only when reaching a certain age could be treated as humans in every sense of the word. To that end, they had frequently to survive educational systems quite similar to those of animal training. This noxious attitude, which may be understood as part of our 'civilization and its discontents' based on deep psychic splitting, sometimes leads people to prefer an image of childhood not yet threatened by any kind of knowledge, 'innocent' in the strict sense of the word; and at others, it may lead to terrible exploitative practices or even to annihilation in different ways, depending on each culture.

As regards the subject of this chapter, I think it is clear that Freudian and post-Freudian analytic discoveries have greatly contributed to the endeavour to improve this state of affairs, and for this reason we may feel satisfied. However, we may face obstacles in our own field: our shortcomings may distort the theories available to us owing to the intellectual and affective commitments we are involved in, given that we formulate statements related to mental functioning with the only tool available to us – our mind – which in turn is dependent on inner and outer pressures.

Inasmuch as we are aware of this problem, we attempt to scrutinize our countertransference in our clinical practice so as to make our interpretations more accurate. But sometimes, when we theorize in our patients' absence, we forget to be cautious and are prone to believe that we are able to propose theoretical hypotheses devoid of any subjective component.

So, the choice between directly observing infantile neurosis and being satisfied with the reconstructed child of adult analysis is crucial; it may either foster significant obstacles or help in avoiding them when we theorize: we know that empirical data help to validate certain theoretical hypotheses or, by refutation, they may compel us to give them up. Freud himself has set the example of his interest in empirically corroborating his theories, but sometimes he has given proof of how theories can prevail over clinical data (Freud, 1909; Etchegoyen, 1988). Similar difficulties can still be noticed in the current competing accounts of the earliest stages of psychic development, thought development and the role of language, all these problems being closely connected to the antinomy narcissism–object relations.[2] In this context, the study of IST becomes especially significant since they clearly show the interrelationship between the data used to generalize hypotheses, the (psychic) conditions under which these hypotheses are obtained and the structure and quality of the outcome. The above issue coincides with what the epistemologists study as the contexts of discovery and of justification of theories; both contexts are as relevant for them as they are for us; hence an interdisciplinary approach to it seems to be an appropriate one.

Freud and Bion are outstanding figures of their respective times in their attempts to specify the succeeding steps in the structuring of human thought, which at some point of its development will manifest itself through IST. In this chapter, I shall deal with only some of the hypotheses introduced by them, inasmuch as they become necessary to point out the course I intend to follow. On the other hand, Money-Kyrle (1971, p. 448), whose endeavour was to 'bridge the gap between psychoanalysis and ethology' (an aim I find both essential and legitimate), sees human cognitive development from a viewpoint attuned to Darwinian and post-Darwinian theories in which Freud was already interested when writing his Project (SE 1: 303). I also hope that the introduction of certain notions arising from genetic epistemology will turn out to be useful in this interdisciplinary dialogue, enabling a general reflection on the construction of theories, which may include psychoanalytic theories as well.

---

[2] See 'Erna and Melanie Klein', paper presented in collaboration with RH Etchegoyen, T. de Bianchedi, N. de Urman, U. de Moreno at the IPA Congress, Santiago de Chile, 1999. In the section 'Erna and the Wolf Man' I deal with the concept of the *après-coup* (*Nachträglichkeit*) and with the influence that his argument with Jung could have on Freud's implementation of this concept. IJPA, 84, 6 (1999), 1587.

Freudian developments

Freud's paper 'On the Sexual Theories of Children', which according to Strachey constituted the first complete and coherent presentation on this subject, was published in 1908. This paper appeared only a year after 'The Sexual Enlightenment of Children' (1907) and some months before the 'Little Hans' case history, although that work was probably already in proof in 1908. We can agree with Strachey's opinion as to the existence of some references to IST in 'The Interpretation of Dreams' and that the concept was not added to the 'Three Essays on a Sexual Theory' until 1915. Freud circumscribed the primal facts children endeavoured to theorize to the origin of children, birth, the nature of coitus, the differences between sexes and castration. His interest in laying solid foundations for his new ideas on human sexuality (1905) led him to compile and explain the theories of children. Freud hypothetically defined them as the outcome of 'thinking . . . that goes on operating as a self-sustained instinct for research', which becomes inhibited by the adults' lies (SE 9: 213). If we take into account his further remarks on the natural sexual curiosity of children (1910a, SE 11: 126-7), we shall see that a strong link is created between children's curiosity and humanity's spontaneous interest in research, knowledge and creation.

A careful reading of the 1908 paper suggests the development of divergent lines of thought. In a paragraph preceding the already quoted reference to the 'self-sustained instinct for research', Freud had stated that the child's interest in the existence of two sexes 'does not in fact awaken spontaneously . . . it is aroused under the goad of the self-seeking interests that dominate him, when – perhaps after the end of his second year – he is confronted with the arrival of a new baby' (1908b, SE 9: 212). A few pages later (1908b, SE 9: 223) he wrote: 'These seem to be the most important of the typical sexual theories that children produce spontaneously in early childhood, *under the sole influence of the components of the sexual instincts*' (emphasis added).

Then it would seem that, on the one hand, Freud believed that children build their theories on the basis of the deceitful replies of adults (and stimulated by their self-seeking interests); but, on the other hand, there arises another view, according to which they appear as the outcome of spontaneous infantile intellectual activity. Thus, in a correlative way, from the perspective of their epistemological value, two opposing views seem to be present. According to the first, the focus of these theories would have more to do with pathology whereas the second would emphasize their importance in the building of knowledge. In brief, children create false theories as a result of either lack of information or distorted information, although 'each one of them contains a fragment of real truth' (p. 215). Freud also held that: 'This brooding and doubting, however, becomes the prototype of all later intellectual work directed towards the solution of problems, and the first failure has a crippling effect on the child's whole future' (p. 219). But if 'what is correct and hits the mark in such theories is to be explained by their origin from the components of the sexual instinct which are already stirring in the childish organism' (p. 215), such theories would be necessary steps in the acquisition of real knowledge about sexual facts, as part of a more extensive development of an intellectual capacity, always open to the inevitable conflicts inherent in mental functioning.

However, following Freud in cases such as that of Little Hans or the Wolf Man, we may understand that the patients' pathological phantasies he met with, when repression was defeated, were just versions of the sexual theories he had discovered and described.[3] This would imply that there exists some divergence in the understanding of the phantasies, primal phantasies and sexual theories and their mutual relationship because, according to one of the Freudian views, sexual theories are built with material supplied by adults, whereas primal phantasies are, and have always been, unconscious and exist beyond any personal experience.

But analogies between (primal) phantasies and sexual theories may be established, and Laplanche and Pontalis say in *The Language of Psychoanalysis*:

> If we consider the themes which can be recognised in primal phantasies, the striking thing is that they have one trait in common: they are all related to the origins. Like collective myths, they claim to provide a representation of and a 'solution' to whatever constitutes a major enigma for the child. *Whatever appears to the subject as a reality of such type as to require an explanation or 'theory'*, these phantasies dramatise into the primal moment or original point of departure of a history. (1973, p. 332; emphasis added)

In their 1968 essay 'Fantasme originaire, fantasmes des origines, origine du fantasme', Laplanche and Pontalis had already maintained that these primal phantasies may be of the order of a myth of origins; in fact, what Freud was attempting to grasp, when giving the myth a figurative representation, was the precise moment in which desire arose.

It would be convenient to remember that both Laplanche and Pontalis, and Strachey, in his introductory remarks to 'Hysterical Phantasies and their Relationship to Bisexuality', underline the fact that 'the subject of phantasies seems to have been very much in Freud's mind at about the date of this paper' (Freud, 1908a). A related subject which also was in Freud's mind at the time was that of the family romances, dealt

---

[3] Freud himself had already become aware of this (cf. quote p. 1).

with in another paper (1909, SE 9: 235), which was first published with Otto Rank's book, *Myth of the Birth of the Hero*. For Marthe Robert (1990, pp. 52-4):

> The Oedipus legend remarkably combines the theme of the abandoned child who is found, the innocent and in some way pre-sexual child with those of parricide and incest, in which Freud discovered the confirmation for his analyses of psychic unconscious facts. Oedipus is the son of a king, but he was raised by shepherds, therefore his birth remains as an enigma for him.

Robert further states (pp. 62-3) that 'like the universal human validity of the Oedipus Complex, every work of fiction, or representation or artistic image constitutes some sort of veiled illustration of this structure. In this sense, "romances" are nothing else but another manifestation of the Oedipal conflict' (my translation).

In short, from what has been expounded up to now, we may conclude that if we follow the leading thread in Freud's thought, as it was shown in several papers between 1908 and 1909, including 'Creative Writers and Day-dreaming', there is a close relationship between apparently different phenomena, such as fantasies, infantile sexual theories, the neurotic's family romance, daydreams and creative literary works.

In this last mentioned paper, after establishing the continuity we may find between child's play, day-dreaming and creative writing, he added: 'I cannot pass over the relation of phantasies to dreams' (SE 9: 148), and then in 'Formulations on the Two Principles of Mental Functioning' (1911, SE 12: 219-22), he put forward some other mutually implied problems when he wrote: 'It is probable that thinking was originally unconscious, in so far as it went beyond mere ideational representations and was directed to the relations between impressions of objects, and that it did not acquire further qualities, perceptible to consciousness, until it became connected with verbal residues' and that 'phantasying . . . abandons dependence on real objects'.

The introduction of these interrelated problems to psychoanalytic studies and later theoretical contributions, particularly those dealing with object relations, gave rise to the formulation of new hypotheses.

IST and unconscious phantasy: Klein and her followers

There is no doubt that Klein enlarged our knowledge about IST by endowing her descriptions of them with the incredible realism and detail with which she observed they were displayed in the sessions.

When presenting her paper 'The Nature and Function of Phantasy' (1948) in the course of the *Controversial Discussions* in London

(1941–44), Susan Isaacs gave shape and methodological support to this concept, which was already present in Klein's works. We know that the Kleinian group wanted to validate their concept of unconscious phantasy, which was different from the one Freud had proposed (though loyal to his thought according to its members). This concept had been developed on the basis of recording child and adult manifestations, both verbal and behavioural, and no other could substitute for it in clinical practice because it paved the way for the construction of hypotheses about the underlying psychic reality. At this point, closely following Freud, there was agreement as to the role of psychic reality in symptom-formation and in the choice of neurosis.

From an epistemological viewpoint, it can be stated that by using the concept of unconscious phantasies in this way (equivalent to IST and to psychic reality) as the basis for interpretation, it takes the place of the presupposed theory in the interpretive hypotheses. This approach implies a profound theoretical change, without which many further developments would not have been possible; however, it is necessary and fair to emphasize that the Kleinian and post-Kleinian approach to unconscious phantasy continues to be more or less exclusive to the Kleinian school. This holds especially with regards to the rigorous method with which the concept of unconscious phantasy is applied in clinical practice, and despite the attempts to reconcile it with similar ones coming from other schools.

Elizabeth Bott Spillius thoroughly examines the concept in both Freud's and in Klein's works and in her final conclusions states:

> In summary, I think Freud's idea is that the prime mover of psychic life is the unconscious wish, not phantasy. The 'work' of making phantasies and the 'work' of making dreams are parallel processes in which forbidden unconscious wishes achieve disguised expression and partial fulfilment. For Freud himself, especially in his central usage, and even more for his immediate followers, phantasies are conceived as the imagined fulfilment of frustrated wishes. Whether they originate in the *system conscious* or the *system preconscious*, they are an activity of the ego and are formed according to the principles of the secondary process. That is not the whole story, however, because phantasies may get repressed into the *system unconscious*, where they become associated with the instinctual wishes, become subject to the laws of the primary process, and may find their way into dreams and many other derivatives. For Freud and for French psychoanalysts particularly, there are the primal phantasies, 'unconscious all along', of the primal scene, castration and seduction, also capable of being directly incorporated into dreams and expressed through other derivatives. (2001, p. 361)

Thus, the ontological and meta-psychological status of both types of unconscious phantasy would be left open. The Kleinian school seems to solve this issue when defining unconscious phantasies as the unconscious contents of *all* psychical activity, even of dreams, because they 'play the part that Freud assigned to the unconscious wish' (Bott Spillius, 2001, p. 371), thus becoming a more inclusive concept up to the point of acknowledging their existence as previous to verbal language acquisition and capable of being expressed through bodily channels. In this way, a point of view is shaped according to which there is a psyche that, no matter how primitive it may be, operates from the beginning of life; it recognizes objects and tries to regulate its relations with them, starting from meanings ascribed to them. Hence, we would have access to psychical contents through the knowledge of unconscious phantasies surmised from *all and any* of its productions.

We could reasonably maintain that IST express the scenarios of certain unconscious phantasies that create psychical reality at any given time, and whose study is relevant because they account for both the development of sexuality (by emerging as such in the transference) and cognitive development. The latter could accordingly be considered as the unavoidable and concurrent correlate of instinctual activity.

Following one of the many paths opened by Freud, enquiries into the child's early interactions with its environment, as well as the child's objects' performance in both facilitating and hindering the child's acquisition of knowledge, become especially important. Moreover, this subject is studied not only by cognitive researchers but also by those psychoanalysts associated with some of the existing object relations theories.

Bridging the gap between psychoanalysis and ethology

I should now like to continue with the analysis of IST from the perspective of object relations theory by recalling Money-Kyrle's above quoted words (1971), not only because of the synthetic power of his statement but also to pay homage to an author less quoted and remembered than he deserves. What arises from his brief quotation is that not only do psychoanalytic and ethological theories deal with common issues, but these may also help analysts to validate or refute their own hypotheses. This author's works are characterized from the start by a sustained interest in cognitive processes, which, according to him, are present, in addition to object relations, from the beginning of life, in so far as the former are the outcome of the inherent cognitive component of the instinctual drives.

We could maintain that the human infant, as well as other species' offspring, is endowed at birth with some kind of innate cognitive equipment, whose working vicissitudes will determine its further cognitive development. We can support this viewpoint inasmuch as psychoanalytical hypotheses may be compatible with those of ethologists in general when trying to describe and explain animal behaviour, and with the laws proposed by Darwin in his studies on species' evolution and selection; or at least, that psychoanalytic hypotheses do not oppose the latter in an insurmountable way.

Money-Kyrle's extensive work was taken into serious consideration by Bion, and even though it cannot be strictly said that these authors were collaborators, a reading of their respective works conveys the closeness of their ideas and their mutual enrichment.

Money-Kyrle was Moritz Schlick's disciple while he was under analysis with Freud in Vienna. Schlick was one of the founders of the Vienna Circle and Money-Kyrle took from him the idea that knowledge consists in the use of an (innate) capacity to recognize something (an object) as belonging to a class. In two of his best papers (1968; 1971), he combines this hypothesis with Bion's theory of thought development (Bion, 1962).

The forceful idea that Money-Kyrle introduces is the existence of innate knowledge. This knowledge does not involve objects themselves, but those characteristics that are recognizable by the subject and that allow their being assigned to a class. Thus the human infant – without ignoring its initial immaturity – is appropriately included in a view of our species that is more compatible with its belonging to the animal kingdom and being in some ways subject to the general laws of evolution, which give importance to the possession of early cognitive capacities, obviously necessary for adaptation and survival.[4]

Money-Kyrle put forward some of his ideas on this topic in both papers. In 'Cognitive development' (1968, p. 418), he proposed that 'whether these [innate preconceptions] are thought of as the product of some kind of racial memory or cerebral variation and selection is perhaps psychoanalytically irrelevant. Personally, I think of them as products of variation and selection'. Next, in 'The aim of psychoanalysis', he wrote:

> Our phylogenetic inheritance, then, contains class notions which we cannot imagine though we can recognise their members. *This is the cognitive part of the innate response which precedes the affective and conative. Variation and selection may be expected to have laid down an immense amount of potential information in this way, which probably comes into being in stages, mainly during the first few weeks or months of post-natal life (not counting what develops before).* (1971, p. 443; emphasis added)

---

[4] In a very interesting paper by McGill University researchers (Onishi and Baillargeon, 2005), the authors state: 'we assume that children are born with an abstract computational system that guides their interpretation of others' behaviour'.

It is tempting to go on quoting at length; however, the above seems to be enough to indicate the compatibility between the developmental biological approach and the psychoanalytical theories of human thought, which maintain that cognitive development is based on the recognition of just what phylogenetic heritage has prepared us to recognize. If this process fails because the preconception of an object mates with a 'spurious' object, a 'misunderstanding' – as Money-Kyrle defines it – will emerge. It is very likely at this point that the distortions observed in IST are rooted.

Let us synthesize what has been expounded up to now:

1. In the context of his wider view of human sexuality and the part it plays in the aetiology of neuroses, Freud placed IST in a new context and recognized their relevance in connection with at least three different viewpoints: infantile sexuality, transference phenomena and creative activity.
2. On account of the relationships between IST and other forms of phantasy life, based on formal resemblance and meta-psychological understanding, we are led to pose the question of the nature of conscious and unconscious phantasies in general and to state their participation in various types of psychic products, including abstract thought and scientific theories. This latter fact would reveal the cognitive aspect of instinctual activity.
3. We have considered the possibility of taking the Kleinian concept of unconscious phantasy (the mental expression of instincts, the primary contents of unconscious mental processes) as a common denominator, as the leading thread that allows us to understand the whole sequence of different mental productions, from the less complex to the more sophisticated.
4. The acknowledgement of the cognitive aspect of instinctual activity, on one hand, requires a review of the part played by objects (according to what has already been explained, their favouring or hindering role in the achievement of the infant's earliest 'realizations'). On the other hand, it constitutes a central question for object relations theories, in spite of which they never reach any agreement about the first stages of object relationships (narcissistic object relations versus objectless narcissism). We should also take into account the theoretical change involved in the passage from the conception of an epistemophilic impulse to the idea of a cognitive component in every instinctual activity.
5. Therefore, IST may be viewed as part of childhood sexuality, partly conscious, partly containing important fragments of truth. Their defensive function (at the service of the Pleasure Principle) and their

poor explanatory structure cannot be ignored, but it follows from my line of argument that their epistemological value, the part they play in the development of thought, as well as their contribution to creative and theorizing activity in general are outstanding. Moreover, the role played in IST by deceitful or distorted information provided by adults is restated, *vis-à-vis* the hypothesis of an innate knowledge inclusive of some basic data of biology and sexuality. This early knowledge then turns out to be exposed to opposing tendencies: knowing and not knowing (the K and -K links described by Bion). It may be posited that the above restatement became explicit through a more objective consideration of the role attributed to children's sexual enlightenment as carried out by adults in the early stages of psychoanalytic practice.

6. The idea that unconscious phantasies, with the exception of the primal ones, are unconscious just because they were once repressed seems to give way before the above-presented hypotheses to the possibility of thinking of even the id, the instinct reservoir, as including an inherent cognitive component. This way of thinking, more in agreement with the ethological hypotheses, suggests that IST should be conceived as spontaneously triggered by an infantile mind 'developmentally endowed to that end'. The possibility arises of granting IST the epistemic value of scientific theories *in statu nascendi* even from their origins, and of describing the child as 'a little researcher'.[5] The child's theories are just that, and are expressed with whatever degree of coherence and adjustment to reality that he has been able to achieve at every stage of development.

Thus if we consider these IST as a specific case of what theories are in general, it may be useful to introduce some of the ideas springing from genetic epistemology, as proposed by Piaget and García (1982).

Psychoanalysis and genetic epistemology

First, I should like to raise two questions that may seem naïve: Are IST real theories? And, does their infantile nature lie in their contents or in their structure?

To answer the first question, it may be useful to appeal to the opinion of a well-known epistemologist, Gregorio Klimovsky (1994, p. 29), who assigns various meanings to the term 'theory'. However,

---

[5] Freud (1909, SE X, 11, fn 3) referred in this text to certain 'young enquirers', who in speaking about their little sisters, expressed their judgement that their 'widdlers' would get bigger when the girls grew up. However, I think I use this expression in a somewhat different way.

they all refer to a hypothesis or set of hypotheses, or it may be an initial hypothesis and all the hypotheses springing from it. IST may also constitute a formulation dealing with empirical regularities or the statement of laws reflecting the generalization of such regularities. According to these definitions, we could consider IST as just another case. Regarding their infantile nature, I think that we may recognize this in both their inner structure and in their contents. They would be hypotheses and generalizations of hypotheses based on empirical material provided by child observation on the one hand, and by adults' explanations on the other.

As the reader may have noticed, we are dealing with a development whose characteristics allow that it be included in the field of genetic epistemology. As Bléandonu underlines (1990, p. 150, n 1), the concept of genetic epistemology may be applied to both Bion's theory of thought and the work of Jean Piaget. Bléandonu explains that Bion never referred to an author whom he most probably knew, by pointing out that their approaches and theoretical backgrounds were very different. From my own perspective, and without disregarding the existing differences, I think that certain aspects of Piaget's work may be very useful.

I would especially like to refer to the book written by Jean Piaget in collaboration with the Argentine epistemologist Rolando García (1982) in which they not only analyse the inner logical coherence of theories, but also describe the existence of significant analogies between the individual building of knowledge and the history of scientific development in general. Piaget and García depict cognitive growth as constituted by stages, though these do not form a simple linear series in which each is overthrown by the next once its aim is achieved; but they see these stages as consecutive reorganizations in which the already existing materials are 'reflected' and become reformulated elements of a higher level. They write:

> ... according to common sense, the child does not invent anything and receives through education everything he learns. However, the best way to prove the falsehood of this thesis is the marvellous development that takes place in the course of the first eighteen months of life, when the child does not yet speak and has at his disposal only a few patterns of behaviour. Nevertheless, the progress of his/her intelligence, the construction of space, of permanent objects, of causality, etc., bear witness to a surprising multiplicity of inventions and discoveries. It so happens that *from this time onwards, we have to deal with the problem of learning whether these are consecutive innovations, whether it has to do with the performance of an inherited programme, or even with the realisation of possibilities implied from the start within certain a priori synthetic intuitions.* (1982, pp. 19-20; emphasis added, my translation)

Piaget and García further maintain that 'pure' perceptions or experiences do not exist; the reading of experience means the application of cognitive tools that make it possible.

It is important to emphasize that given the correspondences that this approach (genetic epistemology) establishes between the individual and the general levels, some problems may arise when the vicissitudes of individual learning are mistaken for the proposal of a scientific theory which claims general validity. When this takes place, two important consequences may be expected in psychoanalysis, of which the first is the intra-theoretical confusion between developmentally distorted concepts drawn from certain facts and the analyst's theoretical statements of the laws that supposedly govern these facts.[6] Not infrequently, this may be seen in the generalizations the contents of some IST undergo. The second – which may be defined as an inter-theoretical consequence – may emerge at the clinical level, when the interpretations of theories developed by patients in the transference meet with those theories that shape the analyst's frame of reference. Up to now, IST have been studied as generators and the expression of some kind of pathology. But their 'theoretical' value – or their condition as theories that may be refuted, which would mean steps in the direction of knowledge more congruent with reality – in my view has not been sufficiently underlined in psychoanalytic theory.

These observations have briefly shown some points of contact between certain psychoanalytic hypotheses and those of Piaget and García's genetic epistemology, even the possibility of considering cognitive development as depending on the existence of an inherited programme up to a certain extent (an idea also held by Money-Kyrle).

I should now like to deal with the problem of the contexts of discovery and justification. This problem is thoroughly examined from a genetic view by Piaget and García (1982, Chapter IX) and, within the boundaries of what he appropriately calls 'logic of psychoanalytic research', by Jorge Canestri in recent papers (Canestri et al., 2002; Canestri, 2003).[7]

To put it simply, the possibility to keep both contexts carefully apart when it comes to considering any given theory – as is Popper's and

---

[6] In the Barcelona version of this paper, I quote Diego and Amalia Rapela's paper '¿Mujer o varona? Psychoanalysis of femininity and infantile sexual theories' (1994), in which they maintain that Freud did not approach the subject of female sexuality in a clear enough way. This I consider compatible with the ideas here discussed.

[7] As is known, the introduction of a distinction between both contexts was first made by Hans Reichenbach and this differentiation is considered and discussed in one way or another by most epistemologists. It has been Popper perhaps who has more insisted on the convenience of separating them and giving privilege to the context of justification.

many other epistemologists' wish – is opposed to psychoanalytical knowledge and experience. Moreover, such an opposite view of the same problem might have been to Popper's great dismay, comprehensible especially in such a cultivated man who approached the study of psychology only to dismiss it later on scientific grounds. But to us psychoanalysts, as to any analysed person, the evidence of a permanent interaction between conscious and unconscious processes is impossible to set aside. It will be useful at this point to quote Didier Anzieu on interpretation to explain my viewpoint: 'The interpretation framed by the psychoanalyst belongs to secondary process permeated by primary process and . . . the patient, understands the interpretation at this double level alike' (Anzieu, 1972, p. 255). In these words Anzieu stated his opposition to the existence of a non-conflicting autonomous psychic area from which interpretation would emerge (and to which it would be addressed) as well as to 'a conception of psychoanalytic practice at the frontiers of psychoanalysis without interpretation' (by which he means Lacanian psychoanalysis). It is worthwhile noting the simultaneous double level and their mutual permeation because this entails the following: if this is the way in which the human mind continuously works, any of its productions will have to reflect it to a greater or lesser degree. A brief review of the psychoanalytic literature may allow us to verify that Anzieu's transcribed opinion is not at all isolated. In fact, almost 20 years earlier, Money-Kyrle (1956, p. 324) had introduced a similar viewpoint when asserting that 'instinct in the main creates our first world *which survives in the unconscious*, and that the common sense world is developed from it under the influence of a few months' experience' (emphasis added).

But, if we are to consider 'common sense', its absence in unconscious processes and their coexistence, it would be very appropriate to refer to Matte-Blanco's vast work (1975; 1988), in which he defines this coexistence as the 'fundamental antinomy' (1988, p. 70). To understand this author's line of thought, which is most pertinent here, I think it convenient to quote his transcription of a dialogue between Albert Einstein and the French mathematician Jacques Hadamard. The latter was interested in the psychology of invention in the field of mathematics. Einstein wrote to him about 'signs and more or less clear images', and added that 'the desire to arrive finally at logically connected concepts is the emotional basis of this rather vague play with above mentioned elements'. In his further comments Matte-Blanco maintains:

> we may also say that the unconscious, which respects so little the laws of logical thinking is nevertheless the father of logical thinking. And again we find here the *co-presence of the two incompatible modes of being: the fundamental antinomy which, in this case, we see at work and as the*

source and the expression of the highest creative activity. (1988, p. 98; emphasis added)[8]

In brief, to resume the essential argument of this chapter, different psychoanalytic sources show the many efforts to bridge the gap between the psychological conditions under which a theory is developed and the latter's inner logical coherence. If we returned to an exclusively Freudian approach, we could claim that unconscious functioning, at the service of the Pleasure Principle, has possibly more bearing on the context of discovery. When drawing the distinction between the different mistakes in judgement in the 'Project for a scientific psychology' (Freud, [1895] 1950a, SE 1: 384, 387), Freud already attributes these errors to the intense facilitations of the cathexes of certain neuronal complexes. On the other hand, the functioning of the Pc. Cc. systems can be seen as more closely linked to the context of justification owing to the type of logic they exhibit.

In the above mentioned papers, Canestri, following Lakatos, states: 'But Popper, who laid the foundations of this (fallible) logic of discovery, did not deal with the meta-question of what the nature of this enquiry was and did not notice that it is neither psychology nor logic, it is an independent discipline, the logic of discovery, heuristics.' (Canestri *et al.*, 2002, p. 139)

In dealing with this problem, Klimovsky (1994, p. 29) writes: 'The frontier line between these two contexts (ie discovery and justification) is neither well-defined nor legitimate, because there would be close links between the problem of justifying a theory (and its logical qualities) *and the way the theory was constructed on the particular occasion of its emergence*' (emphasis added).

A useful illustration, though not the only possible one related to the subject we are dealing with, which shows the existence of such links and their bearing on the final outcome may be Etchegoyen's (1988) revision of the Little Hans case history. The author thoroughly examined this case history and discovered that Freud insistently omitted data in this patient's clinical material that would have enabled him to recognize that the boy was quite aware of the existence of female genitalia with their own characteristics. It may be assumed that if this omission had not been made, the theory of the phallic phase would have been formulated in a quite different way.

Let us return to Piaget and García's ideas regarding the importance of the use made of available cognitive tools to account for reality (a perspective quite compatible with that of projective identification theory).

---

[8] In Argentina, Etchegoyen and Ahumada (1999) have been thorough readers of Matte-Blanco's work.

After extensively examining and comparing, among other authors, the ideas of Popper, Lakatos, Kuhn and Feyerabend on the problem of both contexts, Piaget and García write:

> Neo-positivists adopted an *a priori* position on the irrelevance of the process of discovery to what they judged as the fundamental aim of the philosophy of science: to justify the validity of scientific knowledge. *There is a flagrant inner contradiction in their not looking for any empirical basis for their dogmatically adopted assertions*. (1988, p. 243: emphasis added)

This statement, which strongly supports the position of genetic epistemology, explicitly refers to Popper ([1934] 1959), who claimed through the separation of both contexts to achieve the 'elimination of all psychologism' to devote himself exclusively to the inner logic of theories. There may be well-grounded arguments to deny the existence of any connection between the two contexts, but here we encounter the difficulties confronted by those who, in adopting this position, can only put forward 'logical' arguments which have no need to take into account *'the way the theory was constructed on the particular occasion of its emergence'*.

However, it may be stated that the 'way' and the 'particular occasion' are for psychoanalysts nothing else but the expression of the author's subjectivity when he designs his theories and its influence on the creative act. How can we attempt to reconcile what seem to be unyieldingly divergent epistemological views? Perhaps by underlining that nobody would reasonably attempt logically to justify a theory purely on the basis of the 'way' or the 'particular occasion' of its creation, yet the impact this may have on the logical structure of the final product should not be overlooked without proof enough. I conclude that it is possible (though difficult) for psychoanalysts to contribute to solving this problem. From the vantage point of this chapter, the subject of IST, we could draw on a plethora of empirical data and theories to approach this work.

As previously argued, based on Freud's own ideas, IST operate in the phenomenon of transference and their 'theoretical' framing clearly reveals the interactions between both contexts; that is, between their inner logic and the (psychological) conditions of their production. Let us also recall the possibility of considering both the patient's utterances and the analyst's interpretations as theoretical formulations expressing, although differently, the 'way' and the 'particular occasion' on which they were produced. All things considered, this constitutes in fact the transference–countertransference relationship. In referring to the way both theories are contrasted in the analytic session so that one of them may be refuted, Etchegoyen (1986, p. 637) asserts that the patient's ostensive insight occurs when he or she precisely perceives that his or her own theory has not been able to pass the test of its being refuted.⁹

At this point some questions, some of them disturbing, have to be put forward. Shall we be able to follow this thread while examining theories and satisfy the exigencies of this task? And: shall we be able to apply this approach to our own theories?

To conclude, I would like to say that, as regards the first question, this is one of the several responsibilities we have in the face of the scientific community. As psychoanalysts we should be expected to provide the data and knowledge essential to reach a deeper comprehension of theoretical production and for a more fruitful restatement of an uncalled-for confrontation between epistemological positions. And let me clarify that I am saying 'several' because we have similar responsibilities in the intersection with other disciplines. The attempt to be listened to in fields distant from our specific one is not at all easy, but the time may come when our efforts will be rewarded and the 'Claims of psycho-analysis to scientific interest' (Freud, 1913c) may show their enduring force.

As to the second question, I think that we, as analysts, are now in debt to ourselves. The struggle to elucidate and improve our theoretical language and the inner coherence of our theories, as well as their subsequent use in clinical practice, should be closely linked with the study of the psychological conditions under which (psychoanalytical) theories are generated in our own minds, where our own IST are also present. This may be inferred legitimately from Freud's opinion, when he pointed at the study of countertransference as one of the technical innovations along the path of the 'future developments of psychoanalysis' (Freud, 1910b, SE 11: 139). Because what else could be said of countertransference but that it is an emotional and psychological condition of the analyst that may be very disturbing to his work, but, insofar as he succeeds in thinking about it in logical verbal terms, and in integrating it into his 'theory' of clinical facts liable to be registered in the analytic situation, he may express it through an interpretation as devoid of his own subjectivity as it can be?

In Argentina, David Liberman (1970–72) maintained that before turning to theories with the highest levels of abstraction, it would be appropriate to begin with those close to our empirical basis, when working 'under fire' in the session, since in this way we may contrast them once and again and next go through them in detail in the interval between sessions. To this end he began working systematically with

---

⁹ A paper by Sanchez Grillo (2001) on the analysis of a six-year-old boy clearly illustrates the presence of these type of privileged moments and the subsequent changes they introduce.

several groups of analysts, but this endeavour came to a premature end because of his unexpected death. In the following years some of his disciples[10] trying to follow his steps, devoted themselves for a long time to the study of anonymous analytic sessions to attempt to ascertain the type of relationship holding between the analyst's formulations and the (psychoanalytic) theories that may be supporting them.

Similar projects seem at present to attract interest in different regions. This seems to point to the fact that there are concurrent concerns and parallel theoretical and practical needs in the psychoanalytic community, a situation that corroborates the vitality of our discipline and permits to have a reasonable hope to be able to state similarities and differences that are inevitable among different analytic cultures. With the intention of collaborating to this end I have put forward in this chapter my ideas on the importance of IST, approached from an interdisciplinary point of view based on psychoanalysis, ethology and genetic epistemology.

---

[10] See, for instance, Lancelle *et al.* (1990, p. 83).

10
The search to define and describe how psychoanalysts work: preliminary report on the project of the EPF Working Party on Comparative Clinical Methods

DAVID TUCKETT

It has been difficult to know what does and does not constitute competent psychoanalytic work and so equally difficult to assess when it is being practised and when it is not. Within and outside the International Psychoanalytic Association[1] there is in most countries an overwhelming range of contradictory theories and techniques held dearly and jealously by their adherent groups, but all broadly claiming to base their practice

---

[1] Founded to establish Freud's wish that there be some degree of authority and standardization (Wallerstein, 2003).

Psychoanalysis: From Practice to Theory. Edited by J. Canestri. © 2006 Whurr Publishers Ltd (a subsidiary of John Wiley & Sons Ltd).

on Freud's ideas.[2] I have introduced the issue in relation to competence. Eisold (2003) summarizes it in terms of identity: 'the common identity of psychoanalysts is largely a fiction, an illusion that protects us from experiencing the full extent of the dissolution and fragmentation that has occurred. Our common identity is a remnant of the past, and possibly a hope for the future.'

The great differences among us and the way they are growing point to the fact that while we have more or less given up dogmatic assertions of superiority, we have not found a methodologically adequate way to say no to theories or, as I shall focus on in this chapter, techniques. By methodologically adequate I mean the ability to state a proposition in a confident and supported way such that it can create an uncompelled consensus. The consequence of this lack is that ideas about how to practise psychoanalysis have proliferated unchecked, so that few if any clinical practices given the name psychoanalysis can be securely regarded as untrue or invalid and then discarded. It is hard to have more confidence in one idea about practice than another. In effect, but with the possible exception of gross financial or sexual exploitation of the patient, in psychoanalytic practice at this moment it can seem anything goes.

My concerns about the general problem began when I was Editor of the *International Journal of Psychoanalysis*. At that time I realized how hard it was to judge the merit of papers putting forward psychoanalytic ideas in a fair way. I also realized the extent to which people were accustomed to making judgements on the basis of charisma, authority or politics rather than argument and support. In response I initiated a debate on what could be considered clinical facts (Tuckett, 1994) and then with my colleagues at IJPA went on to develop a way to judge arguments and the way they were supported (Tuckett, 1998). These concerns about the need to develop a critical and constructive peer culture also informed my recent work for the EPF (Tuckett, 2002; 2003; 2004).

I have contended that a main reason for the difficulty psychoanalysts have in being perceived advantageously (even by each other) is caused by the fact that we are not really confident in judging the merit of what we each do and have underdeveloped the capacities to be so. One result is that within our institutions there is an underlying suspiciousness and defensiveness about what we do, how different ways of doing it actually work or what their effect is. I think these have a quite deeply corrosive effect on our perceptions of ourselves and are a main cause of the suspiciousness and defensiveness there is about how we each work –

---

[2] See, for instance, Arbiser (2003); Eisold (2003).

whether because it leads to opaque judgemental criteria in which anything goes or to divisive conflict in which institutions effectively split.

In 2000 the EPF Council established a new scientific policy. Five EPF working parties and several European Forums and Ad Hoc groups were created to try to build a more critical, more knowledgeable and ultimately more securely based and confident peer review culture for our psychoanalytic discipline. The various entities exist to sponsor ongoing work. They meet each year at the annual conference and in between those meetings.

The EPF working party on comparative clinical methods

One working party the EPF formed was on Comparative Clinical Methods. Its task is to see what might be done about the difficulty defining what is and is not practised as psychoanalysis and how we communicate to each other about what we do.

The simple answer to questions about what we do in psychoanalytic practice is to say that we seek to establish a psychoanalytic process. But what is that? As long ago as 1947 a distinguished committee of the American Psychoanalytic Association was unable to agree on what constituted psychoanalysis and also to note a strong resistance to any investigation of the problem (Rangell, 1954). Several subsequent investigations did no better (see Vaughan *et al.*, 1997; Schachter, 2004) and an empirical study found that candidates in American institutes were often unclear about what they needed to master to qualify as analysts. They did know they should avoid serious disagreements with their supervisors and should keep their patient in treatment. While they reported a belief that what mattered was to establish a psychoanalytic process, they found themselves mostly unable to define the meaning of psychoanalytic process or to state what their supervisors would say it meant (Cabaniss *et al.*, 2003). In the United States these difficulties have now been recognized as so significant that some argue that the American IPA group should provide courses, supervision and experiences that need to be completed, but abolish the Board that judges whether candidates presenting work can practise properly (Renik, 2003).

If we cannot define psychoanalytic process or determine when people who say they are practising psychoanalysis actually are doing so, the difficulties I have mentioned at the beginning of this chapter will intensify. It has seemed to me, therefore, that a further effort to describe what psychoanalysis might be is worthwhile.

In considering the task, I took the view that one facet of the difficulty has been political and another methodological. The political problem is a great deal of unwillingness to accept both that there are fundamental differences between forms of analytic practice and a great deal of desire to assert rather than to study the merits of one form over another. The methodological problem has been an over-reliance on abstract definitions that leave a great deal of latitude[3] and an under-reliance on grounded empirical study. Taking these problems together I thought, therefore, that rather than trying to define a single psychoanalytical approach it would be more useful to start by enquiring what reputable psychoanalysts actually do and then to have the argument about legitimacy and relative merits later.

To establish what reputable colleagues in Europe were actually doing in their practice, representatives from societies were asked to invite colleagues reputed within their society to be clinically skilled to present their work within small mixed discussion groups (drawn from several societies) meeting for a number of hours. The task within these discussion groups was to use the resources available – good quality presentations and different viewpoints and norms about how to work – to create the conditions to understand the presenters' assumptions and method and compare presentations in depth. Using this approach I hoped that although we might end up no further along the path of describing the way to do psychoanalysis, we might perhaps be able to achieve describing and comparing some ways.

Three problems came up when, with Haydee Faimberg leading the project, we tried out this approach when 120 colleagues met in ten groups in Prague to see how far they could get. First, it proved very difficult to focus on the presenter's method. Instead, and despite an attempt to anticipate the difficulty, there was a strong tendency to supervise and approve or disapprove how it had been done from the listener's point of view. Second, communication within groups was difficult because the same psychoanalytic terms had different but implicit meanings in different cultures. Nearly everyone thought psychoanalysis required an understanding of transference, for instance, but there were clearly many contradictory ways to define it and especially to use it in interpretations. Third, there was no commensurable framework for comparison (Bernardi, 2002) – no way to ask the same question of each presentation and then compare answers. Groups did try to find items against which

---

[3] Some of the problems faced by our American colleagues seem to me to have started with the attempt to approach matters theoretically rather than empirically and from the quite disastrous impact Hartmann's thinking had on the valuation of clinical material as data for scientific enquiry (see Edelson, 1986).

to compare cases, but in doing so they arrived at a very long list of some 40 variables of very different logical orders.[4] After Prague, Faimberg continued trying to find ways to manage the first two problems. The WPCCM was formed with the Prague moderators at its core to deal specifically with the third problem.

Detailed feedback was provided to the working party group from the Prague meeting and a year later, in Sorrento, I attempted to construct a preliminary comparative typology, based on what analysts said to their patients, which was intended to provide an instrument to take further the task of seeing how far we could describe what an analyst was doing so we could make formal comparisons between different methods of conducting psychoanalysis. This typology method worked to a degree. It was mostly successful in getting the groups who took part to focus on what the presenter was actually trying to do and could sharpen and sometimes deepen the lines of discussion. But in other ways it was far from being satisfactory. It did not always produce a very good experience. Some colleagues reacted very negatively to the idea of a restricted discussion and formal classification, which could be experienced in a concrete, reified fashion. One contributing factor was that the instrument was quite loose and members of groups were not well prepared: categories were too many and not well enough defined. Another problem was that even the five or so hours provided to discuss each presentation was insufficient. There was not always time both to go into detail and to allow the group to feel they had got a sense of the analyst's work, etc. Another problem seemed to be that the whole idea of formalization and comparison (perhaps interacting with some characteristics of some of the cases discussed) created complex emotional processes in groups. Finally, although the groups discussed only two cases, only one group attempted the task of comparison in any depth – the results were interesting and have been used in the next development but they were not based on the typology and the group's discussion did not suggest it had been much use to them for its specific comparative purpose

---

[4] The variables ranged widely. One moderator commented: 'We had to grapple with not only a multiplicity of models/viewpoints/ assumptions, but also with a multiplicity of levels . . . some of the ideas under discussion belonged in fact to different logical classes. For instance, "is it useful and even permissible, to not have a tight control over the expression of one's emotion?" belongs to a different class than "is it useful to interpret the enactment of family relationship in the transference?". On the other hand, the "importance of reaching emotionally the patient" may be classed with "privileging the importance of free-associations" or "enabling patients to symbolize their mental processes" and [all three] belong to a separate class – let's call them basic assumptions regarding psychoanalysis – from technical concepts such as projective identification or reconstruction . . . [and] to the multiplicity of levels, or classes, we must add the multiplicity of models within the class.'

(beyond the typology's general value in creating a different focus for discussion).

I had never expected that something as affectively coloured and polysemic as an analytic interpretation could be placed absolutely in a single category or, similarly, that a complex, 50-minute session in a long-term psychoanalysis could be examined intervention by intervention without some element of artificiality. Theoretical development requires the conceptual generalization and categorization of uniquely experienced instances and, like language itself but more so, is restrictive. Through abstraction and categorization there is loss, which produces ambivalence. The hope is that there is also gain.[5] None the less, I had not expected the emotional response that some people had to the Sorrento task – some even stating that an effort was afoot to kill psychoanalysis – and this in itself was interesting: evidence perhaps of unfamiliarity with empirical research and the fragility of the psychoanalytic identity at the present time.

In Sorrento the WPCCM moderators struggled to maintain a focus on what we were attempting and thus on the group's purpose. It was not easy, but groups did manage to become task-oriented rather than to denounce it or to avoid it by doing something else. Within one group the debate and discussion led to an important formulation – the grid, so-called – which could be used instrumentally (i.e. as a function, in a process); or used as an instrument (i.e. as a structure, a support). There is an important difference between the two ways. If the grid is used as a structure, an instrument, then it could indeed become a dangerous monster within. But used instrumentally, functionally, it did – as we came to see – help us psychoanalytically (Matthis, 2003). In other words, what is being proposed when we count the number of interventions in different categories is one method (among others) to help thinking not something which is an end in itself.

I was also aware by participating in one Sorrento group how the scheme we had was too complicated. I had made too much effort to try to accommodate subtle differences in advance of knowing what would be useful. I myself could never remember each of the 13 categories easily and so quite obviously they were not easy to internalize. The number of possible categories into which an analyst's interventions could fall needed to be reduced (from 13 to something like five) so that the dif-

---

[5] This is perhaps an example of the psychological sequelae of growth. In order to go forward, something is lost. This loss must be worked through within a containing structure before there is any certainty that the new situation will be valued. Future efforts need to recognize this situation and address the issue of containment from the start.

ferentiations could more easily be held in mind. The detail lost by this – increasing the likelihood that different approaches might get classified as the same – would have to be replaced in a different way once we knew what the problems were.

All the feedback from the Sorrento meeting was discussed in the working party some months later. With this formulation we could see what the next round of meetings would need to face directly. The preparatory documents and the moderator's opening remarks in each group would need to stress that the aim of the discussion to allocate numbers to interventions was not to create reified categories and check boxes, but to facilitate the most rigorous debate we could manage, grounded in what the analyst was actually doing.

Discussing the Sorrento groups we also realized that to compare analysts' ways of working we needed to go beyond the typology of interventions and for this purpose required a list of some core elements of psychoanalytic practice against which people would differ. In a long discussion, working with some of the cases we had from Sorrento and with other examples freely introduced into the discussion, we established a long list of possibilities.

Over the next few months, the WP chair, working with a research assistant,[6] examined clinical reports from the Prague and Sorrento meetings as well as cases reported in the *International Journal*'s Psychoanalyst at Work series. Using ideas generated from the list created at the WP meeting and seeking to organize those ideas we attempted to compare the way the different analysts worked by looking at how they listened to material (what they listened to, what they seemed to think was the unconscious level in the material, etc.), how they conceived it psychoanalytically and what they seemed to be trying to do with their interventions.[7] A long list of possible variables was established within each category and then each session was carefully considered. For example, one of the items that a psychoanalyst might listen for would be signs of unconscious infantile sexual conflicts; and/or an analyst might listen to signs of ambivalent phantasies about the relationship to the analyst, etc.; and/or an analyst might listen at a meta-level to how the patient listens to him, etc. In the inadequate circumstances of an incomplete case report and without the possibility to question the analyst further, we tried to see if comparisons along these lines were possible and also possibly

---

[6] I am grateful to Naama Ben Yehoyada for her assistance in trying to analyse systematically some 25 published or unpublished case reports and to the Research Advisory Board of the IPA for the financial support to make this possible.
[7] These organizing categories had come to mind as part of the EPF Working Party on Education project trying to work out the criteria used to differentiate the clinical work of candidates approaching qualification; see Tuckett (2005).

enlightening. We also looked at the extent to which interventions were saturated or not – that is to say either had a clear conscious meaning or left things more open for development and introduction of meaning – and at the ways various dimensions such as the here-and-now relationship was conceived and interpreted.

Although there were significant difficulties with the comparisons we had been able to make, I now felt we had gone far enough to propose to the WP that future group discussions could comprise two steps: one step using a simplified typology of interventions, the other using an additional and so far provisional typology assessing some key dimensions of the way psychoanalysts work: how they listen, how they conceive what they listen, etc.

We tried out this new, two-step approach at the next meeting of the working party and at some other meetings organized by different moderators and this is what we then took to Helsinki.

This time, group discussion would first focus again on debating how to classify the interventions an analyst made in a session and so aim to profit from the advantages introduced in Sorrento. But groups would be prepared more so that the classifications and objectives were circulated in advance and it was made rather clearer than before that classifying interventions was intended to be an instrumental task not a reified activity. We stressed classification was not in itself of interest except insofar as the task could help to make more precise the search for indicators as to which of several different approaches an analyst might be adopting.

But above all we stressed how the first step was now an aid to a second discussion step. When discussing each intervention and the category into which it fell, the idea was that such elements of practice as were privileged when listening, what methods are used to further the process and how transference is understood and interpreted could be examined. I will now describe the arrangement and experience of the Helsinki groups in more detail.

The Helsinki method of group discussion

The effort I had made with a research assistant to try to classify different analysts' published clinical presentations demonstrated how difficult it is to make sense of psychoanalytic material. The meanings that strike one are in large part situationally influenced – that is, they depend to a great extent on what is in one's mind at the time. This means that when confronted with someone's material it is often hard to think and feel one's way into what that analyst is trying to do. This problem is extreme if the analyst is not there to present the session verbally with all the significations that makes possible and when he is not there to be questioned. It is a frequent experience in meetings that our sense of a pre-circulated written presentation often appears to diverge from what we experience when we hear the analyst actually talk. But when the analyst is there, things are not easily better – particularly if one accepts the premise that the analyst's technique is implicit and only partly conscious, which is not easy for the analyst to accept.

However, we also have the experience that well-managed group discussion with a psychoanalyst of his clinical material can bring the material alive and can be used to bring out the implicit assumptions in a presenter's work (Tuckett, 1993). The potential of the groups at the EPF meetings, therefore, was to go considerably beyond what I could do with a research assistant. We would have all the advantages of a group. For Helsinki we arranged for eight, well-respected and reputed analysts[8] to take part in a group discussion of two or three detailed sessions they presented. The groups were formed so that between eight and twelve experienced analysts from several traditions made up each one. Two groups spoke in French; the others used English. Because differences in tradition tend to create differences in focus, the composition of the groups was designed to facilitate a discussion of implicit assumptions: about procedures, the meanings of terms, etc.

After the case presentation there was time for a fairly free and unstructured discussion of the sessions. As mentioned, the formal discussion that followed was intended to take place at two conceptual levels. Step 1 involved detailed consideration of each intervention; Step 2 sought to move beyond this to consider the analyst's overall approach against a number of common axes.

Step 1: classifying interventions

In Step 1 we went through each intervention in detail and one by one, asking in each instance into which one of five types each one might fit:

1. Interventions directed at maintaining the basic setting.
2. Interventions aimed directly at facilitating a psychoanalytic process – but not through drawing direct attention to the situation with the analyst in any saturated[9] way (which is 3 below).

---

[8] Most of them were training analysts. To preserve the confidentiality of their patients none of the analysts is mentioned in this report. All names in the report are fictitious and all group members and moderators are anonymous. I would like to take this opportunity to thank the presenters and moderators as well as all group members for their untiring efforts.
[9] Saturated – the meaning of interpretations can be left more or less open in a subtle way. A saturated interpretation is one where the meaning of the interpretation seems likely to be quite precise. An unsaturated interpretation is one where the interpretation is likely to have several meanings or affective possibilities – to be polysemic, particularly in the unconscious. The idea has been developed by Ferro, among others, who makes an interesting distinction between strong and weak interpretation, arguing that many patients need to be helped to reformulate before strong interpretation is possible (see Ferro, 2004).

3. Interventions directed at designating the here-and-now emotional and phantasy meaning of the situation with the analyst.
4. Interventions directed at providing elaborated meaning of the here-and-now experience with the analyst of the particular session (whether linked more broadly to other issues or not).
5. Interventions directed at providing elaborated meaning of what analyst and patient are discovering but not particularly closely based on the here-and-now experience of the analyst in the particular session.

Step 2: Discerning the underlying model

As mentioned, during the discussion of how to classify each individual intervention the idea was that group members should have a second step in mind: the aim to identify where each analyst might be placed, compared to others, according to (another) five core components which we apply to the analyst's work as a whole and eventually discuss one by one.[10] These five components again exist as a device to ask the group discussing the case to consider the underlying model and to think about examples of the analyst's way of working. They have no other purpose.

1. *The analyst's ideas about listening for unconscious content.* What does the analyst seem to hear (sense) as relevant in this patient's material today? For instance, how far does he look for: responses to impulses; shifts in resistance; the relation to the analyst; emotional turmoil and fragility; implicit historical scenes, movements towards increased toleration of affect; unconscious phantasies; listening to listening (Faimberg, 1996); patterns in the patient's outside life, etc.? In theory analysts agree with many of these objectives. But the issue to be decided was what seems to be privileged in practice; judging from what the analyst tells the group and what seemed to stimulate his interventions and his reasons for them.
2. *The analyst's ideas about how to further a psychoanalytic process.* The idea is to derive some idea as to what this analyst means by a psychoanalytic process and then to see how he thinks he will actually further it. We expected that the study of what the analyst said would quite naturally grow into an understanding of what the analyst thought a process was and how his interventions furthered it.

---

[10] The procedure requires time – in Helsinki we devoted about 15 hours in each group to a single case.

3. *The analyst's ideas about the here-and-now relationship to the patient in the sessions studied.* For some analysts, the analytic process and listening to and interpreting the patient's here-and-now relationship to the analyst (conscious and unconscious) are the same. For others this is not so. There are also significant differences as to how systematically, how directly (how strongly) and at what level of detail the here-and-now relationship is conceptualized by the analyst and then commented on to the patient – particularly with regard to destructive or hating components in the situation. We wanted to differentiate analysts according to whether in the sessions studied (i) they practised systematic or only occasional interpretation *of* the patient's here-and-now feelings and phantasies towards the analyst; (ii) they conceived the here-and-now relationship in terms of more or less detailed constructions, whether they interpreted them or not; (iii) these constructions of the here-and-now were linked to infantile or childhood experiences or fantasies; (iv) they conceived the here-and-now as an (object) relation or as a mental experience; (v) they used countertransference in understanding or interpreting; and (vi) they practised *direct* (strong) interpretation of the patient's angry, destructive, hateful or envious (etc.) relations to the analyst or of his eroticized or loving ones.
4. *The analyst's transformational theory.* We were less clear how to specify this but, following Körner (2002), wanted each group to think about how the analyst posited what was happening in the sessions would produce what sort of change in the patient.
5. *The analyst's theory of pathology.* Again, we were not very clear, but we wanted to know what exactly it is about the particular patient's mental (or other) life that the analyst believes he or she is trying to help or change.

Some results: how the group discussions were further explored

The group discussions in Helsinki do seem to have worked and to have taken us forward. Perhaps because of the prior preparation and in no small measure due to the determination and good will of the moderators, the experience was better. The groups were well mixed, with members from six or more societies in every group. Each case and every assumption was therefore questioned from many points of view. At the review meeting on Sunday and since then members of the groups have commented that the formal framework of the two steps seemed to allow quite a sharp and rigorous debate about the detail of what an analyst was actually doing from which the analyst's thoughts, feelings and conceptualizations could be discerned in some depth (Foresti, 2004).[11]

As an experience the groups worked well. They were also tape-recorded. In this way they produced a great deal of data about highly complex processes. The problem became how to develop a valid and reliable method to analyse and make best use of the data which we then had. This report is based on the preliminary reports of some of the moderators, supplemented by detailed analysis of one tape-recorded group. Each group's discussions are being transcribed and analysed along similar lines and the summaries of each case (together with the transcript) will be circulated to group members (including the presenter) for comment. As the project progresses the descriptions will be revised after consideration by each moderator.

As mentioned, each group discussed one case within the formal structure of the two steps. To draw some preliminary conclusions in Helsinki as moderators, we then met for an hour and a half and briefly described the cases to each other. This was far too little time, but we wanted to give the groups some feedback.

I will now give some preliminary idea of what it may be possible to achieve by way of comparative descriptions by describing three of the cases against the common template made possible by the two-step method. My summary is the outcome of all kinds of compromises and simplifications, but I hope it provides some opportunity to begin to see how we might gradually refine a typology with which to compare psychoanalytic models of working. In each case I have aimed to build a comparative model of the psychoanalyst's approach based on the five components of Step 2. In each instance, I will begin by summarizing the sessions the analysts reported and then the formulation achieved by the groups using the new method.

Case 7: the sessions

Three sessions were presented from the case of a man almost 60 years old (P7). He had presented with a severe agitated depression, some sexual problems and difficulties with business partners, along with a tendency to become panicky. The analysis has now been going on for some years. P7 is much better, except in the sexual area and termination is

---

[11] A well-known and respected colleague from Geneva, Danielle Quinodoz, has summarized in a couple of phrases her ideas about the working party group method. At the beginning of this experience, she said, 'I was convinced that the method being utilized was too artificial and would not work. But after taking part in one of the groups using it I have changed my mind and now believe this grid is really useful and makes possible an interesting and far from artificial work' (Foresti, 2004; translated from the Italian).

beginning to be envisaged. The sessions are immediately before an unusually long break. A7 felt under pressure in these sessions and that he had sometimes enacted rather than interpreted – he does not intend this, but it is part of his expectation this will happen from time to time and will then be considered. In his view he and P7 have been working towards allowing P7 to reach a deeper emotional capacity – particularly to acknowledge and contain ambivalent (and particularly hostile) feelings to A7 and internal objects.

The first session contained four interventions by A7. P7 had begun by saying he was gloomy and depressed like the weather, reporting that he had not dreamt and that he thought he was preparing for the break and eventually for the end of analysis. He had been to a party with his friends with whom he was planning to take a holiday and for which he must miss some analytic sessions. He says he does not think he is rebelling, but does notice he is now gloomy. He wonders if he is wise to go away rather than stay at home with his wife and be taken care of. At this point there is a silence and A7 reported he did not speak – which the group assessed as an intervention in the form of a deliberate silence (1.1). P7 then talks at length about the situation in G where a male relative who is separating from a female relative has behaved intrusively and insensitively and there are various social and emotional messes. This reminds him of his father, and at some length he tells A7 how his father found new friends and behaved like a hippy and sat naked on the beach with him, his sister and a new girlfriend shortly after his mother's death. Mother was hardly dead! A7 (1.2) suggests it was difficult for P7 to tolerate ambivalence, which in some way is comparable to his relationship with his analyst. P7 agrees. He said he feels his analyst is friendly to him but that he (P7) treated A7 badly when in his mind he felt triumphant at reading a critical article about psychoanalysis in a newspaper. He then made an ambiguous remark about holidays and his analyst's dogmatism before talking about how his sister felt very upset at his father's mean behaviour when he would not let her study abroad. A7 reported that at this point he was struck by P7's arrogance, which he realized was making him angry. Meanwhile P7 went on to compare favourably his relative W's behaviour to a young man (T) with his father's behaviour to his sister. At this point A7 intervened to point out that P7 is concerned for W, but that his own situation when his mother died was worse. ['But your situation was even more distressing. Your mother had just died.' 1.3.] P7 agreed and wondered about how old he was then, making some comments comparing himself and T. A7 reported that at this point (knowing the session is shortly to end), he had a feeling that something was being left out. He did not comment directly (i.e. at the meta-level), but tried to bring P7 back to his depressed mood and to make a link to his feelings when his mother died. ['What about your mood today and the weather lying heavily on your soul? This has something to do with your dead mother?' 1.4.] This brought P7 to his need to appear tough and then back to his worries about going away.

The second session contained seven interventions. It began with P7 describing a fantasy that he had seen an Arab terrorist in the street and noticed that nowadays he is more worried about security and his bank accounts than he was in the past. A7 reminded him that he once used to sympathize with terrorists and links this to an often expressed wish to blow up a competitor's home and his triumphant feelings reading about attacks on psychoanalysis in newspapers in yesterday's session (2.1). P7 then tells A7 he dreamt last night about flying in a wooden house and being in a tender erotic situation having sex. He wonders if he is now feeling inferior to his analyst and like a terrorist, linking this to how he avoids discussing psychoanalytic theory with his analyst because he does not want to feel inferior, and also acknowledges how he can feel scornful and ironic. This prompts A7 to wonder if 'Perhaps you fear the contrary too: that I reveal myself as weak and inferior' (2. 2), to which P7 says, 'Yes, This could be', to which A7 responds, 'What if we would meet equal to equal, the same height? Is that what you fear most?' (2.3). Again, P7 sort of agrees and then talks about the woman (X) from his dream and his wish for fusion, wondering if this is connected to the possible end of his analysis. Reflecting on this he wonders if it is all a trick to avoid sexuality and states that he is a mighty masturbator, but avoids appearing to take the lead in public, as on the forthcoming ski trip for which he will miss some sessions. He then says (in opposition) that his analyst is not his mother and wonders out loud what he was wanting to experience. To this A7 asks, 'But how do you feel bringing such feelings into the session and talking about them? Do you feel enough space?' (2.4). P7 claimed not to understand and becomes a bit dull. A7 noticed this, but did not comment on it directly.[12] He asked a similar question more directly: 'When you talk about X and Y [another woman] the way you did today, is this difficult? Do you feel here to be in an atmosphere to elaborate on these topics?' (2.5). The patient responds that it is diffuse with X and that he feels like a worm. It reminds him of his experiences with drugs. 'There is your dream and the flying house,' says A7 (2.6), with which the patient concurs, but offering a comment about the wooden house as linked to an Internet search for buying a house. A7 is taken aback

---

[12] This is a useful opportunity to show technical variations: A7 notices that P7 responds by going dull. In this sense he listens to the listening, but does not theorize about the origin of the resulting mental state or comment directly at a meta-level (e.g. 'You had some difficulty with what I just said?'). Instead, A7 effectively repeats his earlier comment in a different way.

now and uncertain, and asks 'Why?' (2.7), to which the patient replies that he just got interested. [Immediately after his presentation A7 volunteered that in this session that he felt he had been over-persecuting at the beginning, but by the end he thought the situation recovered and the patient was emotionally preparing for the end of analysis.]

The third session contained about four interventions, beginning with the patient becoming concerned about sounds from A7's new toilet, which he had just used and which did not seem to stop flushing. A7 quickly reassures him this is normal (3.1), whereupon P7 talks about being confused about A7's holiday plans and various things which will be happening because analyst and patient will both be away but at slightly different times. P7 is explicit in wondering what all this means about the way they are treating each other, and then recalls a fragment of a dream in which he lost his backpack, as he has dreamt on previous occasions. After saying he has no associations, he talked about not finding his altimeter at first when packing, when finally it fell into his hands. He then mentioned a successfully negotiated property sale, but said how the good feeling does not last long. He continues that stock markets too can fall, and how going away and leaving the markets makes him anxious. Here A7 mentions that this time A7's holiday dates are *particularly* unusual – using a word to imply they are impossibly intrusive to the sessions (3.2). P7 immediately states that that is true but he could not have told A7. He then admits he is furious, while immediately adding that his analyst treats him honestly and decently. To this A7 replies that he is torn by ambivalence and frightened of his feelings becoming too intense, as he was frightened about the noise of the toilet flush, which he wanted to stop (3.3). P7 concurs and makes the remark 'this is typical of a postwar child'. A7 reported he heard this remark both as superficial and as conveying something deeper. P7 then talks about how the elation at selling the property does not last because he somehow feels he has no right to it – a very old feeling. The next association is to his buying a resort map for the place he is visiting, which shows where the ski-runs go. The runs do not continue into adjacent valleys and are blocked by mountain tops. Somehow analyst and patient then talk about the parallel with the end of his analysis, which eventually leads A7 to interpret 'These holidays are a separation, too', foreshadowing the final separation (3.5). P7 responds by talking about how it is comfortable to come regularly to analysis and how it structures his week. He recognizes this could easily continue after the holidays even for another seven years. He then says he feels he had been hiding behind the property-sale story, which was a diversion. He knew he had been furious and defending against his wish to rebel, which would show stamina – here he uses a specific word with a strong allusion to a sexual erection. A7 now reminds him of a dream, which has been in A7's mind several times since it was dreamt in the last week or so in which P7 actually had an erection (3.6). To this the patient responds that he could have been clearer about when A7 was planning to go on holiday earlier and thought more about what he was feeling before making his own plans. (A7 stressed how these were new remarks for this patient and the session ended for the holidays. A7 also noted that in this session the patient had spoken very quickly and that he had felt strongly overwhelmed by feelings that were hard to contain – represented by the flushing toilet.)

The three sessions included a total of 18 interventions which were each discussed in detail and in the context of the week's work. It emerged that the group thought A7 mainly used interventions of types 2 (facilitating) and 3 (designating here-and-now), but sometimes elaborated by linking things rather more so that there were some five interventions (linking but not in relation to the here-and-now).

In the first session all four interventions were judged to be type 2 – unobtrusive attempts by A7 to open up the patient's experience and feelings in the first session of the last week before a holiday. We realized this was a particular quality of type 2 in which the focus is on opening up affects and particularly awareness of affective conflicts (ambivalent loving and hating feelings) rather than symbolic content. The second session was more varied and has a different ambience. A7 made several here-and-now interventions aimed at designating the feelings the patient had about being with A7 but somewhat indirectly. He particularly sought to help the patient to recognize his difficulty acknowledging more negative feelings to his analyst: four interventions were judged to be type 3, two considered type 2 and one assessed as type 5. The third session began with a type 1, and then contained three type 2s, one type 3 and one type 5. It was marked by a small mutual enactment (flushing away angry feelings) at the beginning of the session, which A7 eventually recognized in himself and brought together with it being the last session (3.3; 3.4; 3.5). A feature of this session was that the various comments seemed to come together through the patient's work, so that in one sense it was the patient who seemed to complete the interpretive work.

Case 7 – formulation of the analyst's way of working

The group discussing these three sessions with A7 thought it could identify a consistent thread running through A7's ideas about listening for unconscious content, his efforts to further the process (as indicated by his interventions and by their discussion) and his approach to the here-and-now relationship. Together, these seemed to form a specific transformational theory relevant to this patient's pathology.

This analyst focused his *listening* on his countertransference perception of his patient's emotional state in the session and particularly on his assessment of the patient's current capacity to move in the direction of allowing himself to experience and know here and now about a wider range of his feelings – particularly psychic pain and his negative feelings towards his analyst and his internal father and mother. For example: In session 1, after initial associations, there is a lengthy account of a complex social and sexual situation which stimulates memories of the time when P7's mother died and his father surrounded himself with many young women. P7 then said, 'I do not want to think of my father like that.' A7 (based on his sense that P7 has mentally turned away) heard this remark as a defensive movement away from ambivalent experience. It was this that prompted what was his first verbal intervention of the session – 1.2).

For A7, *furthering analytic process* could be defined in terms of trying to facilitate affect development by recovering affective splits – trying to engage P7 with becoming aware of what for him were his too overwhelming feelings of love and hate and trying to help him gradually to elaborate these feelings both in his here-and-now relationship with A7 and by working over of his remembered relationship to his mother and father. To bring about such a psychoanalytic process we can see A7 works at different levels. At one level he tries to verbalize any missing affects he senses the patient might sense (but does not yet acknowledge) and he tries to help him elaborate these missing affects into a better integration (for example 1.2; 1.4; 2.1; 2.4, etc.). At another level it was clear that in this way of working P7 is helped to integrate his conflicting feelings through A7 first working over these feelings intuitively and to a large extent unconsciously in his own mind – positive and negative feelings, but with the emphasis on difficulty experiencing aggressive hate and its derivatives. (For instance, describing session 1, A7 told the group he recognized he had himself to hold on to an irritated feeling the patient was being dismissive. A7 also told the group about several past incidents where he had not been able to hold on and had betrayed irritation with his patient instead.)

It seemed to follow from this discussion that how analysis works for A7 is centred on providing a containing setting in the here-and-now for the experience of dangerous, particularly destructive, feelings. The *here-and-now* is conceived as a relationship between persons and maintained (1) through A7's countertransference working through of *here-and-now affects* and particularly his struggle to recognize them and find ways to talk about them so they are opened up for recognition; and (2) through A7's care (even caution) about maintaining a situation he described as two adults talking together and which has some similarities with what is otherwise called the working alliance. Affects are verbalized. By contrast, verbal articulation of unconscious phantasy content or direct interpretation of transference process (what the patient is phantasizing, doing, etc.) plays a smaller part. It seemed to the group that this approach was particularly suited to depressive pathology understood as resulting from object-relational conflicts between love and hate.

A7's view of P7's *psychopathology* was that he was depressive – in effect suffering from classic ambivalence: difficulties due to the conflict of his unconscious hate and love (and related feelings), which then prevented him loving. His *transformational theory* underlay his view of how to do psychoanalytic work with this patient. He was clearly aiming to seek to modify the pathological situation through work on the patient's capacity for affect in the here-and-now: based on trying to help him see what he was feeling (like launching a terrorist attack) and how this affected him and his potency.

In potential comparison with other analytic practices we noted that in practice (though not necessarily in his explicit theory) A7 is not particularly active in recognizing and then attempting detailed translation either of phantasy or dream content, the meaning of particular words or detailed transference reconstruction. His approach to the here-and-now is carefully indirect: he stresses feelings and emotions and, although not opposed to interpreting underlying transference phantasies and actions when he sees them, does not see understanding them as a normal and essential part of the daily work. He would thus have been quite happy to take up with P7 some of the detailed unconscious phantasies the group hypothesized about the primal scene material provoked by his holiday break in the first and second sessions, but had not seen it at the time. He can get along without such detailed conceptualization and verbalization. In fact, he had felt the situation between himself and P7 and was particularly impressed by the progress he sensed when P7 was able to talk with real feeling about being like a terrorist, despite the difficulty elaborating it further.

Case 2: the sessions

P2 is a young man in a very early stage of his analysis. He has a psychiatric history which includes breakdowns and a previous history of breaking off psychotherapy after a very short while. He began with A2 face to face and twice a week, initially rejecting her offer of analysis. The sessions presented come after some months of twice weekly meetings: the first analytic session (when he arrived and put himself on the couch for the first time), the 13th session some four weeks later after a week's holiday interruption, and the 17th session a few days later. A2 describes P2 as having narcissistic and borderline psychopathology. He behaves in a quite superior way and tends to have paranoid reactions that develop in response to a narcissistic wound and often take a grandiose form. The analyst commented that he describes his breakdowns as times when he was depressed. Her feeling is that they were breakdowns in his narcissistic personality and that when talking about being depressed, depressive affect is often missing. Generally, he presents a mixture of cold distance and over-sensitivity: getting in touch with his fragility and vulnerability is difficult.

The first session begins with P2 walking over to lie on the couch for the first time. He then announced, after implying he was dissatisfied with earlier sessions making speeches at each other, that he has spent his weekend thinking and wishes to be more involved. He complains about his father who doesn't understand him when he behaves affectionately towards him; then recounts three dreams at considerable length. In the first *he was on a modern bus which turned into a flying object from which one looked down. A boy advises him to take a tablet and the bus-flying object lands near a pile of broken stuff.* In the second, *he is at a professor's house and suddenly having to take an examination. There is a discussion about history in which the professor is knowledgeable but reminds P2 of people who look as though they know everything but have actually only learned the lesson by heart* (sic) – *like a teacher someone else knows. Such theories are now out of date.* There are many other details. In the third dream *there is a big screen and a message he cannot read. Then there is a large chair at a three-dimensional angle.* P2 is silent and A2 stays silent too (1.1). P2 still does not speak and so A2 asks for associations (1.2). He remains silent. A2 then comments at length that this is the first time P2 has brought dreams and links the chair (in the third dream) to the chair he has been sitting in before, which he has come to know from all angles: 'Maybe you need to know how it works. That is to say, maybe you feel as in the dream about the professor: in a state of expectation, curiosity to know how the analysis works, how we proceed with dreams . . . as if you were expecting me to explain to you the development of the situation. Lastly, starting the analysis might be as training for a sort of examination . . .' (1.2). P2 giggles and says he doesn't know if it is important. In any case, the boys in the first dream do not look like people with psychological troubles. He also says the dream is stylized and does not look real. To this the analyst makes a further, quite long, intervention suggesting that 'We could think that he is dreaming of two parts of himself – one that needs a cure, some medicine, and the other one that advises him how to behave concerning the cure.' She goes on to suggest that the decision he has taken to lie on the couch and to increase the frequency of sessions is connected with what happened in the last session when they had talked about grandiose aspects – showing him how this is represented in the dream (1.3).

P2 agrees that it is true, 'I am at the top, but before I was using public transport.' A2 interrupts to point out a helicopter is elitist (1.4), which the patient concedes with a nervous laugh. He refers to being linked with both the boys. The analyst again intervenes at some length discussing the inner dialogue in the patient and suggests that his decision to ask for (proper) psychoanalysis can be seen in the dream about the flying object: 'You have been thinking a lot about what to do after the last session, in which we had seen that depression is linked to grandiose thoughts . . . grandiose thoughts that had found a strong, convincing image in the idea of [your fantasy of] living in a tower represented in the dream scene about the flying object' (1.5). P2 recalls this, but states at some length that it was not a fantasy of what he planned but a daydream.[13] After a pause he talks about his idea that stories release him. A2 responds, again at some length, that he does seem to be looking for a way to approach his problems, but one which is not too different from what he already knows and over which he has control. 'Maybe you are curious to see what happens in this scene here,' she says, 'a scene in which your own representations are put on stage! But certainly here there also is a problem to be faced: that you are not the only one to decide the meanings of things, what attracts you and worries you in the same time, as we said in the previous session, you are not alone here . . .' (1.6). P2 giggles.

The *second session* is taken from the fourth week of full analysis after a week's break. P2 begins in silence and then talks about how he is frustrated. When at home he has complex negative thoughts, but when he comes to analysis he can no longer remember them. He falls silent. A2 tries to encourage him to continue (2.1). He is hesitant with nervous laughter and apparent circumlocutions, but then talks about how his parents have been annoying him – wanting to know what he has been doing and making demands. He then wonders why he feels so compelled to talk with them and then speaks about sleeping late (to 2 pm) and working in his garden, which put him in a good mood. After a silence he says that last week there was a difficult moment when he was bored and talked to his mother. She wanted to talk about her seriously ill brother and he fears he was a bit brusque and that his call was not appreciated. He apologized and thinks he should only talk to her when in a good mood because she cannot give him psychological support. He has to rely on himself and fortunately he now feels better. A2 says: 'Maybe you perceive that you need some psychological support, that is to say in this

---

[13] 'It was my imagination! What was amusing me was to imagine what people who were down below could think. I was picturing this scene . . . I often cry as well. Three to four years ago, in the first crisis, my imagination helped me a lot. Thus, although I tell to myself that spending too much money makes me anxious, I accepted the idea of doing more psychotherapeutic sessions!'

place here, in which you can say how you feel when you are depressed or bored' (2.2). P2 says it might be like that but he does not remember now how he was feeling last week. There is then a long silence, broken by the analyst asking if the patient has been dreaming (2.3). P2 is not very responsive and A2 explains something of her reason for asking. In the remainder of the session P2 does not elaborate very much, and A2 makes a further 22 interventions, most of which are short questions apparently aimed at trying to bring him out.[14]

The *third session* presented took place the following Monday. P2 again begins by talking about the thoughts that come to his mind when there are no sessions, but which he forgets now he is here. A2 comments that it seems he has an inner dialogue when not with her (3.1), to which he assents. He says in fact he did not sleep much last night because of the dialogue – many requests to which he must respond and which he cannot stop. A2 responds: 'Maybe those thoughts belong to a very private scene, kept secret from yourself, that in some manner you are ashamed of. And they disappear like that when you are here. Maybe you have more familiarity and confidence in me when you are alone, in a private conversation with yourself, than when you are here with me, with a real me' (3.2). P2 thinks this may be so and responds by telling her of a television programme about murderers and a comparison he has made between their mental state and his own. He talks about being caught up in inhuman and meaningless murderous logic. A2 responds that one can be inside this logic and outside at the same time (3.3). P2 says he thinks he behaved in a similar manner with his ex-girlfriend. A2 draws attention to the unilateralism of that love affair (3.4), to which P2 responds by reflecting on reality and absolutes. A2 says, 'One could also say that this perception of reality, different from the perception of sound people, is an emotional access to reality. This is a simple or simplified way of getting to reality, a way that makes you see things as either black or white' (3.5). P2 responds with a long association reflecting on his relationship to his girlfriend and his mental state of getting into a maze. A2 intervenes with a quite lengthy comment about reasoning and emotions (3.6), to which P2 responds by discussing his feelings of being stressed. There are two further interchanges of a similar kind.

---

[14] 'What motivational aspect . . . What motivational aspect are you talking about?' (2.4). 'When you started the analysis, you told several dreams . . . maybe at that point there was a motivational aspect?' (2.5). 'Maybe at that point you were motivated to start the analysis – or maybe the opposite, you had dreams and thought it was better to analyse them on the couch, an analysis was needed' (2.6). 'Do you speak X as well as Y (dialect of analysis)?' (2.10). 'What dialect do you express yourself best in?' (2.11). 'So you seem to be more flexible, agile, when you talk to your mother than to your father' (2.14). 'Too few . . . ? What does it mean? . . . few . . . regarding the people you are thinking about?' (2.17). 'Aha! And this idea should help you out of the depression, as it seems to me that it happened to you during the first depression . . .' (2.20).

To summarize, A2 makes perhaps 36 interventions in the three sessions: six in the first (plus at least one in the form of a silence), 25 in the second, and eight in the third. Most of these are aimed at trying to help the patient to associate or to make links – interventions are assessed as mostly type 2 or 5 with some 3s.

Case 2: formulation of the analyst's way of working

In the discussion that followed this presentation, I think the group was able to discern a pattern running through what A2 was attentive towards, her ideas about a psychoanalytic process and how to further it, her approach to the here-and-now, her transformational theory and her notion of the pathology she was seeking to transform with it.

A2 focused her *listening* attention along five related pathways: P2's mental state; the degree of mental isolation she felt P2 to be experiencing; the extent to which P2 seemed to be engaged in a shared reality; how P2 was managing separation (moment to moment, between sessions or over formal breaks); and the state of P2's relations to his own thoughts. For example, in both sessions 1 and 2, P2 tells A2 how many things were going on in his mind while they were apart, but now that he is back he can recall none of them. But some things do then come to mind, including his experience of his parents making demands on him. Listening to this, A2 feels P2 is communicating how he is withdrawing here and now from contact and is in an isolated mental state. Similarly, A2 volunteered she was attentive to how P2 had shaken hands with her; seeming to her to remove his hand as he was doing so, and to A2 indicating a state of mental withdrawal.

In general, the way A2 talked to P2 (and about P2 to the group) revealed a delicate style of listening and more broadly of sensitivity to different levels of communication (often left at an unconscious level) between them. This focus on the patient's mental state came through and was elaborated many times in discussing A2's interventions: for example, in session 2, A2 asked a lot of quite prompting questions. She had sensed the patient had withdrawn from contact and tried to encourage him to share his thoughts and his reality. When, later in the session, P2 mentioned a project concerning a journey to China, A2 was unsure whether to hear it as a reference to a state of being deluded or not: she responded by trying to ask him (2.19).

A2's focus on P2's mental state was consistent with her view of his borderline pathology, which, it appeared to the group, she saw as capable of transformation through a psychoanalytic process that focused on the development of the patient's observing ego; a shared process between analyst and patient, helping him to verbalize his thoughts and bring them together in his mind.

In fact, the need to develop a balance between P2's observing and experiencing ego was crucial to A2's ideas as the group formulated A2's *transformational theory*. To help P2 achieve a balance between observing and experiencing, A2 believed she needed to work at obtaining conscious observing co-operation from him and also to ensure his emotional presence in the session. Thus, she aimed at elaborating a (conscious) narrative continuity with P2 (to develop his observing ego) in order to develop his capacity to sustain his emotional experiences. P2's conscious ideas about the analysis and what is going on in his mind as well as his emotional and affective co-operation were, therefore, often the focus of interventions. In this way A2 tried to build a particular quality of therapeutic alliance, one where P2 would be able to reveal his intimate experiences and find the support to do so in the analysis.

Because it was so important to A2 to maintain P2's cooperation at a conscious level,[15] she consistently related to her patient at a secondary process level (see especially the second session). Her interpretations in that session were directed to P2's conscious (or perhaps preconscious) level, but never directly to the unconscious. The same idea seems to have informed the attention A2 paid to trying to help P2 to disclose fantasies and so to internalize the analyst as an observing ego, able to give space to the emotional experiences that are contained in fantasies.

A further important part of this analyst's working method (implying a further transformational theory centred on a specific way of building a therapeutic alliance) was identified by the group. In a complex discussion, some members had suggested that A2 was perhaps unconsciously enacting being P's intrusive father, particularly with her many questions to P2 to elaborate fantasies and thoughts. In response, A2 clarified that she thought it was part of her approach: she works to present herself as an object differentiated from the parental objects. The group understood this as an effort to enact (L. *agir*) being the new object[16] (not just to interpret doubts or phantasies about herself as a bad or unreliable object; nor an unconscious enactment prompted in some way by P2).

As noticed before, when A2 heard a potential withdrawal in her patient, she went intentionally to some lengths to be active in seeking

---

[15] In this model dreams were conceived as representing an intermediate space between primary and secondary processes.
[16] Perhaps we may contrast this way of working with a method which listened to the unconscious material in the form of enacted infantile or other sexual or aggressive phantasies, etc., and then interpreted these phantasy configurations of the patient's inner world in order for the analyst to be experienced as new.

to engage him. She would ask a question rather than allow too much silence. For instance: 'Have you had any dreams?' (2.3). She would also ask about dream content or phantasy content (2.4; 2.5; 2.19). Much of the second session – in which A2 made 25 interventions – illustrated this approach forcibly.

Interventions such as these reveal how A2's transformational theory has implications for both her approach to the here-and-now and her way of viewing and *furthering psychoanalytic process*. Her main way to further the process is by trying to bring P2 consciously and emotionally into contact with his thoughts and feelings, including by drawing attention to relations between his thoughts and his conscious and unconscious life. For example, she interprets what she sees as P2's internal mental workings in his dreams: 'We could think that it could be a matter of two aspects of yourself . . .' (1.3); or, regarding the thoughts he was having outside the session he could not recall in the third session, 'There is a sort of inner dialogue between you and me when there are no sessions' (3.1).

The group noted that in comparison to some other analysts, A2 speaks quite often and some of her interventions are quite long. It was clear she also does not speak like a distant oracle, and what she does say by way of interpretation is often preceded by a comment about what P2 said aimed to help him follow her thoughts. The analyst also showed the group that she gives P2 a lot of space. For example, at the beginning of the session she let him freely choose the chair. The group also noticed the way in which she asked many questions, and the style of interpreting indicated how A2 was giving P2 the possibility to choose the meaning and the procedure most important to him. For example: 'That is to say? . . . Maybe at this point you were motivated to analyse your dreams . . .' (2.6). In her approach she greatly emphasized the (pre)conscious links created with P2. The analytical work includes the building of a narrative that should contain and elaborate a shared and public (in the analysis) memory of P2's life and fantasies. Thus A2 asked P2 questions about the dialect he prefers (2.12; 2.13), and the journey he is planning (2.11, 2.15, etc.). She also reminded him about the analytical past: 'Yes, for two sessions you have told four or five dreams' (2.7).

In such ways it was clear to the group, and fully confirmed by the analyst, that the active and conscious participation of P2 in the psychoanalytic process is regarded as essential for it to develop further. Some analysts might interpret such efforts on the part of a patient to be controlling or even hostile. In contrast, on one occasion A2 was happy to let herself be jostled by P2 – reasoning that if, by her own participation, she could achieve P2's participation, this was useful. For example, in session 2, when P2 had said he did not understand a common expression used by the analyst, A2 simply answered with an explanation (2.9).

A2 made many more comments aimed at helping P2 to open up and bring into contact for thinking important mental contents. For example, in her second intervention A2 said: 'Maybe these thoughts [that he has mentioned that now he is in the session he has forgotten] belong to a very private scene, kept secret from yourself, that you feel in some manner ashamed of . . .' (3.2).

To summarize how A2 furthered the process, the group judged many of the analyst's interventions, based on discussion with the analyst,[17] to have had two main aims. First, many of the comments were designed to do what A2 called to accompany (*sic*) P2: as we have noted, this accompaniment involved contacting P2 at several levels: conscious cognitive, mental state, feeling state – all of which could be said to amount to providing a particular quality of empathic framework for a therapeutic alliance. Second, A2 worked to help P2 make public (between them) what is private (only known to him). To achieve that end we have seen that A2 asked many specific questions to try to discover these thoughts and build a shared conscious narrative of P2's experience.

Based on such observations we might say that, for A2, the psychoanalytical process is very much seen in here-and-now relational terms, conscious and unconscious: for her the analyst is someone who offers a new relational possibility in which the patient may find a new way of functioning in the sessions and of relating to his own thoughts. This view of process informed how A2's work might be characterized in terms of her approach to the here-and-now.

The analyst's attention was focused on the relational situation of the patient with her in the here-and-now. She did not regularly designate the situation between them directly and so worked more *in* the transference than in making interpretation *of* the transference. Also she did not interpret evident signs of the negative transference. In her opinion, this would have been traumatic and inaccurate, particularly because in A2's opinion P2 was lost more than aggressive. The second session took place after a one-week break. During the session A2 paid much attention to the possibility that her patient might retreat into himself and become inaccessible, perhaps because of the disruption, but she did not talk to him about the disruption or how his negative feelings towards her (perhaps as a counter to his decision to try to be more involved) might be part of it. Nor did she construct this response as an historical infantile fantasy-based enactment of some kind. Interestingly, when she did make a direct des-

---

[17] In these discussions it is the group's function to arrive at a conclusion as to the analyst's model, but on the basis of questioning the analysts as carefully as possible.

ignation of the here-and-now relationship she did so by bringing up P2's unconscious fears about the analyst's possible negative intentions, she did so by saying he feared she would be just like his parents: 'Maybe you are afraid I could raise your hopes and you could be again the victim of somebody who would be mistaken concerning you, of somebody who would not be able to understand you – like your parents' (3.7). Similarly, in interpreting a dream (1.2; 1.3) A2 clearly has the phantasy relationship to the analyst in mind, but interprets in an unsaturated way leaving the situation and any resulting anxiety very open. In the dream an appointment with a professor, made to discuss the circumstances of his forthcoming examination, turns into an examination. The professor was described by P2 in a definitely ambivalent way. A2 tells P2: 'Maybe you need to know how it [the analysis] works as in the dream about the professor . . . is in a state of expectation, curiosity', and so on (2.2).

The group noted that A2 used countertransference extensively and intuitively – almost all the time she is watching her relationship with P2 to discern his state of mind and possible retreat into himself.

Case X – the sessions

PX is a 35-year-old married woman, with two children. She described herself as imposed on by her husband in a variety of ways, but also worked for him at home. She had probably married her husband to get away from home. As a couple they were angry with each other, sexually dissatisfied and mutually frustrated. This made her feel guilty and she was perpetually dissatisfied, impatient and irritable. She had an eating disorder. She had sought treatment with another analyst after recognition of the marital difficulties, but left quickly as she felt that analyst was rigid and too interventionist.

The two sessions presented were from the second year of an analysis (three times a week) which was completed after two or three further years. The termination was, in AX's view, slightly premature but at the same time he felt it important that it was her decision and did not oppose it. At termination, PX had left her husband and had begun a new and satisfying sexual relationship. In a whole variety of ways she was more outgoing and more involved in her life, and had become a published writer. Her eating disorder had resolved. AX considered his work in these sessions to reflect his way of working and to be the kind of work that led this patient to change.

In the first session PX began immediately by telling a dream she had before the weekend. She was *on a river bank with the water up to midthigh and she catches a big silver eel. She holds it in her hand and then puts it back into the water. The eel swims and suddenly bites the front of her left thigh with its razor-sharp teeth. She is paralysed with fear and does not dare move. The eel does not let go.* She woke up. (It seemed that at the slightest movement the teeth would tear her skin.) She now thought about another dream in which another very threatening fish appeared. *She was cooking; a river flowed through the garage of her childhood house. She was fishing with a green bean when something horrible suddenly appeared which gobbled up everything – something which also had a mouth full of teeth and a shining silver body. She was very surprised. She did not think this fish would be so nasty, or that it could have such long, pointed teeth.* She now wondered if she had drawn a dangerous catch from psychoanalysis. She also thought of her husband in this waiting phase in which she feels blocked and afraid of moving. AX asked her if she could link the eel to something male (1.1). She hesitated. Maybe, she does not know, but this big mouth makes her think more of something female. A big voracious mouth! AX said, 'Indeed!' (1.2). She says she has the impression of being cautious here with AX, of being careful about what she says, maybe she could none the less be surprised. She mentions that she sleeps better now that she dreams. AX was thinking of the dream and asked her if this fish could be like something she has no hold over (1.3). 'Absolutely,' she replied. 'Even though I thought I could control it.' She said she really had the impression it hated her. 'It really is an attack,' AX told her (1.4). She now said that she thought she has a text that would be suitable for this year's short story competition. She still thinks this although she was dismayed when she read it through again. It must be completely rewritten. She was a bit discouraged, then started on it and to her astonishment it is going well. It seems so easy to her. For once her text is too long. She must cut it and it is much easier. She also wants to simplify her style, whereas before she always tried to complicate it on purpose. Basically, things are as usual for her at the moment! She goes on to mention there is another short story that she is probably also going to rework. It is a short story about battered babies. She had forgotten about it as it was hard for her, but as things are going well with her children, she can now cope with it.

In the second session PX began by thinking about the summer holidays and again about a caravan tour in Z with her uncle and aunt when she was eleven or twelve. She has decided now strictly to limit holidays taken alone with her husband. There will be a fortnight with the family, then a week with a girlfriend. She has many holiday plans without the family. There are friends who are divorced or separated to be with. In some aspects it is as if, at times, she and her husband are also separated. He takes the children on holiday at Easter and they both go out on their own. That is what she wanted, but it seems strange. On Sunday, they had a lie-in and made love. It had not happened for several weeks. She was astounded to see how far they were apart – much further than she had imagined. She had thought they only needed to come together for everything to be as it was before. She wondered if there was any hope that things could be the same again. AX now asked her if she means to have things the same as before or to evaluate her present choices and wishes (2.1). She responds that in any case it seems strange. Her husband was different, much less needy and greedy, whereas before she had always had the impression he wanted to devour her. It flattered but repelled her at the same time. In the same way, when he shows too much physical desire to her taste, she does not feel anything any more. She does not know why. It is as if there were no more place for it. This time he seemed more passive, waiting for something. She felt better but, at the same time, it was rather worrying, she felt less loved.

She remembers a discussion she had with a girlfriend who asked her whether she did not risk harming herself by living like that. She did not really understand, but it worried her. However, she went on, it was a good morning, then her husband went out on his motorbike in the afternoon. And things were fine with the children. AX now asked whether 'you can link what you say about these devouring experiences to the dream you told the day before' (2.2). 'Indeed,' she said, there is a kind of oppression and love that she sees as devouring in her husband. Something that holds, grasps, constricts her when he squeezes, catches her. She thinks of *The Naked Ape* by Desmond Morris and to the connection he makes between a kiss and a bite. She sometimes feels attacked by her husband's marks of love. Why did she choose to get married? Why did she rush into it? AX now reminds her she told him she had had the dream before the weekend. So could these be aspects of herself she had just discovered in psychoanalysis? (2.3). She now says that for the other dream it was very clear, obvious, even if everything was formless – as for this one, she had not thought about it.

In all, AX made seven quite brief interventions – four in the first session and three in the second. All the interventions were succinct and relatively unsaturated – i.e. indirect and apparently opening up meaning via introducing alternative ideas and so prompting in PX, as in the group, many different possible thoughts about the underlying meaning. In fact, in discussion in the group many meanings could be read into the comments. The comments were not directly designating the here-and-now (type 3) and we eventually decided that in terms of the five-point rating scheme all but the last interpretation were properly rated (type 2) – interventions apparently aimed directly at facilitating an unconscious representational process. The last interpretation (2.3) could also be a type 2 but is also perhaps a type 5 as it was both somewhat more saturated than the others and linked several ideas together in a more direct way. Although that comment referred to the analytic relationship, it does not specifically designate an aspect of the here-and-now of the relationship in that session.

Case X – formulation of the analyst's way of working

This was the first presentation on which we tested the new two-step method. Because of time constraints group discussion was more truncated and the formulation has relied on construction by the author rather than through discussion and consensus in the group. None the less, I think enough was achieved in the meeting for me to give a picture of AX at work as described by the new method.

AX *listened* for information within PX's material which told him about her libidinal impulses and her representational and creative capacity to manage them and her unconscious conflicts. This, for example, is how he listened to the dreams told in the first session. The first featured an eel which bites her, and this reminds her of the second in which a horrible gobbling something with teeth appeared. He hears this material as a representation of her oral voracious impulses. Her dream is thus a statement about what he calls mental mechanisms in her mind. He is not bothered about what screen memories might be represented, or the state of internal object representations or any here-and-now transference relation to him. Later in the first session he hears the subsequent account of PX's entry for a coming short story competition and her dismay at realizing it must be completely rewritten as confirmation of growing representational capacity (forward movement in the session itself) and an increased capacity for self-critical reflection which it is not for him to interrupt – in particular when she says she feels she had deliberately over-complicated her writing. AX listens to the short story material and that about her children (etc.) without any need for translation of meaning into the here-and-now, past history or any particular phantasies, and also without feeling the need for further interpretation: hearing all this as PX elaborating her thoughts in a less complicated, more direct, more communicative and less phobic way. He is thus attentive to the evolution of her creative psychic potential and the music of elaboration in her associations. The symbolic content is not a focus of his attention, and he makes no effort to decode or think about what is said in that way. In AX's mind her improved mental capacity is linked to what he has heard from her: the appearance in the dream of the eel mouth, demonstrating an increased capacity to represent her unconscious impulses of which she had been phobic.[18]

---

[18] The analyst did not formulate in his listening an explicit account of the way his intervention was heard – he did not, for example, revise interpretations; recognize the meaning of his interpretation through the patient's response, etc. He focused on the patient's relationship to her own mental products. Nor did he interest himself in possible ways he might have blocked association (defensive association).

To stress again, neither the dream nor other associations are heard as a here-and-now commentary of the analytic relationship or as expressions of a specific unconscious fantasy which might be decoded to elaborate meaning. (Group members had all kinds of ideas, including that PX had an unconscious rape fantasy, but these were not what AX had in mind.) Rather, the capacity to dream and the associations that follow are heard as an evolutionary step in representational capacity – particularly related to the capacity to symbolize the conflicts of infantile sexuality at the oral level (relating to sexual and creative inhibition).

The way AX listens is linked to the way he interprets and to his implicit ideas about a *psychoanalytic process and how to further it*. For him the process seems to be about an internal mental elaboration occurring in PX in the presence of AX as a kind of witness – AX stresses the value of acknowledgement to reduce disavowal. Hence: 'It *really* is an attack' (1.4). He also stresses the value of linking – enabling PX to bring together what is happening to her in her mind (interpretation 1.1 and 2.2). As one group member put it: 'He listens for broken links in the associational chain and disavowal. He seeks to widen associations and to avow signs of developing psychic life.'[19] For AX, although he would not make a translation interpretation, the manifest dream has the latent meaning that PX is able to represent herself as attacked by her own impulses in the form of a mouth. This attack is heard empathically as creating a phobic predicament and a potential resistance. AX gradually verbalizes what he takes to be the link to the underlying phobic situation, but not in a saturated or explanatory way – 'A big voracious mouth!' (1.2); 'something you have no hold over' (1.3) and 'It *really* is an attack' (1.4). Then he sees PX associates freely and to his mind in a forward or creative direction. He has no need to say more from his view of analytic process so long as she continues her development in his presence.

All four brief comments in the first session and the three in the second are made in one style – indirect and unsaturated; sensing the underlying instinctual phobia and opening and elaborating multiple additional meanings to facilitate an unconscious representational process. It is not necessary in this approach to verbalize what is happening, to translate meaning for the patient or to make direct comments. Rather, as mentioned, the interventions are designed to facilitate the making of new links. I think that the question of links is very important for him, that he

---

[19] 'I thought he is listening to the question if the patient is stepping forward or backward, to the question if she is going into an illusion, or she is thinking of it as a new experience. This is not focusing on erotization, for example, but it is focusing on an illusion or more contact to reality or to a new experience.' (I ask her if she means to have things the same as before, or to elaborate her present choices.)

feels that either explicitly or, more importantly, implicitly and unconsciously, PX is invited or helped to make links and that that is the way of the comments. One participant, thinking of Winnicott, said this was a squiggling method. In that way AX's comments, like Winnicott's addition of the odd line to a child's squiggle, create a potential space for PX to make and elaborate affectively meaningful links. For instance, in the first session AX says only: 'It *really* is an attack!' (1.4). This seems to facilitate PX's own elaborations, with a strong emphasis on acknowledgement of the difficulty and aiming to minimize intrusion. In this way, in this model it is PX who is seen as doing much of the work. AX is unobtrusive, but with a positive countertransference disposition: making contributions which are infrequent and brief. In this way AX's work is done silently and affectively, albeit focused on developing representations – words, dreams, links.

This approach has implications for how we describe how AX uses the *here-and-now*. He is present and works with his feeling in the transference–countertransference situation, which is conceived within an ongoing phobic–counter-phobic disposition, which he sees as at the core of this patient's difficulties based on infantile oral conflicts. (AX mentioned to us PX's first dream after one week of sessions. In it a baby boy was found inside a thermos. AX emphasized that he saw links in this to both the marital sexual difficulties and her eating disorder as well as the underlying transference and had kept it in mind for a long time.) Based on these ideas he conceived his position in the transference as potentially intrusive. His approach is not to interpret that directly in a saturated way,[20] but to respond to it by a subtle adjustment and with deliberate caution. His role is to be non-obtrusive and to create the space for PX to develop in his presence. In general, he does not need to tackle in direct words any specific here-and-now anxieties she might have with him unless they prevent PX associating. And the anxieties she does have are viewed in instinctual terms (in terms of her capacity to manage her instincts), not within an object relationship (e.g. a fear he wants to get her with his teeth and hold onto her, even rape her). This means he is not an analyst who works on moment-by-moment consideration of what is happening between analyst and patient in sessions or between sessions and there are no type 3 interventions: direct interpretations of anxiety or action in the relationship between them (you feel me trying to intrude myself, etc.). Similarly, although AX has his own ideas about PX's family structure (mother, father and grandmother) he does not attempt to translate material from the session into an understanding of the way the history is represented in the present fantasies nor to elaborate or con-

---

[20] E.g.: 'You find me intrusive!'

struct the here-and-now experience and phantasies in any detail or to verbalize to PX hypothesized infantile or oedipal experiences or inner parental relationships. Nor is this approach one which conceives or uses interpretation of PX's angry, destructive, hateful or envious relations to AX.

The *transformational theory* to which this analyst subscribes and the kind of *pathology he will treat* may be inferred from the above description. PX is viewed as instinctually impulsive and inhibited – as tending to be compelled to act particularly with her husband and children. She has been unable to represent and so manage her oral appetite which has led to sexual, eating and work inhibitions, as well as to problems expressing herself potently, managing her family and progressing her projects. In sum, her problems are seen in terms of libidinal inhibition rather than in terms of conflicts with destructive aspects or anxieties about destructiveness. Analysis proceeds in part through acknowledgement – helping PX to realize that she is impulsive and so reducing disavowal. Also, by providing an opportunity to develop her capacity to represent her impulses through associations and recovered links she can develop her representational creative capacity so that, so to speak, she can elaborate her psychic life and her sexual wishes more extensively and grow. PX's problems are not seen as played out in the here-and-now relationship to AX, or if they are this is not the focus for seeking to address them. Phantasies about AX's relationship to PX and vice versa are not a central focus either. Thus in this approach the here-and-now creates a setting for an internal developmental process rather than an object relationship.

Some preliminary results: beginning to discern some models?

I hope this very sketchy outline of the three cases gives some idea of the work on comparative clinical methods that is going on and what it may make possible. The task of comparative description has been difficult. First, there is the problem of finding a commensurable framework – which is what the two-step typologies are meant to provide. But second, there is at least one major further challenge facing us: how to convey in a few pages and in a convincing manner the rich and detailed emotional understanding of a way of working gained in long hours of work in one group and then compare it with the work of several others. I hope something of interest has been conveyed.

Meanwhile, for the sake of showing what the method may eventually make possible and with tongue in cheek, I will make some preliminary comparisons of the way sessions presented by three analysts show them listening to the unconscious, furthering the process, and conceiving and interpreting the transference, as well as what might be inferred about each analyst's model of psychoanalytic transformation and treatable pathology, based on the cases presented.

Although one can discern commonalities, which I will mention in a moment, it seems to me that in the work of A2, A7 and AX we are considering three rather different models, which in interesting ways differ from other models we can expect to find. To simplify greatly perhaps, we might describe A2's method as the new object approach; AX's might be termed squiggling; and A7's as perhaps containing ambivalence.

For A2 the emphasis in the psychoanalytic process is relational and on being perceived consciously by the patient as different to past objects, particularly the parents. A great deal of attention is given to working with the patient's consciousness. This is in contrast to Ax, who pays little attention to that level of communication and works with a process aimed at unconscious representations of libidinal drives. A7 is different again. He is the only one of the three analysts to be explicitly very concentrated on the problem of hatred (more generally the negative transference) and of affects, as they are experienced between persons.[21] While, like A2, he does pay some attention to the patient's conscious capacity and, like AX, his representational development, his main emphasis is on containing ambivalent affects – recognizing them in himself and his patient and allowing them to be talked about and tolerated. His model of analytical process is based on seeking to perceive, to contain and to draw the patient's attention to his ambivalent feelings and their consequences – particularly the anxieties introduced by his hatred. In terms of historical construction A7 does have a constant picture of the patient's childhood experience and oedipal relationships in his mind, but he does not seek to create a process which works with more complex fantasy constructions which other analysts might seek to unravel. Meanwhile, A2 and AX had only very general ideas, in these specific cases, about the role of infantile fantasy and infantile history in the present.[22]

In terms of the enormous emphasis in psychoanalytic theory (and ideology) on the role of infantile fantasy content (Oedipus complex, primal scene, etc.) and its detection though the transference during psychoanalytic process, this pattern seems both interesting and surprising; worthy of more investigation.

Turning to what was common: all three analysts work in a very subtle manner with their feelings – particularly judging meaning and how propitious it is to intervene on their intuition of the patient's feelings at that

---

[21] For AX, affects are the product of internal rather than object related impulses.
[22] It was, of course, very early days for A2.

moment. Psychoanalytic process involves the analyst's intuitive feelings. They all work in the here-and-now countertransference in that sense.

All three analysts are also more prone to furthering the process through unsaturated rather than direct or saturated interpretation. Thus A2's approach is similar to some aspects of the approach to transformation described by Ferro (2004), when he discussed the difficulty with many modern patients in making more direct transference or even fantasy translation interpretations. Certainly, none of the three analysts attempts very systematic interpretation of the meaning of transference phenomena or direct interpretation of its enactment in the here-and-now. There is little minute examination of action in the here-and-now and of its unconscious phantasy components in the manner of Joseph (1985). Nor did the three analysts use detailed consideration of the minute effects of the analyst's interpretation on the patient – whether discussed in Joseph's way or in the listening-to-listening of Faimberg (1996). Turning to another prominent school of European thought, nor did they describe anything in presenting their sessions and their thinking to suggest they work with historical fragments and memories to construct – with the associational material and in the here-and-now experience – past conflicts or repressed traumatic difficulties in the manner described by Green (2001) or Fedida (2001).[23]

---

[23] Such approaches might be difficult to describe in a few recent sessions – discoveries of the scale and kind these authors narrate are not everyday events. However, it was not apparent from the three ways of working described that something like that was in the analysts' minds.

Bibliography

Abend S (1979) Unconscious fantasy and theories of cure. J. Amer. Psychoanal. Assn. 27: 579-596.
Ahumada JL (1991) Logical types and ostensive insight. Int. J. Psycho-Anal. 72: 683-691.
Ahumada JL (1994) What is a clinical fact? Clinical psychoanalysis as inductive method. Int. J. Psycho-Anal. 75: 949-962. Reprinted in The Logics of the Mind: A Clinical View. London: Karnac, 2001.
Ahumada JL (1997a) Counter-induction in psychoanalytic practice: epistemic and technical aspects. In JL Ahumada, J Olagaray, AK Richards, AD Richards (eds.) The Perverse Transference and other Matters. Essays in Honor of R Horacio Etchegoyen. Northvale, NJ, Jason Aronson.
Ahumada JL (1997b) Towards the epistemology of clinical psychoanalysis. J. Amer. Psychoanal. Assn. 45: 507-530.
Ahumada JL (1997c) Disclosures and refutations: clinical psychoanalysis as a logic of inquiry. Int. J. Psycho-Anal. 78: 1105-1118.
Ahumada JL (2001a) The rebirth of the idols: the Freudian unconscious and the Nietzschean unconscious. Int. J. Psycho-Anal. 82: 219-234.
Ahumada JL (2001b) Presentation of 'The Rebirth of the Idols'. The Freudian unconscious and the Nietzschean unconscious. Bulletin of the British Psycho-Analytical Society 37 (3): 1-4.
Ahumada JL (2004) Objectivity in the clinical setting: the double work on the evidences. Panel on idea and observation: can clinical observation evaluate interpretations and theories? Chaired by Charles Hanly. IPA Congress New Orleans, March.
Althusser L (1974) Philosophie et philosophie spontanée des savants. Paris: Editions F. Maspéro.
Anzieu D (1972) Dificultad de un estudio psicoanalítico sobre la interpretación. Revista de Psicoanálisis, Asociación Psicoanalítica Argentina, Vol. XXIX.
Arbiser S (2003) A brief history of psychoanalysis in Argentina. J. Amer. Psychoanal. Assn. 51 (Supplement): 323-335.
Arlow JA (1979) Metaphor and the psychoanalytic situation. Psychoanal. Q. 48: 363-385.
Arlow JA (1980) Object concept and object choice. Psychoanal. Q. 49: 109-133.
Arlow J (1981) Theories of pathogenesis. Psychoanal. Q. 50: 488-514.
Ayer AJ (1956) The Problem of Knowledge. London: Macmillan.
Bach S (1998) Two ways of being. Psychoanal. Dial., 8: 657-673.
Bateson G (1979) Mind and Nature: A Necessary Unity. Toronto: Bantam, 1988.
Bellone E (2003) La stella nuova. L'evoluzione e il Caso Galilei. Torino: Einaudi.

Beres D, Arlow JA (1974) Fantasy and identification in empathy. Psychoanal. Q. 43: 26-50.
Bernardi R (2002) The need for true controversies in psychoanalysis: the debates on Melanie Klein and Jacques Lacan in the Río de la Plata. Int. J. Psycho-Anal. 83: 851-873.
Bion WR (1962) Learning from Experience. London: Heinemann.
Bion WR (1992) Cogitations. London: Karnac Books.
Blackburn S (1984) Spreading the Word. Groundings in the Philophy of Language. Oxford: Clarendon Press.
Bléandonu G (1990) Wilfred R. Bion, La vie et l'oeuvre. Paris: Dunod.
Boesky D (2005) Psychoanalytic controversies contextualized. Journal of the American Psychoanalytic Association 53: 835-863.
Bolton D (1999) Postempiricism and psychological theory. Journal of Clinical Child Psychology 28: 550-552.
Bott Spillius E (2001) Freud and Klein on the concept of phantasy. Int. J. Psycho-Anal. 82, 2: 361-373.
Bouveresse J (1991) Wittgenstein Reads Freud. The Myth of the Unconscious. Princeton, NH: Princeton University Press.
Brenner C (2000) Observations on some aspects of current psychoanalytic theories. Psychoanal. Q. 69: 597-632.
Breuer J, Freud S (1895) Studies on Hysteria. SE 2.
Brierley M ([1943] 1991) Memorandum on her technique by Marjorie Brierley: memorandum on valid techniques for the training committee, 24 October 1943. In P. King and R. Steiner (eds.) The Freud-Klein Controversies, 1941-1945. London and New York: Routledge.
Bucci W (1997) Psychoanalysis and Cognitive Science: A Multiple Code Theory. New York: Guilford Press.
Busch de Ahumada LC (2003) Clinical notes on a case of transvestism in a child. Int. J. Psycho-Anal. 83: 293-313.
Cabaniss D, Schein JW, Rosen P, Roose S (2003) Candidate progression in analytic institutions: a multicenter study. Int. J. Psycho-Anal. 84: 77-94.
Campbell K (1982) The psychotherapy relationship with borderline personality disorder. Psychotherapy: Theory, Practice and Research 19: 166-193.
Campbell NR (1920) Physics: The Elements. Cambridge: Cambridge University Press.
Canestri J (1993) The logic of Freudian research. In D Meghnagi (eds.) Freud and Judaism. London: Karnac Books, pp. 117-129.
Canestri J (1999) Psychoanalytic heuristics. In P Fonagy, AM Cooper, RS Wallerstein (eds.) Psychoanalysis on the Move. London and New York: Routledge.
Canestri J (2003) The logic of psychoanalytic research. In M Leuzinger-Bohleber, AU Dreher, J Canestri (eds.) Pluralism and Unity? Methods of Research in Psychoanalysis. London: International Psychoanalysis Library.
Canestri J, Bohleber W, Denis P, Fonagy P (2002) Mapping private theories in clinical practice. Paper presented at the Annual Congress of the European Psychoanalytic Federation, Prague.
Caper R (1999) A Mind of One's Own: A Kleinian View of Self and Object. London: Routledge.
Churchland PS, Ramachandran VS, Sejnowski TJ (1994) A critique of pure vision. In C Koch, JL Davis (ed.) Large-Scale Neuronal Theories of the Brain. Cambridge, MA: MIT Press, pp. 23-60.

Cicchetti D, Cohen DJ (1995) Perspectives on developmental psychopathology. In D Cicchetti, DJ Cohen (eds.) Developmental Psychopathology: Theory and Methods, Vol. 1. New York: John Wiley & Sons, pp. 3-23.
Cooper AM (1989) Concepts of therapeutic effectiveness in psychoanalysis: a historical review. Psychoanalytic Inquiry 9: 4-25.
Davidson AI (2001) The Emergence of Sexuality: Historical Epistemology and the Formation of Concepts. Cambridge, MA: Harvard University Press.
Donnet J-L (1995) Le Diran Bien Tempéré. Paris: PUF.
Dreher AU (2000) Foundations for Conceptual Research in Psychoanalysis. London and New York: Karnac Books.
Dyson FJ (1998) Science as a craft industry. Science 280: 1014-1015.
Edelson M (1986) Heinz Hartmann's influence on psychoanalysis as a science. Psychoanal. Inq. 6: 575-600.
Edelson M (1989) The nature of psychoanalytic theory: implications for psychoanalytic research. Psychoanalytic Inquiry 9: 169-192.
Eisold K (2003) Towards a psychoanalytic politics. J. Amer. Psychoanal. Assn 51 (Supplement): 301-323.
Etchegoyen RH (1986) Los fundamentos de la técnica psicoanalítica. Buenos Aires: Amorrortu.
Etchegoyen RH (1988) The analysis of little Hans and the theory of sexuality. Int. Review Psycho-Anal. 15: 37.
Etchegoyen R, Ahumada J (1999) Bateson y Matte-Blanco: bio-lógica y bi-lógica in Descubrimientos y Refutaciones. Madrid: Biblioteca Nueva.
Faimberg H (1996) 'Listening to listening'. Int. J. Psycho-Anal. 77: 667-677.
Fairbairn WRD (1958) On the nature and aims of psychoanalytical treatment. Int. J. Psycho-Anal. 39: 374-385.
Fedida P (2001) Constructing place: the supervision of a psychoanalytic cure. Psychoanalysis and Psychotherapy. EPF Bulletin, 56: 17-28.
Fenichel O (1941) Problems of psychoanalytic technique. New York: Psychoanalytic Quarterly Inc.
Fenichel O (1945) The Psychoanalytic Theory of Neurosis. New York and London: Norton and Routledge.
Ferenczi S (1909) Introjection and Transference in Sex in Psychoanalysis (Contributions to Psychoanalysis). New York: Dover, 1956.
Ferenczi S (1914) The nosology of male homosexuality (homoerotism). In Sex in Psychoanalysis (Contributions to Psychoanalysis). New York: Dover, 1956.
Ferenczi S (1985) Journal Clinique. Paris: Payot.
Ferraro F (2001) Vicissitudes of bisexuality: crucial points and clinical implications. Int. J. Psycho-Anal. 82: 485-499.
Ferro A (2004) Interpretation: signals from the analytic field and emotional transformations. Int. For. Psychoanal. 13, 1-2: 31-38.
Feyerabend P (1987) Farewell to Reason. London and New York: Verso.
Fleck L ([1935] 1979) Genesis and Development of a Scientific Fact. Chicago: University of Chicago Press.
Fonagy P (1982) Psychoanalysis and empirical science. Int. Review Psychoanalysis 9: 125-145.
Fonagy P (1989) On the integration of psychoanalysis and cognitive behaviour therapy. British Journal of Psychotherapy 5: 557-563.

Fonagy P (1996) The future of an empirical psychoanalysis. British Journal of Psychotherapy 13: 106-118.

Fonagy P (2003) The development of psychopathology from infancy to adulthood: the mysterious unfolding of disturbance in time. Infant Mental Health Journal 24, 3: 212-239.

Fonagy P, Kachele H, Krause R, Jones E, Perron R, Clarkin J, et al. (2002) An Open Door Review of Outcome Studies in Psychoanalysis (2nd edn.). London: International Psychoanalytical Association.

Fonagy P, Moran GS, Edgcumbe R, Kennedy H, Target M (1993) The roles of mental representations and mental processes in therapeutic action. The Psychoanalytic Study of the Child 48: 9-48.

Fonagy P, Steele M, Moran GS, Steele H, Higgitt A (1993) Measuring the ghost in the nursery: an empirical study of the relation between parents' mental representations of childhood experiences and their infants' security of attachment. J. Amer. Psychoanal. Assn. 41: 957-989.

Fonagy P, Target M (1996) Predictors of outcome in child psychoanalysis: a retrospective study of 763 cases at the Anna Freud Centre. J. Amer. Psychoanal. Assn. 44: 27-77.

Fonagy P, Target M (2003) Psychoanalytic Theories: Perspectives from Developmental Psychopathology. London: Whurr.

Foresti G (2005) Playing with indisciplined realities: Osservazioni sull'esperienza dei gruppi clinico-teorici della FEP. Rivista di Psicoanalisi, Vol. LI, 4 (in print).

Fraiberg SH, Adelson E, Shapiro V (1975) Ghosts in the nursery: a psychoanalytic approach to the problem of impaired infant-mother relationships. Journal of the American Academy Child Psychiatry 14: 387-422.

Freud A (1926a) Four lectures on child analysis. In The Writings of Anna Freud, Vol. 1. New York: International Universities Press, pp. 3-69.

Freud A (1965) Normality and Pathology in Childhood: Assessments of Development. Madison, CT: International Universities Press.

Freud A (1974) A psychoanalytic view of developmental psychopathology. In The Writings of Anna Freud, Vol. 8. New York: International Universities Press, 1981, pp. 119-136.

Freud S (1895) Studies on Hysteria. SE 2. London: Hogarth Press.

Freud S (1900) The Interpretation of Dreams. SE 4-5. London: Hogarth Press.

Freud S (1901) The Psychopathology of Everyday Life. SE 6. London: Hogarth Press.

Freud S (1904) Freud's Psycho-analytic Procedure. SE 7. London: Hogarth Press.

Freud S (1905) Three Essays on the Theory of Sexuality. SE 7. London: Hogarth Press.

Freud S (1907) The sexual enlightenment of children. SE 9: 131. London: Hogarth Press.

Freud S (1908a) Hysterical Phantasies and Their Relationship to Bisexuality. SE 9. London: Hogarth Press.

Freud S (1908b) On the Sexual Theories of Children. SE 9. London: Hogarth Press.

Freud S (1909) Analysis of a Phobia in a Five-year-old Boy. SE 10. London: Hogarth Press.

Freud S (1910a) Leonardo da Vinci and a Memory of His Childhood. SE 11. London: Hogarth Press.

Freud S (1910b) The Future Prospects of Psychoanalytic Therapy. SE 11. London: Hogarth Press.

Freud S (1911) Formulations on the Two Principles of Mental Functioning. SE 12. London: Hogarth Press.
Freud S (1912a) The Dynamics of Transference. SE 12. London: Hogarth Press and the Institute of Psycho-Analysis.
Freud S (1912b) Recommendations to Physicians Practising Psycho-analysis. SE 12. London: Hogarth Press.
Freud S (1912-13) Totem and Taboo. SE 13. London: Hogarth Press.
Freud S (1913a) On Beginning Treatment. SE 12. London: Hogarth Press.
Freud S (1913b) The Occurrence in Dreams of Material from Fairy Tales. SE 12. London: Hogarth Press.
Freud S (1913c) The Claims of Psycho-analysis to Scientific Interest. SE 13. London: Hogarth Press.
Freud S (1914) Remembering, Repeating and Working-through. SE 12. London: Hogarth Press.
Freud S (1915) The Unconscious. SE 14. London: Hogarth Press.
Freud S (1916) Introductory Lectures on Psycho-analysis. SE 15-16. London: Hogarth Press.
Freud S (1919) Lines of Advance of Psycho-analytic Therapy. SE 17. London: Hogarth Press.
Freud S (1920) Beyond the Pleasure Principle. SE 18. London: Hogarth Press.
Freud S (1921) Group Psychology and the Analysis of the Ego. SE 18. London: The Hogarth Press.
Freud S (1923a) The Ego and the Id. SE 19. London: Hogarth Press.
Freud S (1923b) Two Encyclopaedia Articles. SE 18. London: Hogarth Press.
Freud S (1926) The Question of Lay Analysis. SE 20. London: Hogarth Press.
Freud S (1927) Fetishism. SE 21. London: Hogarth Press.
Freud S (1933) The Question of a Weltanschauung. In New Introductory Lectures on Psycho-Analysis - Lecture XXXV. SE 22. London: Hogarth Press.
Freud S (1937a) Analysis Terminable and Interminable. SE 23. London: Hogarth Press.
Freud S (1937b) Constructions in Analysis. SE 23. London: Hogarth Press.
Freud S (1938) Splitting of the Ego in the Process of Defence. SE 23. London: Hogarth Press.
Freud S (1950 [1895]) Project for a Scientific Psychology. SE 1. London: Hogarth Press.
Gabbard GO, Gunderson JG, Fonagy P (2002) Psychoanalytic treatments within psychiatry: an expanded view. Archives of General Psychiatry 59: 499-500.
Gedo JE (1979) Beyond Interpretation. New York: International Universities Press.
Giorello G (1976) Introduction. In I Lakatos (1976) Italian Edition (1979) Milan: Feltrinelli.
Goldfried MR (1995) From Cognitive-Behavior Therapy to Psychotherapy Integration. New York: Springer.
Goldfried MR (2001) How Therapists Change. Washington, DC: American Psychological Association.
Gooding D (1992) Putting agency back into experiment. In A Pickering (ed.) Science as Practice and Culture. Chicago and London: University of Chicago Press.
Green A (1975) The analyst, symbolization and absence in the analytic setting (on changes in analytic practice and analytic experience), in memory of DW Winnicott. Int. J. Psycho-Anal. 56: 1-22.

Green A (1993) Le travail du négatif. Paris: Editions de Minuit.
Green A (1997) Intuitions of the negative in playing and reality. Int. J. Psycho-Anal. 78: 1071-1084.
Green A (1998) The primordial mind and the work of the negative. Int. J. Psycho-Anal. 79: 649-665.
Green A (2000) The intrapsychic and the intersubjective in psychoanalysis. Psychoanal. Q. 69: 1-39.
Green A (2001) The central phobic position. Int. J. Psycho-Anal., 81: 429-451.
Gribinski M (1994) The stranger in the house. Int. J. Psycho-Anal. 75: 1011-1021.
Grossman WI (1967) Reflections on the relationships of introspection and psychoanalysis. Int. J. Psycho-Anal. 48: 16-31.
Grossman WI (1995) Psychological vicissitudes of theory in clinical work. Int. J. Psycho-Anal. 76: 885-899.
Grossman WI (2000) The 'Hartmann Era': on the interplay of different ways of thinking. In: MS Bergmann (ed.) The Hartmann Era. New York: Other Press, pp. 117-142.
Grossman WI (2002) Hartmann and the integration of different ways of thinking. J. Clin. Psychoanal., 11: 271-293.
Grubrich-Simitis I (1986) Six letters of Sigmund Freud and Sandor Ferenczi on the interrelationship of psychoanalytic theory and technique. Int. Rev. Psycho-Anal. 13: 259-277.
Hacking I (1983) Representing and Intervening: Introductory Topics in the Philosophy of Natural Science. Cambridge: Cambridge University Press.
Hacking I (1992) The self-vindication of the laboratory sciences. In A Pickering (ed.) Science as Practice and Culture. Chicago and London: University of Chicago Press.
Hanly C (1992) Inductive reasoning in clinical psychoanalysis. Int. J. Psycho-Anal. 73: 293-301.
Hardin HT, Hardin DH (2000) On the vicissitudes of early primary surrogate mothering. II: Loss of the surrogate mother and arrest of mourning. J. Amer. Psychoanal. Assn. 48: 1227-1258.
Hartmann H (1951) Technical implications of ego psychology. Psychoanal. Q. 20: 31-43.
Holmes J (1998) Defensive and creative uses of narrative in psychotherapy: an attachment perspective. In G Roberts, J Holmes (eds.) Narrative and Psychotherapy and Psychiatry. Oxford: Oxford University Press, pp. 49-68.
Hopkins J (1992) Psychoanalysis, interpretation, and science. In J Hopkins, A Saville (eds.) Psychoanalysis, Mind and Art: Perspectives on Richard Wollheim. Oxford: Blackwell. pp. 3-34.
Isaacs S (1943) The nature and function of phantasy. In P. King, R. Steiner (eds.) The Freud-Klein Controversies: 1941-1945. London: Routledge, 1991.
Isaacs S (1948) The nature and function of phantasy. Int. J. Psycho-Anal. 29: 73-97.
Jacobson E (1954) A contribution to the mechanism of psychotic identi-fications. J. Amer. Psychoanal. Assn. 2: 239-262.
Jones E (1953) The Life and Work of Sigmund Freud, Vol. III. New York: Basic Books.
Joseph B (1985) Transference: the total situation. Int. J. Psychoanal. 66: 447-454.
Kantrowitz J (2004) Tell me your theory. Where is it bred? A lesson from clinical approaches to dreams. J. Clin. Psychoanal., in press.

Kazdin AE (2000) Psychotherapy for Children and Adolescents: Directions for Research and Practice. Oxford: Oxford University Press.

Kernberg O (1975) Borderline Conditions and Pathological Narcissism. New York: Aronson.

Kernberg O (1984) Technical strategies in the treatment of narcissistic personalities. In O Kernberg (ed.) Severe Personality Disorders. New Haven, CT: Yale University Press.

Kernberg OF (1989) The narcissistic personality disorder and the differential diagnosis of antisocial behavior. Psychiatric Clinics of North America 12: 553-570.

Kernberg OF et al. (1972) Psychotherapy and psychoanalysis: final report of the Menninger Foundation Psychotherapy Research Project. Bulletin Menninger Clinic 36: 3-275.

Kernberg OF, Selzer MA., Koenigsberg HW, Carr AC, Appelbaum, AH (1989) Psychodynamic Psychotherapy of Borderline Patients. New York: Basic Books.

Kihlstrom J (1987) The cognitive unconscious. Science 237: 1445-1452.

King P, Steiner R (1991) The Freud-Klein Controversies: 1941-45. London: Routledge.

Klein GS (1976) Psychoanalytic Theory: An Exploration of Essentials. New York: International Universities Press.

Klein M (1927) Symposium on child analysis. In Love, Guilt and Reparation: The Writings of Melanie Klein, Vol. I. London: Hogarth Press, 1975, pp. 139-169.

Klein M (1946) Notes on some schizoid mechanisms. Int. J. Psycho-Anal. 27: 99-110.

Klein M, Heimann P, Issacs S, Riviere J (eds.) (1946) Developments in Psychoanalysis. London: Hogarth Press.

Klimovsky G (1994) Las desventuras del conocimiento científico. Buenos Aires: A•Z editora.

Kohut H (1971) The Analysis of the Self. New York: International Universities Press.

Kohut H (1977) The Restoration of the Self. New York: International Universities Press.

Kohut H (1984) How Does Analysis Cure? Chicago: University of Chicago Press.

Körner J (2002) Structuring case reports to promote rational debate. A new model of presentation. Presented at the Berlin Conference of the Deutsche Psychoanalytische Gesellschaff. December, 2002.

Kris E (1952) Psychoanalytic Explorations in Art. New York: International Universities Press.

Kuhn TS (1962) The Structure of Scientific Revolutions. Chicago: University of Chicago Press, 1970.

Lakatos I (1970) Falsification and the methodology of scientific research programmes. In I Lakatos, A Musgrave (eds.) Criticism and the Growth of Knowledge. Cambridge: Cambridge University Press, 1994.

Lakatos I (1976) Proofs and Refutations: The Logic of Mathematical Discovery. Cambridge: Cambridge University Press.

Lakatos I (1999) Lectures on scientific method. In I Lakatos, P Feyerabend, For and Against Method. Edited by M Motterlini. Chicago and London: University of Chicago Press.

Lancelle G, Lerner H, Nemirovsky CD, Frágola AO (1990) Identificaciones propias e impropias en el psicoanalizar. Psicoanálisis, XII, 1: 83-103.

Laplanche J, Pontalis J-B (1967) The Language of Psychoanalysis. Translated by D. Nicholson-Smith. New York: Norton, 1973.

Laplanche J, Pontalis J-B (1968) Fantasme originaire, fantasmes des origines, origine du fantasme (Phantasy and the origins of sexuality), Int. J. Psycho-Anal. 49.

Laplanche J, Pontalis J-B (1984) Fantasía originaria, fantasía de los orígenes, orígenes de la fantasía. In El Inconsciente Freudiano y el Psicoanálisis Francés Contemporáneo. Buenos Aires: Nueva Visión.

Liberman, D. (1970-1972) Linguistica, interaccion comunicativa y proceso psicoanalitico, Vols. I-III [Linguistics, Communicative Interaction and Psychoanalytic Process]. Buenos Aires: Galerna-Nueva Vision.

Loewenstein R (1963) Some considerations on free association. J. Amer. Psychoanal. Assn. 11: 451-473.

Luborsky L, Diguer L, Seligman DA, Rosenthal R, Krause ED, Johnson S, et al. (1999) The researcher's own therapy allegiances: A 'wild card' in comparisons of treatment efficacy. Clinical Psychology: Science and Practice 6: 95-106.

Luborsky L, Luborsky E (1995) The era of measures of transference: the CCRT and other measures. In T Shapiro, R Emde (eds.) Research in Psychoanalysis: Process, Development, Outcome. New York: International Universities Press, pp. 329-351.

Mahler MS, Pine F, Bergman A (1975) The Psychological Birth of the Human Infant: Symbiosis and Individuation. New York: Basic Books.

Matte-Blanco I (1975) The Unconscious as Infinite Sets. London: Duckworth.

Matte-Blanco I (1988) Thinking, Feeling and Being. London: Routledge.

Matthis I (2003) To play or not to play with a grid. EPF Conference, Sorrento; and EPF website.

Meissner WW (1989) A note on psychoanalytic facts. Psychoanalytic Inquiry 9: 193-219.

Mill JS (1852) A System of Logic, Ratiocinative and Inductive. 4th Edition. New York: Harper.

Mill JS (1859) On Liberty. London: Penguin, 1985.

Modell AH (1976) 'The holding environment' and the therapeutic action of psychoanalysis. J. Amer. Psychoanal. Assn. 24: 285-307.

Money-Kyrle R (1956) The Collected Papers of Roger Money-Kyrle. Edited by D Meltzer. Perthshire: Clunie Press.

Money-Kyrle R (1965) Success and failure in mental maturations. In The Collected Papers of Roger Money-Kyrle. Edited by D Meltzer. Perthshire: Clunie Press, 1978, pp. 397-406.

Money-Kyrle R (1968) Cognitive Development. In (1978) The Collected Papers (The Ronald Harris Educational Trust Library). London: Karnac Books.

Money-Kyrle R (1971) The aim of psychoanalysis. In (1978) The Collected Papers (The Ronald Harris Educational Trust Library). London: Karnac Books.

Money-Kyrle R (1978) The World of the Unconscious and the World of Common Sense. In (1978) The Collected Papers (The Ronald Harris Educational Trust Library). London: Karnac Books.

Ogden TH (1994) The analytic third: working with intersubjective clinical facts. Int. J. Psycho-Anal. 75: 3-19.

Ogden TH (2001) Reading Winnicott. Psychoanal. Q. 70(2): 299-323.

Onishi KH, Baillargeon R (2005) Do 15-month old infants understand false beliefs? Science, 308, 255, 8 April.
Parsons M (1992) The refinding of theory in clinical practice. Int. J. Psycho-Anal. 73: 103-115.
Peirce CS (1883) The general theory of probable inference. In Philosophical Writings of Peirce. Edited by J Buchler. New York: Dover, 1955. pp. 190-217.
Piaget J, García R (1982) Psicogénesis e Historia de la Ciencia. Mexico: Siglo XXI.
Polanyi M (1966) The Tacit Dimension. Garden City, NY: Doubleday.
Popper K (1959) Realism and the aim of science. Postscript to the Logic of Scientific Discovery. Italian edn. Milano: Il Saggiatore, 1984.
Popper K (1979) Objective Knowledge: An Evolutionary Approach (rev. edn.). Cambridge: Cambridge University Press.
Popper K ([1934] 1959) The Logic of Scientific Discovery. London: Hutchinson.
Porder NS (1987) Projective identification: An alternative hypothesis. Psychoanalytic Quarterly 56: 431-451.
Quine WVO (1953) Two dogmas of empiricism. In WVO Quine (ed.) From a Logical Point of View. Cambridge, MA: Harvard University Press.
Quine WVO (1957) Carnap and logical truth. In The Ways of Paradox and other Essays (rev. edn.). Cambridge, MA and London: Harvard University Press, 1976, pp. 107-132.
Quine WVO (1964) Implicit definition sustained. In The Ways of Paradox and other Essays (rev. edn.). Cambridge, MA and London: Harvard University Press, 1976, pp. 133-137.
Rangell L (1954) Similarities and differences between psychoanalysis and dynamic psychotherapy. JAPA, 2: 734-744.
Rangell L (1963) Structural problems in intrapsychic conflict. Psychoanal. Study Child 18: 103-138.
Rapaport D (1951) The Organization and Pathology of Thought. New York: Columbia University Press.
Rapaport D (1960) The Structure of Psychoanalytic Theory: A Systematizing Attempt. Psychological Issues, Vol. II (2). New York: International Universities Press.
Rapela D, Giorgi de Rapela A (1984) Mujer o varona? Psicoanálisis de la feminidad y de las teorías sexuales infantiles. Presented at 1er Congreso de psicoanálisis de niñas y adolescentes de la FEPAL. Carlos Paz, Córdoba, Argentina.
Reed GS (1994) Transference Neurosis and Psychoanalytic Experience: Perspectives on Contemporary Clinical Practice. New Haven, CT: Yale University Press.
Reed GS (1997) The analyst's interpretation as a fetish. J. Amer. Psychoanal. Assn. 45: 1153-1181.
Reed GS (2001) The disregarded analyst and the transgressive process: discontinuity, countertransference, and the framing of the negative. J. Amer. Psychoanal. Assn. 49, 3: 909-931.
Reed GS, Baudry F (1997) The logic of controversy: Susan Isaacs and Anna Freud on f(ph)antasy. J. Amer. Psychoanal. Assn. 45: 465-490.
Reichenbach H (1947) Elements of Symbolic Logic. New York: Macmillan.
Reichenbach H (1938) Experience and Prediction: An Analysis of the Foundation and the Structure of Knowledge. Chicago: University of Chicago Press.
Reichenbach H (1951) The Rise of Scientific Philosophy. Berkeley: University of California Press.

Renik O (2003) Standards and standardisation. Plenary Address. American Psychoanalytic Association. J. Amer. Psychoanal. Assn. 51 (Supplement): 43-55.

Robert M (1990) Roman des origines et origines du roman. Paris: Gallimard.

Rose N (2000) Biological psychiatry as a style of thought. Written for Workshop on Metaphors and Models in the Human Sciences. Princeton, NJ: Princeton University, December.

Roth A, Fonagy P (1996) What Works for Whom? A Critical Review of Psychotherapy Research. New York: Guilford Press.

Roussillon R (1999) Actualité de Winnicott. In A. Clancier, J. Kalmonovitch (eds.) Le paradoxe de Winnicott: de la naissance à la création. Paris: Centre National du Livre, pp. 9-26.

Russell B (1911) Knowledge by acquaintance and knowledge by description. In Mysticism and Logic. London: Unwin Paperbacks, 1989.

Russell B (1967) The Problems of Philosophy. Oxford: Oxford University Press.

Sandler J (1983) Reflections on some relations between psychoanalytic concepts and psychoanalytic practice. Int. J. Psycho-Anal. 64: 35-45.

Sandler J, Dreher AU (1995) What do Psychoanalysts Want: Problems of Aims in Psychoanalytic Therapy. London: Routledge.

Sandler J, Sandler A-M (1983) The 'second censorship', the 'three box model' and some technical implications. Int. J. Psycho-Anal. 64: 413-425.

Schachter J (2004) Psychoanalytic process, psychoanalysts and standards. ApsA Openline Internet Posting.

Schafer R (1997) Vicissitudes of remembering in the countertransference. Int. J. Psycho-Anal. 78: 1151-1163.

Searl MN (1936) Some queries on principles of technique. Int. J. Psycho-Anal. 17: 471-493.

Searle J (1992) The Rediscovery of Mind. Cambridge, MA and London: MIT Press.

Spillius EB (1994) Developments in Kleinian thought: overview and personal view. Psychoanalytic Inquiry 14: 324-364.

Stein S (1991) The influence of theory on the psychoanalyst's countertransference. Int. J. Psycho-Anal. 72: 325-334.

Steiner J (1993) Psychic Retreats: Pathological Organisations in Psychotic, Neurotic and Borderline Patients. London: Routledge.

Stern DN (1994) One way to build a clinically relevant baby. Infant Mental Health Journal 15: 36-54.

Terman DM (1989) Therapeutic change: perspectives of self psychology. Psychoanalytic Inquiry 9: 88-100.

The New Shorter Oxford English Dictionary 1 (1995) Oxford: Oxford University Press.

Tuckett D (1993) Some thoughts on the presentation and discussion of the clinical material of psychoanalysis. Int. J. Psychoanal. 74: 1175-1189.

Tuckett D (1994) The conceptualisation and communication of clinical facts in psychoanalysis - Foreword. Int. J. Psycho-Anal. 75: 865-870.

Tuckett D (1998) Evaluating psychoanalytic papers: towards the development of common editorial standards. Int. J. Psycho-Anal. 79: 431-448.

Tuckett D (2002) The new style conference and developing a peer culture in European psychoanalysis. Presidential Address, Prague. EPF Bulletin 56.

Tuckett D (2003) A ten-year European scientific initiative. Presidential Address, Sorrento. Bulletin of the Federation of the European Psychoanalytic Federational 57. October.

Tuckett D (2004) Building a psychoanalysis based on confidence in what we do. Presidential Address, Helsinki. EPF Bulletin, 58.

Tuckett D (2005) Does anything go? Towards a framework for the more transparent assessment of psychoanalytic competence. Int. J. Psycho-Anal. 86: 31-49. Earlier version available on EPF website in English and French.

Tully RE (1995) Logic, informal. In The Oxford Companion to Philosophy. Edited by T Honderich. Oxford and New York: Oxford University Press, p. 500.

van IJzendoorn MH, Juffer F, Duyvesteyn MGC (1995) Breaking the intergenerational cycle of insecure attachment: a review of the effects of attachment-based interventions on maternal sensitivity and infant security. Journal of Child Psychology and Psychiatry 36: 225-248.

Vaughan S, Spitzer R, Davies M, Roose S (1997) The definition and assessment of analytic process: can analysts agree? Int. J. Psycho-Anal., 78: 959-973.

Vygotskij LS (1934) Myšlenie I reč', Moskva–Leningrad. Italian translation. L Mecacci, Pensiero e Linguaggio. Roma–Bari: Laterza, 1990.

Wallerstein R (1998) The new American psychoanalysis: a commentary. J. Amer. Psychoanal. Assn. 46: 1021-1043.

Wallerstein RS (1986) Forty-two Lives in Treatment: A Study of Psychoanalysis and Psychotherapy. New York: Guilford Press.

Wallerstein RW (2003) The intertwining of politics and science in psychoanalytic history. J. Amer. Psychoanal. Assn. 51 (Supplement): 7-21.

Weiss K (2003) Ludwik Fleck and the art-of-fact. Evolutionary Anthropology. 12: 168-172.

Westen D (1999) The scientific status of unconscious processes: is Freud really dead? J. Amer. Psychoanal. Assn. 47, 4: 1061-1106.

Whewell W (1849) Mill's logic. In William Whewell, Theory of Scientific Method. Edited by RE Butts. Indianapolis and London: Hackett, 1989, pp. 265-308.

Whewell W (1850) Criticism of Aristotle's account of induction. In William Whewell, Theory of Scientific Method. Edited by RE Butts. Indianapolis and London: Hackett, 1989, pp. 311-321.

Whewell W (1858) Novum organon renovatum. In William Whewell, Theory of Scientific Method. Edited by RE Butts. Indianapolis and London: Hackett, 1989, pp. 79-249.

Whittle P (2000) Experimental psychology and psychoanalysis: what we can learn from a century of misunderstanding. Neuro-psychoanalysis 1: 233-245.

Williams M (2000) Epistemology and the mirror of nature. In RB Brandom (ed.) Rorty and His Critics. London: Blackwell.

Winnicott DW (1945) Primitive emotional development. In Through Pediatrics to Psycho-Analysis. New York: Basic Books, 1975, pp. 145-156.

Winnicott DW (1951) Transitional objects and transitional phenomena. In Through Pediatrics to Psycho-Analysis. New York: Basic Books, 1975, pp. 229-242.

Winnicott DW (1953) Transitional objects and transitional phenomena. In Playing and Reality. London and New York: Routledge, 1989, pp. 1-25.

Winnicott DW (1971) Playing and Reality. New York: Basic Books.

Wisdom JO (1967) Testing and interpretation within a session. Int. J. Psycho-Anal. 48: 44-52.

Wittgenstein L (1938) Lectures and Conversations on Aesthetics, Psychology and Religious Belief. Edited by C Barrett. Berkeley and Los Angeles: University of California Press, nd.

Wittgenstein L (1980) Culture and Value. Edited by GH von Wright. Chicago: University of Chicago Press.

Wollheim R (1995) The Mind and its Depths. Cambridge, MA: Harvard University Press.

Working Party on Theoretical Issues (2002, 2003) Mapping Implicit (Private) Theories in Clinical Practice. Introduction. EPF webpage.

Wright GHv (1957) The Logical Problem of Induction. New York: Macmillan.

Wright GHv (1971) Explanation and Understanding. Ithaca, NY: Cornell University Press.

Young JE (1999) Cognitive Therapy for Personality Disorder: A Schema-Focused Approach (3rd edn.). Sarasota, FL: Professional Resource Press/Professional Resource Exchange.

Zysman S (1998) Théories sexuelles infantiles et sexualité enfantine. La Psychiatrie de l'enfant. XLI, 2.

Index

abandonment 36
Abend, S. 89
action vector 4, 27, 38-9
 behaving 39
 formulating 39
 listening 38
 wording or interpretation 39
Adelson, E. 75
aggression 34
Ahumada, J.L. 8, 139, 162
Althusser, Louis 24-5
anaclitic depression 62
analytic listening 4
analytic space 109, 119-22, 123, 124
anxiety 34
Anzieu, Didier 161
Arbiser, S. 168
Aristotle 127, 138, 139, 141, 142
Arlow, J.A. 89, 110, 115, 116
'as if' personality 65
attachment theory 40-1, 62, 65
attunement 65
authenticity 65
Ayer, A.J. 138

Baillargeon, R. 156
Bateson, Gregory 141
Baudry, F. 108
Bellone, E. 20
Beres, D. 115
Bergman, A. 79
Bernardi, R. 170
Bion, Wilfred R. 1, 9, 14, 17, 18, 119, 148, 150, 156
Blackburn, S. 143
Bléandonu, G. 159
Bolton, D. 83

Bott Spillius, Elizabeth 154, 155
Bouveresse, J. 141
Brenner, C. 108, 109
Breuer, J. 78, 87
Brierley, M. 95
Broglie, Louis de 21
Bucci, W. 75
Busch de Ahumada, L.C. 131

Cabaniss, D. 169
Campbell, K. 75
Campbell, N. 18
Canestri, J. 24, 26, 84, 160, 162
Carnap, Rudolf 140
castration anxiety 36
Chandrasekhar, S. 21
Churchland, P.S. 84
Cicchetti, D. 79
Claparède, Edouard 21
classical model 7
client-centred approach 85
clinical theories 72
cognitive asceticism 81
cognitive neuroscience 78
cognitive therapy 85
Cohen, D.J. 79
coherence vs contradiction vector 4, 41-2
combinatory play 23
commitment 134-5
common-sense psychology 14, 31
communities of thought 6
Complexity of Causes 141, 143
Comte, August 139
conceptual change 21
conceptual generalizations 36
conceptual negotiation 26
conceptual patchwork 41

conceptual vector 4, 35-8
  clinical concepts 36
  clinical generalizations 36-7
  psychoanalytic process 37
  theories of change 37-8
  worldview or cosmology 35
conflict theory 7, 108, 117
conjoint objectivity about subjectivity 92-3
conscious 23
conscious judgement 90
consensual validation 92
context of discovery 3
context of justification 3
Cooper, Arnold 73
Copernicus 141
core theory 5, 80, 81, 84
counterinduction 8, 143-5
countertransference 14, 34, 37, 38, 46, 62, 63, 74, 89, 105, 118, 149-50, 164
covering laws 141
creative solutions 42
critical realism 145

Darwin, Charles 8, 127, 139, 140, 141, 142, 143, 156
Davidson, A.I. 99
defence 68
depression 34, 36, 62
development vector 4, 42
developmental theory 5
discipline, concept of 14
discontinuity 117
Donnet, J.-L. 32
dream as metaphor 67
Dreher, A.U. 8, 25, 34, 72, 83
drive/defence model 67
Duyvesteyn, M.G.C. 75
Dyson, F.J. 101

eclecticism 33
Edelson, M. 71, 170
ego 115, 116, 117
Einstein, Albert 23, 161
Eisold, K. 168
emotional contact 63
environmental defect 5

envy 5, 36, 39, 80
epistemological status of clinical theory 71-2
epistemology 8
equi-finality 79
erotic transference 35
Etchegoyen, Dr R. Horacio 127, 150, 162, 163
ethology 155-8
European Psychanalytical Federation 10
  Working Party on Comparative Clinical Methods 10, 11, 167-200
  Working Party on Theoretical Issues 2, 11, 15, 17
exhibitionism 62

factor K 9
Faimberg, Haydee 31, 170-1, 176, 200
Fairbairn, W.R.D. 73
false self 36, 65
falsificationism 138
family therapy 85
fantasy 108
Fedida, P. 200
Fenichel, O. 73, 76
Ferenczi, Sandor 1, 14, 24, 128, 132
Ferraro, F. 137
Ferro, A. 175, 200
Feyerabend, P. 140, 163
First Topography 77
Fleck, Ludwik 93, 98-9
Fonagy, P. 69, 74, 75, 79, 82
Foresti, G. 178
formal logic 138
formal theory 8, 138, 141
formula-theories 8, 140
formulating 38
fragile self 65
Fraiberg, S.H. 75
Frame of the Frame 32
frame-theories 8, 140
free association 37, 72, 74, 137
Freud, Anna 72, 76, 79
Freud, Sigmund 3, 5, 8, 21, 22, 24, 35, 71, 73-4, 76, 78, 79, 80, 82, 87, 92, 93, 96, 97, 115, 117, 119, 139, 150, 167, 168

on analytic neutrality 129
on free associations 137
on identification in groups 99
on infantile sexual theories 9, 148-9, 151-3, 154, 155, 157, 162
on non-conscious intentionality 84, 90
on scientific thinking 127, 142, 143, 164
on thing-presentations 128
on transference neurosis 116
on the unconscious 109
Fuchsian functions 22
fundamental antinomy 161

Gabbard, G.O. 75
García, Rolando 10, 158, 159, 160, 162, 163
Gedo, J.E. 73
genetic epistemology 160
genuineness 65
gestalt 85
Giorello, G. 21, 23
Goldfried, M.R. 80
Gooding, D. 140
Green, Andre (1975) 7, 109, 110, 116, 119, 120, 121, 122, 200
Gribinski, M. 128
Grillo, Sanchez 164
Grossman, W.I. 89, 93, 96, 98, 117, 124, 125
Grubrich-Simitis, I. 24
Grünbaum, A. 139, 141
Gunderson, J.G. 75

Hacking, I. 140
Hadamard, Jacques 21, 22, 23, 161
Hanly, C. 145
Hardin, D.H. 137
Hardin, H.T. 137
Hardy, G.H. 21
Hartmann, H. 88, 93, 170
Hegel, G.W.F. 66
helplessness 34
history of science 10
Holmes, J. 81
homooeconomicus 15
homosexual ideation 49

hopelessness 33
Hopkins, J. 78
human subjectivity 81
Hume, David 83

Ilahi, Nasir 117
implicit function 16, 19
implicit psychoanalytic knowledge base 83
implicit theories 2, 6, 7, 15, 66, 67, 95
implicit, private and preconscious 16, 25
inductivism 138
inescapable objectivity 89-90
infantile sexual theories 9, 147-65
inferential method 143
informal logic 138
informal theory 8, 138
insight 74
insufficient self-realization 62
integration of theories 66
intellective passions 23
inter-generational transmission 6
interpretation 74
intersubjectivity 92
inter-systemic conflict 117
intra-scientific element 25
introspection 91
irreducible subjectivity 89
Isaacs, Susan 108, 109, 154

Jacobson, E. 117
James, William 32
Jones, Ernest 143
Joseph, Betty 65, 200
Juffer, F. 75
Junktim 8

Kazdin, A.E. 79
Kernberg, O. 72, 75, 76, 117
Kihlstrom, J. 78
King, P. 77
Klein, Melanie 7, 9, 72, 77, 79, 93
on infantile sexual theories 153-5
on paranoid-schizoid universe 115, 118
on unconscious phantasies 6, 109, 153-5, 157

Klimovsky, Gregorio 18, 148, 158, 162
knowledge by acquaintance 128
Koerner, J. 177
Kohut, H. 1, 14, 65, 73, 97
Krypton effect 132
Kuhn, Thomas 19, 99, 138, 163

Lacan, Jacques 18
Lakatos, I. 19, 21, 23, 24, 80, 138, 143, 162, 163
Lancelle, G. 165
landscape 26-8
language 33
Laplanche, J. 72, 117, 152
'leavable' object 137
legislative postulation 140
Liberman, David 164
listening to the patient's listening 31
listening with the third ear 65
live theory 29
lived theory 4, 29
Locke, John 83
Loewenstein, R. 98
logic of discovery 20
logic of justification 20
logica situs 141-2, 143
logicization 18
Luborsky, E. 75
Luborsky, I. 75

Mahler, Margaret 79
Map of private (implicit, preconscious) theories 4, 7, 9, 15-16-18, 25, 27, 29-43
mapping 6, 26-8
master-pupil relationship 33
mathematical invention 21-2
Matte-Blanco, I. 73, 137, 161
Matthis, I. 172
Mead, G.H. 32, 62
Meissner, W.W. 71
Menninger Foundation Psychotherapy Research Project 72
mental space 110-11
mentalization 65
meta-communication 37
metaphor 33, 41-2, 106-10

metaphorical space 120, 121
metaphors of transition 7, 105
Mill, J.S. 141, 142
Modell, A.H. 73
models of development 76
models of disorder 76
models of the mind 76
Money-Kyrle, R. 9, 140, 150, 155-6, 157, 160, 161
Moran, G.S. 82
Morris, Desmond 194

narcissism 34, 62
narcissistic identity 111-12
narcissistic trauma 5, 80
negative identity 65
negative transference 35
neoclassical theory 15
neo-empiricism 3
Neurath, Otto 140
Newton, Isaac 140
Nietzsche, Friedrich 81
non-conscious intentionality 84
normative reconstructions 140

object relations of knowledge vector 4, 40-1
   attachment theory 40-1
   history of knowledge 40
   internalization of theory 40
   sociology of knowledge 40
   transgenerational influences 40
oedipal rivalry 80
official theories s13
Ogden, T.H. 107, 120
omnipotence in childhood development 64
Onishi, K.H. 156

paradigms 99
paranoid/schizoid position 7
Parsons, M. 64
partial theories, models or schemata 14, 17
pattern-realism 137-45
Peirce, Charles 139
permanent training 6
perverse conflict 117

Piaget, Jean 10, 26, 158, 159, 160, 162, 163
Pine, F. 75
Plato 140-1
play therapy 72
Pleasure Principle 157, 162
pluralism 5, 14
poetic invention 21
Poincaré, Henri 22
Polanyi, M. 17, 23
polymorphous concepts 41-2
Pontalis, J.B. 72, 117, 152
Popper, Karl 3, 8, 19, 24, 26, 138, 139-40, 141, 142, 161, 162, 163
Porder, N.S. 77
post-empiricist epistemology 9, 23, 83
preconscious 2, 14, 17, 19, 23
 see also Map of private (implicit, preconscious) theories
preconscious system of the topographical model 26
private theories 2, 4, 5, 19, 29, 95
 see also Map of private (implicit, preconscious) theories
projective identification 77
pseudo-problems 20
psychic reality 92
psychoanalysis 3
psychoanalytic identity 34
psychoanalytic mode of thought 93
psychogenesis 10
psychosocial point of view 99
psycho-synthesis 128
public theories 4, 5, 95

quasi-empirical 21
Quine, W.V.O. 83, 140
Quinodoz, Danielle 178

Racker, Heinrich 36
Ramachandran, V.S. 84
Rangell, L. 117, 169
Rank, Otto 153
Rapaport, D. 93, 99
Rapela, Diego and Amalia 160
Reed, G.S. 108, 116, 117, 124
Reichenbach, Hans 19, 138, 160
Reik, Theodor 65

Renik, O. 169
repressed ideation 34
resistance to change 64
rights of citizenship 2
Robert, Marthe 153
Rose, N. 99
Roth, A. 74
Roussillon, R. 107, 108
Russell, Bertrand 72, 128, 140

Sandler, Joseph 4, 6, 13, 14, 17, 18-19, 25, 64, 72, 79, 83, 89, 93, 95
Saussure, Raymond de 22
Schachter, J. 169
Schafer, R. 98
schema theory 85
Schlick, Moritz 156
scientific fantasy 22
Searle, John 141
second censorship 25
Second Topography 77
Sejnowski, T.J. 84
self-accusation 62
self-awareness 84
self-disclosure 74
self-disgust 62
self-doubt 62
self-object theory 65
self-observation 91, 96, 97
self-reflection 63, 65, 66
self-understanding 84, 91
separation anxiety 36
separation-individuation conflicts 80
separation theories 63
shame 62
Shapiro, V. 75
simple empathy 62
socialization of thinking 99
space of proximal development 23
spatial metaphor 7, 103-25
Spillius, E.B. 77
Steele, M. 75
Stein, S. 93
Steiner, J. 75
Steiner, R. 77
Stern, Daniel 65, 79
Strachey, J. 151
structural theory of the mind 25, 66

subjectivity 5, 89
superego 34, 38, 115
surreptitious activity 23
Synthesis 24
system conscious 154
system preconscious 154
system unconscious 154

tacit activity 23
Target, M. 74, 79
technical generalizations 36
Terman, D.M. 72, 73
theory, concept 9, 16, 17
theory as countertransference 34
theory as resistance 35
theory, definition 8
theory of groups 22
theory of identity 65
theory of mind 62
theory of omnipotence 67, 68
theory of science 127-45
theory-realism 137-43
theory, splitting of 34-5
thirdness 92
thought collectives 99
thought communities 88, 98-100
thought development 156
thought styles 99
three-box model 25-6
three-component model of theory 29
topographical vector 4, 30-5
  conscious but not public 30-1
  preconscious theories and theorization 31-3
  unconscious influences on the use of theories 34-5
training 6
transference 33, 37, 49, 53, 63, 64, 74, 89
  as 'total situation' 65
transference neurosis 116

transformational theory 184, 189, 198
transitional space, concept of 7
traumatization, theories of 63
true identity 62
true self 62, 64, 65
Tuckett, D. 168, 175
Tully, R.E. 138
typology of intervention 10, 11

unconscious 14, 19, 23
unconscious conflict 80
unconscious phantasies 6, 109, 153-5, 157
unconscious theories 140
unresponsive mother 65

Valéry, Paul 21
van IJzendoorn, M.H. 75
Vaughan, S. 169
Vienna Circle 8, 139, 156
von Wright, Georg-Henrik 8, 143, 144
Vygotskij, L.S. 23, 26

Wallerstein, Robert 1, 167
Weiss, K. 99
Weltanschauungen 14, 35, 95
Westen, D. 75
Whewell, William 142, 145
Whittle, P. 81
Williams, M. 141
Winnicott, D.W. 1, 7, 64, 65, 67, 68, 97, 106-7, 116, 118, 119, 120, 128, 197
Wisdom, J.O. 31
Wittgenstein, Ludwig 80, 139, 141, 143
Wollheim, R. 78
wording 38

Young, J.E. 85

zone of proximal development 26